Parenting Coordination
A Practical Guide
for Family Law Professionals

Debra K. Carter, PhD, is a nationally recognized expert in the area of Parenting Coordination (PC). As an expert consultant to attorneys and courts across the United States, Dr. Carter has played an integral role in the integration of mental health and family law. A frequent lecturer and PC instructor, Dr. Carter has served as an adviser to legislatures, Bar Associations, local courts, and Supreme Courts as various jurisdictions integrate PC into their laws, procedures, and standards of ethical conduct. She has played an integral role in helping to develop legislation governing the practice of PC and ethical guidelines for Parenting Coordinators. A nationally acclaimed speaker who has received numerous awards and honors for her work and contributions to the family law system, Dr. Carter is the Co-Founder of the National Cooperative Parenting Center (NCPC) that provides training, consultation, and supervision to Parenting Coordinators as well as forensic services to attorneys, mental health professionals, and families. Dr. Carter is a Licensed Psychologist, a Certified Family Law Mediator, an instructor, and a clinical researcher, as well as a practicing Parenting Coordinator. She is the author of *Parenting Coordination: A Practical Guide for Parents* and coauthor of *Empirically Based Parenting Plans: What Professionals Need to Know* (2010).

Parenting Coordination
A Practical Guide
for Family Law Professionals

Debra K. Carter, PhD

SPRINGER PUBLISHING COMPANY
NEW YORK

Springer Publishing Company, LLC
11 West 42nd Street
New York, NY 10036
www.springerpub.com

Acquisitions Editor: Jennifer Perillo
Production Editor: Dana Bigelow
Cover Design: Steven Pisano
Compositor: S4Carlisle Publishing Services Pvt. Ltd.

ISBN: 978-0-8261-0647-6
E-book ISBN: 978-0-8261-0648-3

11 12 13 14/ 5 4 3 2 1

The author and the publisher of this work have made every effort to use sources believed to be reliable to provide information that is accurate and compatible with the standards generally accepted at the time of publication. The author and publisher shall not be liable for any special, consequential, or exemplary damages resulting, in whole or in part, from the readers' use of, or reliance on, the information contained in this book. The publisher has no responsibility for the persistence or accuracy of URLs for external or third-party Internet Web sites referred to in this publication and does not guarantee that any content on such Web sites is, or will remain, accurate or appropriate.

Library of Congress Cataloging-in-Publication Data
Carter, Debra K.
    Parenting coordination: a practical guide for family law professionals / Debra K. Carter.
        p. cm.
    Includes bibliographical references and index.
    ISBN 978-0-8261-0647-6 — ISBN 978-0-8261-0648-3 (e-book)
    1. Parent and child (Law) 2. Divorce—Law and legislation. 3. Divorce settlements.
4. Custody of children. 5. Domestic relations courts. 6. Dispute resolution (Law)
7. Parenting. 8. Divorce—Psychological aspects. I. Title.
    [DNLM: 1. Divorce—psychology. 2. Child Custody—legislation & jurisprudence.
3. Parenting—psychology. WS 105.5.F2]
    K705.C365 2011
    346.01'5—dc22

                                                                    2011002328

Special discounts on bulk quantities of our books are available to corporations, professional associations, pharmaceutical companies, health care organizations, and other qualifying groups.

If you are interested in a custom book, including chapters from more than one of our titles, we can provide that service as well.

For details, please contact:
Special Sales Department, Springer Publishing Company, LLC
11 West 42nd Street, 15th Floor, New York, NY 10036-8002
Phone: 877-687-7476 or 212-431-4370; Fax: 212-941-7842
Email: sales@springerpub.com

Printed in the United States of America by Hamilton Printing.

*This book was inspired by the many families
who have come to me adrift on a stormy sea.
They have entrusted me with their fears
and worries, and we have learned together
about the difficulty and possibility that change brings.*

*This book was written for those professionals who dedicate their
lives to helping families navigate the raging tides of parental
conflict. These dedicated professionals model temperate
endurance, plant seeds of hope, and provide a steady hand at
the helm for those who feel despair and see no possibility of safe
passage across stormy seas.*

*Lastly, and most important, this book is dedicated
to my mother, Barbara, who inspired me to want to make a
positive difference whenever possible. She has been a model of
grace, wisdom, and integrity. She is my one true North.*

Contents

Preface

Parenting Coordination (PC) is a new child-centered intervention for divorced or separated parents whose children are at risk for harm due to exposure to ongoing conflict and parents who are distracted by divorce. *Parenting Coordination: A Practical Guide for Family Law Professionals* is written for a multidisciplinary audience of professionals in family law including mental health practitioners, lawyers, mediators, custody evaluators, judicial officers, family court administrators, parenting educators, and parenting coaches. It is also written to inform parents and concerned family members about this new process and the promise it holds.

This book offers a practical guide for this innovative intervention, with references to the science that underlies the process. It will provide you with the essential elements that define this new and innovative process as well as new tools to help you better understand the complexities of working with high conflict families.

Parenting Coordination: A Practical Guide for Family Law Professionals details a systematic approach to help parents develop and implement a successful dispute resolution framework that is designed to stabilize the family unit and shield the children from harm. However, this book cannot stand on its own in helping you acquire the skills and tools you need to assist these complex, dysfunctional families. This book will orient readers to the professional ethics, relevant procedural guidelines, underlying legal standards and procedures, and relevant, peer-reviewed, empirical research that must guide all of our work as family law professionals. Therefore, citations to relevant literature are provided wherever possible as are directions to relevant associations, agencies, and Web sites for additional information and resources.

The characteristics of high-conflict families and the potential for entrenched hostility and nonproductive behavior patterns demands a comprehensive understanding of human beings, human interactions, and options for mitigating interventions if constructive change is to occur and if children are to be protected from the damaging exposure to parental conflict. The blending of skills needed to achieve success with these complex and difficult families brings challenges of both integration and segregation. This book exposes readers to the breadth of experience and depth of knowledge that must be integrated to guide quality PC interventions.

For the untrained practitioner, PC may seem fraught with ethical pitfalls, demanding challenges of an adversarial court system, and angry parents who are eager to blame anyone near for their confusion and distress. *Parenting Coordination: A Practical Guide for Family Law Professionals* is a guide and resource for you, the innovative, forward thinking family law professional, who recognizes that the potential benefits far outweigh the risks for families caught in the web of intractable conflict.

The Introduction describes the evolution of Parenting Coordination and the benefits for parents, children, the courts, and society. This chapter also provides the historical, social, and legal contextual variables that contributed to a significant increase in divorce rates and sounded the alarm for the need to protect children from the potential harmful effects of divorce.

Chapter 1, Parenting Coordination: The Integrated Model, describes the hybrid psychological–legal model of PC, including the professional role, responsibilities, protocol for service, and ethical guidelines. In addition, this chapter outlines the core knowledge base and the specific professional skills that are needed to provide this innovative service. A step-by-step approach to integrating the core knowledge with professional skills to manage families enmeshed in conflict is outlined with an emphasis on differentiating professional roles and application of the integrated skill set.

Chapter 2, Parenting Coordination Procedures; Chapter 3, Getting Started; and Chapter 4, Developing an Intervention Strategy, describe the process and initial phase of PC work. Chapter 2 outlines the legal documents that provide direction and authority to the PC and the process by which a PC may become involved with a family. It also describes elements of the Parenting Coordinator's professional services agreement and how to structure the process. Chapter 3 details the information that must be gathered from parents, court files, and other professionals in order to understand the history of the parenting partnership as well as the history of family dynamics that may be contributing to the ongoing conflict between the parents. This chapter illustrates how to gather this data in a uniform and efficient manner to minimize time and expense. Chapter 4 describes the procedures to screen for risk factors and the process to manage risk factors. This chapter also outlines sources of conflict and the tools to identify parenting interaction and conflict management styles. Finally, this chapter emphasizes the need for a support team for the family and how the PC may secure and manage these other resources for the family.

Chapter 5, Conflict Analysis, Transformation, and Containment, reviews the theory behind conflict evolution and describes the elements necessary to change a parent's approach to resolving conflict. The definition of intractable conflicts is also described in this chapter along with intervention options to help transform conflict.

Chapter 6, Strategies to Disengage From Conflict and Chapter 7, Strategies to Build Consensus focus on specific PC strategies and interventions. Chapter 6 describes the types of co-parenting relationships that can be utilized to help parents disengage from conflict and how to utilize empirically based parent education as an intervention tool. This chapter also introduces the concept of an Intervention Strategy as a definitive guide for working with each family.

Chapter 7, Strategies to Build Consensus, describes interventions designed to increase parent motivation to work toward resolution of conflict and the process of helping parents identify common goals and interests. This chapter also describes the process to help parents move beyond the initial phase of conflict and begin to consider whether forgiveness and moving on is in their future.

Chapter 8, Parenting Plans: Using Research on Child Development and Parenting Styles as a Guide, describes the typical components of a parenting plan and how to select the "best fit" parenting plan based on the particular strengths, weaknesses, and needs of each family unit. This chapter outlines, in summary format, the developmental needs of children and discusses why parenting style matters.

Chapter 9, Intervention Strategies for Families With Extra Challenges focuses on interventions for families, which may include substance abusing or dependent parents and mentally ill parents, and describes the elements to identify alienation, estrangement, and parental alignment which impact time-sharing arrangements between parent and child. This chapter also outlines the process for handling threats of domestic violence and allegations of child sexual abuse.

Chapter 10, Managing the Parenting Coordination Process, describes safety procedures to protect all involved in PC, including the practitioner, and what to do when PC is no longer appropriate for a family. This chapter emphasizes the need to monitor professional boundaries and ethical dilemmas that will inevitably present themselves.

The Appendices include sample orders of referral, sample parenting plans, and resources for the Parenting Coordinator. I have included a comprehensive bibliography for additional resources and useful Web sites to assist the PC practitioner.

The contents of this book evolved over the course of many years as the concepts and process of PC developed. When the outline was first drafted, PC, as an alternative dispute resolution (ADR) process, was in its infancy. There were no clear protocols or standards to follow: only the idea that this new process could bring hope and an opportunity for positive change for families that were caught in a crucible of conflict. PC is still a very new and constantly evolving ADR process. Research to address the utility, efficacy, and outcome of this process are underway, but much work still needs to be done to validate and define this evolving intervention process.

I have used case examples to illustrate the application of PC concepts and interventions. In every instance, the case examples are hypothetical and fictitious. Any resemblance to a particular person or family circumstance is purely coincidental.

Debra K. Carter

Introduction

Parenting coordination is an emerging, new alternative dispute resolution (ADR) process for parents (separated, divorced, or never married) who are unable to resolve parenting disputes and who may, ultimately, seek remedy through the judicial system. The *Integrated Model of Parenting Coordination* incorporates philosophies, perspectives, and skills from the legal, mental health, mediation, education, and consultation professions in an effort to confront the significant and harmful impact on children when parents remain locked in hostile and prolonged conflict with one another.

A primary goal in parenting coordination is to help high-conflict parents develop and implement a successful dispute resolution framework for co-parenting their children. This framework enables parents to acquire the skills and tools they need to disengage, emotionally and behaviorally, from a dysfunctional parenting relationship and develop child-focused communication and problem-solving techniques within the context of a functional co-parenting relationship. A successful framework reduces parental conflict, minimizes stress for children, and encourages parents to resolve their parenting conflicts without litigation. Parenting coordinators often serve as "monitors" for children's best interests and work to ensure that children maintain frequent access to both parents, as appropriate, and have the freedom to maintain a loving relationship with both parents without fear of reprisal or adverse consequences.

Divorce and its impact on children, parents, families, the court system, and the community at large has been an area of study since the divorce revolution emerged in the United States in the early 1970s and in other English speaking countries during this same era (www .divorcerate.org). It is widely accepted that children's exposure to chronic hostility and animosity between their parents is damaging (Johnston, 1995; Johnston, Kline, & Tschann, 1989; Kelly, 2002; Teicher, 2002).

Parenting time arrangements, parenting styles, unresolved parenting conflict, parental health, family support, as well as the age and temperament of the child all impact children's adjustment to their parents' change in living and parenting arrangements. For children who may be exposed to hostility between their parents for prolonged periods of time, parenting coordination offers promise to families and courts as an opportunity to prevent or mitigate long-term damage.

Evolution and Definition of Parenting Coordination

The concept of parenting coordination dates back to the early 1990s. In 1994, two psychologists from a high conflict study group in Colorado, Carla Garrity and Mitchell A. Baris, published a book entitled *Caught in the Middle: Protecting the Children of High Conflict Divorce* where the idea of developing a process to protect children from the plight of exposure to harmful parental conflict was first explored. Their idea, and the work of many others who have worked with parents caught in conflict, gave rise to the development of parenting coordination as a new ADR process. ADR services have expanded rapidly in response to a growing demand for services outside the litigation arena that helps parents, children, and the court address family needs in a cost-effective and constructive manner. Parenting coordination evolved as a multidisciplinary ADR process designed to meet family courts' and parents' needs for consultation and directives from professionals trained to assist with questions regarding parenting plan components and time-sharing arrangements that serve children's interests. Courts may appoint a parenting coordinator at any point during, or after, dissolution of marriage proceedings or any other civil action involving custody or parenting of children. Parents may also request and agree to use parenting coordination services whenever they are unable to resolve parenting disputes without assistance.

A "parenting plan" or custody settlement arrangement is either a temporary or final order of the court setting out the residential living arrangements for the children, the time-sharing arrangements between parents, parental responsibilities, and other parenting issues in separating, divorcing, or never married parents.

Family law or divorce mediation and parenting education programs are relatively common ADR services available to most families. Parenting coordination is becoming more widely available and is specifically tailored to address the complex issues in high-conflict parenting. Many mental health practitioners have worked with domestic relation courts in diverse roles such as custody evaluators, parenting educators, experts in the fields of child development and parenting styles, advocates against domestic violence, and other related areas of forensic mental health expertise. The process and practice of parenting coordination differs widely depending upon locale and whether specific laws have been adopted which defines and provides authority for the process. There is not a uniform definition of parenting coordination across the United States or other parts of the world, but there are generally accepted concepts which guide the parenting coordination process. These concepts include the following:

- ensuring that the parenting coordination process does not place anyone involved at risk for physical harm
- monitoring parents' compliance with court orders, including parenting plans or custody-settlement agreements
- making decisions or arbitrating child-focused disputes between parents with the authority of the court and/or consent of the parents
- educating parents about child development, including the impact of separation or divorce and chronic parental conflict on all family members
- teaching and modeling effective co-parenting communication and conflict resolution techniques
- referring parents or children for interventions (e.g., psychotherapy, psychological evaluation, education programs, etc.) to address children's or parents' individual needs; and
- specialized training requirements for the parenting coordinator.

Parenting coordination offers potential benefits for parents, children, the courts, and other family law professionals.

Benefits for Parents

- helps parents shift their role from marital or intimate/romantic partners to parenting partners
- educates parents about the impact of divorce on children, adults, and families
- educates parents about the impact of parental hostility and conflict on their child's development

- teachs parents how to manage their negative emotions (anger/hostility/frustration) more constructively
- teaches and models effective communication tools
- teaches and models effective conflict resolution techniques
- helps parents identify their contributions to conflict in the parenting partner relationship
- helps parents identify unresolved emotional/relationship issues that interfere with effective co-parenting arrangements
- monitors parents' compliance with the parental responsibility and decision-making arrangements as ordered by the court (or stipulated custody-settlement agreement)
- monitors time-sharing arrangements to ensure children maintain access to both parents in a manner sufficient to sustain healthy attachment and bonding
- assists parents in the development of more detailed agreements in their Parenting Plan as a means of reducing parental conflict and misunderstandings; and
- decreases costs associated with chronic litigation.

Benefits for Children

- increases the likelihood of keeping two active parents in the child's life
- reduces the child's symptoms of distress and dysfunction by helping reduce parental conflict
- creates the opportunity for parents to maintain a more relaxed home atmosphere for the child
- helps children develop effective communication tools in order to assert their needs and wishes
- reduces the effects of chronic loyalty binds
- diminishes the likelihood of future relationship difficulties
- enhances the child's confidence and self-esteem by creating an optimal environment for growth and development; and
- creates an opportunity for parents to model and demonstrate security, stability, and trust.

Benefits for the Court System

- reduces docket scheduling burdens
- enables Judges to attend to matters of law versus parenting matters

▪ prevents Family Law judicial burnout; and
▪ utilizes the authority of the court to educate parents and direct them to services to help stabilize their family.

Benefits for Attorneys/Forensic Financial Professionals

▪ provides a resource for directing parenting matters to appropriately trained professionals
▪ increases ability to attend to matters of law or finance; and
▪ prevents burnout.

Benefits for Society

▪ increases two-parent involvement
▪ reduces likelihood of child neglect
▪ identifies childhood and/or family problems early on that, if undetected or untreated, may lead to more serious individual or family pathologies
▪ builds and reinforces individual and family strengths to create the surest scaffolding for children's optimal development over time
▪ decreases the likelihood of children's involvement in the court juvenile system later in life; and
▪ dispells the myth that children are always damaged by divorce.

To get a better understanding of how and why parenting coordination developed, it is important to create a historical context for how families have been affected by the divorce revolution and the redefinition of "traditional family" in the United States and other regions of the globe where divorce is prevalent.

The Divorce Revolution and Changing Family Constellations

In the late 1960s, American society began a great experiment with the structure and foundation of the family that was unprecedented in modern times. In 1969, California passed the first "no-fault" divorce law, precipitating a surge in the divorce rate that moved eastward throughout the 1970s.

By 2002, only 52% of marriages lasted 15 years and of those marriages which ended in divorce, the median duration was less than 8 years (see Table on the next page).

Marriage and Divorce Statistics (2002)	
Median duration of first marriages that end in divorce	Males: 7.8 years Females: 7.9 years
Median duration of second marriages that end in divorce	Males: 7.3 years Females: 6.8 years
Median number of years people wait to remarry after their first divorce	Males: 3.3 years Females: 3.1 years
Percentage of married people who reach their 5th, 10th, and 15th anniversaries	5th: 82% 10th: 65% 15th: 52%
Percentage of married people who reach their 25th, 35th, and 50th anniversaries	25th: 33% 35th: 20% 50th: 5%

U.S. Census Bureau, National Center for Health Statistics, Americans for Divorce Reform

The State of Our Unions 2005, a report issued by the National Marriage Project at Rutgers University, indicated that only 63% of American children grow up with both biological parents. As of 2003, 43.7% of custodial mothers and 56.2% of custodial fathers were either separated or divorced.

It is important to understand how and why such a revolutionary and pervasive phenomenon has occurred that would begin to account for the increase in the divorce rate. Some of the roots of the divorce revolution can be found in the greater valuing of emotional love in relationships and the pursuit of personal happiness. Mutual unhappiness, written into law as "irreconcilable differences" or statements that "the marriages are irretrievably broken", now provides a way out for thousands of unhappy couples. With this increased tolerance, the old language of divorce has been replaced by the new language of acceptance.

Before 1969 in the United States, one could be granted a divorce only if he or she could establish that one party was at fault by virtue of adultery, desertion, physical or mental abuse, drunkenness or drug addiction, imprisonment, or insanity. The advent of "no fault" in divorce laws reflected many changes already going on in the United States and other industrialized nations. Families had become smaller, moved off of farms and into cities, were much more affluent, and had more education and leisure time. The purpose of having children and marriage changed drastically from the time when children were considered "chattel" or property of the male parent (early 1800s) or when the "tender years doctrine" (late 1800s and early 1900s) of law presumed that mothers were uniquely qualified to parent their young children.

In the late 1960s, a number of significant changes were taking place in U.S. society. The Civil Rights and Women's Movements highlighted the notion that individuals had a right to pursue individual interests in order to cultivate and maximize their potential. The premise was the belief that through the development of "human potential", individuals could experience an exceptional quality of life filled with happiness, creativity, and fulfillment. This came to be known as the human potential movement, and proponents believed that the net effect of individuals cultivating their potential would bring about positive social changes. Women were working in larger numbers. Equality before the law and the easing of sex role stereotypes for women were buzzwords in the 1970s. Furstenberg (1994) suggested that the erosion of gender roles played a large part in the increasing divorce rate since research indicates that gender does not limit a person's ability to create a safe and nurturing environment for children, nor does it correlate with adequacy in performing the tasks necessary to raise them (Whiteside, 1998). Dual career couples also became more of the norm (Coleman and Pencavel, 1993b; Winkler, 1998).

By the mid-1970s, the first judicial opinions in the United States began to be handed down in regard to gender equity—the regarding of mothers and fathers as equal before the law in their petition for custody of their children following a divorce (Derdeyn, 1976). By the mid-1980s, gender equity laws had been passed in most areas of the United States (Wyer, Gaylord, & Grove, 1987). A wave of litigation that began in the mid-1980s still has not begun to abate. Approximately 15–25% of couples divorcing with children now engage in bitter emotional disputes over who will obtain the right to raise the children and to make the most important decisions about their well-being (Maccoby & Mnookin, 1992).

Another societal change occurred with the advent of television, media, and access to the world via the Web. It broadened our knowledge about segments of society whose lives differ from our own and highlighted an evolving definition of family. The traditional definition of family was a fundamental social group typically consisting of one or two parents and their children. Often, the family members shared goals and values, had long-term commitments to one another, and usually resided in the same dwelling place. Today, families may no longer be defined solely as heterosexual, married couples. Family definition can be as varied as individual differences. Family constellations may include children being raised by a single parent, grandparents, extended family members, non-family members, never married parents, and gay, lesbian, or bisexual parents.

Today, the divorce rate in English speaking countries ranges from 43% to 52% with the United States having the highest rate of divorce (Marriage and Conjugal Life in Canada, Australian Historical Statistics and ABS, Office of National Statistics-UK, www.divorcerate.org). In the United States, births to unmarried women set a record high of 40% in 2007 (U.S. Centers for Disease Control and Prevention), representing 1.7 million children. Over half of births to women in their early twenties and nearly 30% of births to women ages 25–29 were to unmarried women ("America's Children: Key National Indicators of Well-Being, 2006," www.childstats.gov). According to the U.S. Census Bureau (2007), approximately 68% of children are living in two parent homes (biological and adoptive parents), 22% are living in single parent homes, 2% are living with grandparents, 1.3% are living with extended family members, 3% are living with never married parents, and 2.5% are living with non-family members (U.S. Census Bureau, Current Population Survey, Annual Social and Economic Supplement, 2007, www.childstats.gov/americaschildrentables/xls/fam1b.xls). In addition, the U.S. Census 2000, the National Survey of Family Growth (2002), and the Adoption and Foster Care Analysis and Reporting System (2004) show that an estimated 6–14 million children have a gay or lesbian parent and that an estimated 65,500 adopted children are living with a lesbian or gay parent.

These statistics tell us that family constellations vary widely. These evolutionary changes in society have had far-reaching impact on parents, children, and the court system. Legal presumptions have been challenged, and the court has had to address issues regarding jurisdiction, public policy, and children's best interests in the context of a changing society.

Legal Presumptions of Parenting After Divorce in the United States

In the legal opinions that were handed down in the late 1800s and early 1900s, the term *tender years* was used often. This term referred to the period of a child's life when they are intensely vulnerable and dependent on the mother, specifically thought to be from birth to about age 7 or 8 years old. The historical presumption of "tender years" held that young children were better off when in the primary care of their mothers, particularly when they were very young. This presumption reflected an awareness of children as developmentally unique human beings rather than simply small adults. This doctrine, which emphasized the importance of the maternal–infant relationship, survived well into the twentieth century. Two legal opinions in U.S. courts, *Chapsky v. Wood* in 1881 and *Finlay v. Finlay* in 1925, laid the groundwork for the concept of *"the best interests of the child"*. Because mothers were already considered uniquely qualified to care for children by virtue of the *"tender years"* doctrine, the *best interests of the child* were automatically assumed to be the placement of the child with the mother.

Several other developments contributed to this legal presumption. Early in the twentieth century, fathers were ordered to pay child support to mothers, thereby allowing women, as single parents, greater financial means to support their children. In addition, with changing attitudes minimizing and eliminating the concept of parental fault, mothers were awarded custody of children almost unchallenged for 70–80 years (http://www.divorcepeers.com/stats17.htm; http://www.cdc.gov/nchs/data/mvsr/supp/mv43_09s.pdf). National estimates in the 1970s and 1980s indicated that mothers had primary physical custody of the children approximately 85% of the time, and fathers retained primary physical custody 10% of the time, with the remaining 5% spread over a variety of custody arrangements, including grandparent, split or joint custody. More recent data sets indicate some changes in child custody awards with 75% of physical custody awarded to the mother, but still only about 10% of child custody awards were made to fathers. The rest of the child custody awards involved some type of joint custody arrangement (National Center for Health Statistics, 1990).

Another change occurred during the 1980s and 1990s when the Full Faith and Credit Clause of the U.S. Constitution was applied to issues regarding child custody. The Full Faith and Credit Clause (Article IV, Section 1) states that: "Full Faith and Credit shall be given in each State to the Public Acts, Records, and Judicial Proceedings of every other State. And the Congress may by general Laws prescribe the Manner in which such Acts, Records and Proceedings shall be proved, and the Effect thereof." This meant that judicial decisions rendered by the courts in one State were to be recognized and honored in every other State. This was intended to prevent parties from moving to another State to escape enforcement of a judgment (e.g., custody arrangement) or to relitigate a controversy already decided elsewhere, a practice known as "forum shopping".

Child Custody determinations had historically fallen under the jurisdiction of state courts, and before the 1970s, other states did not accord them Full Faith and Credit enforcement. As a result, a divorced parent who was unhappy with one state's custody decision could sometimes obtain a more favorable ruling from another state. This was an incentive for a dissatisfied parent to abduct a child and move to another state in order to petition for custody. In response to this situation, the Uniform Child Custody Jurisdiction Act (UCCJA) was adopted by the National Conference of Commissioners on Uniform State Laws in 1968. By 1984, every state had adopted a version of the UCCJA. In 1980, Congress passed the Parental Kidnapping Prevention Act (28 U.S.C.A. § 1738A), which aids enforcement and promotes finality in child custody decisions by providing that valid custody decrees are entitled to full faith and credit enforcement in other states.

Another development in the United States impacting legal presumptions regarding "custody" and time-sharing occurred starting in 2003 when several states began to pass laws allowing same sex couples to marry or establish a "union". This, along with the Full Faith and Credit Clause of the U.S. Constitution, provided the basis for same sex couples to retain their rights as parents for their children, who were products of this union by mutual adoption, after the couple separated.

Current View of Divorce

The tender-years presumption is gone. No studies have shown that mothers are more capable of caring for children due solely to their being born female. The "best interests of the child" is the current prevailing legal standard for court decisions in the United States regarding children, although there are wide variations in how this concept is applied and interpreted by the courts. This principle generally favors the custody or time-sharing arrangement that best meets the needs of the children and one which also fosters normative development. Under the laws of almost all states, mothers and fathers have an equal right to custody. Courts are not supposed to assume that a child is automatically better off with the mother or the father. Of course, judges, like the rest of us, are products of their background and personal experience. Some judges may hold personal beliefs that mothers take care of children better than fathers and that fathers have little experience in parenting or that fathers are better at raising boys. Judges with such biases may apply these views when they decide custody cases, although they are supposed to base decisions on the facts of each case and not on automatic presumptions or personal biases. In some circumstances, the principle of the "least detrimental alternative" is applied. This presumption holds that courts and parenting plan evaluators should be guided by the more realistic notion that all children in separating or divorcing families may be harmed to some extent without careful consideration and adequate arrangements.

Joint legal custody has increasingly become the standard arrangement for parents who are separated or divorced. In 1982, only 32 states had embraced the concept of joint custody with some legislation or case law calling for joint legal custody as the preferred arrangement after divorce (Freed & Walker, 1985; Shulman, 1982). There are now only a couple of states that have laws providing that if everything else is equal, the mother may be preferred. In addition, nearly all states have distinguished between legal and physical custody. Legal custody refers to the parental right to make major decisions regarding the child's health, education, and welfare. Physical custody refers to the living arrangements of the child on a day-to-day basis. There are two basic custody arrangements in the United States: sole custody and joint custody, the most common. Sole custody assigns to one parent all legal rights, duties, and powers as a parent, including the right to make all decisions. In sole custody, the child resides with the custodial parent; the noncustodial parent is given the right to visit the child. The limited rights and privileges of the noncustodial parent have been expanded in most states over the past decade to provide equal legal access to child-related information of an educational and medical nature, and to make medical decisions in emergencies when the child is in the noncustodial parent's care.

Joint physical custody statutes are intended to structure parenting arrangements so that the child lives with both parents on some shared basis with each parent assuming day-to-day parental responsibilities. These statutes do not define how much time the child resides with each parent, and are not interpreted as dictating a 50/50 residential time sharing. Thus, parents may elect joint physical custody, but the child may spend anywhere from 10% to 50% of his time with one of his parents, and the remainder with the other. Parents can agree to either of these legal arrangements but the most common arrangement remains that of joint legal custody and sole or primary physical custody to one of the parents, most often the mother. In very unusual circumstances, with a history of extreme conflict over educational, medical, or religious values, parents may have joint physical custody, but one parent is assigned responsibility for sole decision making for a particular aspect of a child's life.

The legal trend over the past decade has been to favor joint legal custody over joint physical or residential custody. However, there are mixed reviews about the impact of joint legal custody. Bender (1994) and others (Cohen, 1998) assert that joint custody compared to sole custody leads to better adjustment in children, higher compliance with financial child support obligations, better adjustments for mothers, and reduced litigation and relitigation. Bender also suggests that joint physical custody is the preferred option in high conflict situations because it helps reduce the conflict over time—and that is in the best interests of children. However, others (Johnston et al., 1989; Kelly, 1993; Kuehl, 1998; Nelson, 1989) report findings which contradict these assertions and counter with the opinion that joint custody often leads to more litigation, creates economic advantage in negotiations for one parent, results in lower child support orders and jeopardizes the security of children.

From a child development perspective, some research suggests regular sharing of children's overnight care between parents fosters closer and ultimately more enduring parent–child relationships (Lamb, Sternberg, & Thompson, 1997; Maccoby & Mnookin, 1992). Kelly and Lamb (2000) support the view that young children's attachments to their parents are fostered by shared schedules. There are others (Pruett, Ebling, & Insabella, 2004; Solomon & Biringen, 2001; Solomon & George, 1999) who argue against presumptions of shared parenting because of the potentially disruptive nature of this lifestyle for young children where they are faced with increased challenges and risks at a time when children's cognitive, emotional, and social development are reliant on stable, responsible care. Pearson and Thoennes (1990) also documented risks for children including an increase in their loyalty conflicts, exposure to ongoing complexity and conflict in parental decision making, and bearing the burden of the organizational load (i.e., remembering belongings, school work, etc.).

Unfortunately, there is no uniform definition of what constitutes "best interests" for children, and joint physical custody, which was originally hailed as the solution to inter-parental conflict (McIntosh, 2009), has been largely a disappointment for parents who are unable to resolve parenting disputes. The lack of clarity or agreement about what constitutes the "ideal" or "best" parenting arrangement for children breeds conflict for many parents and confusion for the courts.

Modern jurisprudence has also changed the landscape for families in terms of financial arrangements, such that child support is not automatically given from father to mother. In addition, many states in the United States and other jurisdictions have now completely eliminated terms such as "custody" or "primary" parent and reference parenting time and parenting plans instead to underscore the child's need for involvement with both parents and gender equality in parenting ability.

In the last 50 years, the dissolution of marriage and the shifting roles of parents have altered the character of the family court and the rulings that are handed down. The divorce revolution phenomena have caused a flood of acrimonious litigation regarding child custody and parenting never before seen in courts. As a result, parents and courts need help finding solutions to co-parenting disputes so that children are shielded from the adverse impact of divorce.

Impact of Divorce on Children

In the late 1960s and early 1970s, as many countries moved towards more liberal divorce laws, there was a prevalent belief that it was better for children to go through the temporary struggle of their parent's separation than for them to live in a family where one or both parents were unhappy. Parents optimistically assumed that what was good for one or both parents was good for the children. If the marriage was dissolved because of long-standing conflict, then surely the children would benefit from ending the years of conflict.

Until the 1980s, mental health professionals appeared to be divided about whether divorce had long-lasting negative effects on children or whether it was, in fact, a benign or even positive experience for children. Divorce was viewed as a transition in children's lives—a period of stress and instability that required the child to use coping mechanisms and to make lifestyle and adjustments in order to reorganize his or her relationships with significant adults and assess his or her trust in others.

Richard Gardner (1970), a controversial figure known more for his ideas about parental alienation, wrote: "the child living with unhappily married parents more often gets into psychiatric difficulties than the one whose mismatched parents have been healthy and strong enough to sever the troubled relationship." Several clinical studies (Felner, 1984; Felner & Terre, 1987; Peterson et al., 1984; Rutter, 1981) lent support to this position, generally concluding that pre-divorce marital discord may be a more potent negative influence on children's subsequent adjustment than the separation or divorce itself. Rutter (1981) states that child separation from his/her intact family constitutes a potential cause for short-term distress but is of little direct importance as a cause of long-term disorder.

However, studies that portray divorce as a difficult transition period with relatively benign aftereffects for children are in the minority. Forty years into the divorce revolution, most social scientists' conclusion is that the national experiment with divorce has been a failure for the children. In the early 1970s, the general rule about divorce was that it was better to divorce than to subject children to the tension of a chronically unhappy marriage. In the late 1990s, most professionals (Biringen & Howard, 2002; Featherstone, 2004; Garon et al., 2000; Kelly, 2007; Lamb et al., 1997; Pruett et al., 2004) would have to admit that divorce is a transition that may benefit the adults involved but may not benefit the children.

The majority of research studies show that divorce is an extremely difficult period for children and conclude that the immediate and long-term negative outcomes can be very serious. Review of the literature (Stewart, 2001) on outcomes for children and parents who separate and divorce identify risk factors that contribute to negative outcomes. These risk factors include structural/environmental factors, such as changes in neighborhoods, residences and schools; relationship factors, such as loss of time with a parent or members of the extended family, changes in friendship networks, and the introduction of new adult partners; and emotional factors, such as maladjustment to the separation by one or both parent's decreased parenting ability, loss of one or both parents, and increased hostility between the parents. All of these risk factors contribute to a loss of predictability and routine for children, two factors which are critical to children's mental health and well-being.

Short-term and long-term studies (Amato, 1983; Emery, 2004; Kalter et al., 1989; Kelly & Emery, 2003; Stolberg et al., 1987; Wallerstein & Lewis, 1998) of children in separated and divorced families show that these risk factors contribute to a series of negative outcomes for children, including the following:

- poor academic achievement
- poor social relationships
- conduct and social difficulties
- emotional difficulties, including depression, fear, and anxiety
- substance abuse; and
- poor adult relationships.

We now know that children require more time than initially was thought to regain their emotional equilibrium after divorce, perhaps as long as 5 years (Lamb et al. 1997). In addition, the quality of the parent–child relationship, including the emotional tone and socialization style, is important to children's postdivorce adjustment (Whiteside, 1998), and children of divorce do best when their parents are functioning optimally (Kelly, 2007; Lamb et al., 1997; Whiteside, 1998). Recent findings indicate that it is not the frequency or quantity of contact that is important, but the quality of the contact involving children and both parents, that is the significant factor in children's post-separation adjustment and well-being (Cashmore et al., 2008; DeGarmo et al., 2008; Pruett et al., 2004).

Guidelines for Intervention With Families During and After Divorce

Fustenberg and Cherlin (1991) explained that a divorce is not simply one isolated event, but rather a transitional event. It initiates a series of multiple changes in roles and family structure that occur throughout the child's development into adulthood. For many children, the divorce is the first in a series of ongoing losses. For many families, particularly those characterized by ongoing hostility and conflict, professional intervention outside the adversarial legal system is necessary if the goal of protecting children and stabilizing families is to be achieved. Parenting Coordination is one such intervention that holds great promise for helping parents implement a successful dispute resolution framework to reduce parental conflict, minimize stress for the children, and encourage families, whenever possible, to resolve their own parenting issues without litigation.

Acknowledgments

I would like to thank the many people who helped me through the complexities and uncertainties that have surrounded a book on this subject. I owe my deepest gratitude to my muse and early reader—MBS—who helped me think through the organization and structure of the manuscript, persistently nudged me to finish the work, and made my personal life more sane when it was under threat from deadlines and my workaholic tendencies. I also wish to thank countless friends and colleagues who have supported me over the years with their interest, critiques, and love.

I also wish to thank the many students in my training courses and workshops who have helped me clarify early thoughts and ideas by their challenging comments and questions. I have been blessed by others who have given generously of their time, helping with the many aspects of reviewing, organizing, editing, and encouraging. To the following people my sincerest thanks: Terry Lambert, Ray McNeal, Nina Zollo, Edie Deane, Linda Fieldstone, Hugh Starnes, and Kathryn Kuehnle. I also want to thank my friends and colleagues from the Twelfth Judicial Circuit of Florida who have been a source of inspiration and creativity for many years.

Finally, I must thank my children who were patient and grumbled only a little when mom's schedule and work demands had to be considered at every turn in order to complete the writing project and still keep food in the house and clean clothes in the closets.

Parenting Coordination

A Practical Guide
for Family Law Professionals

1

Parenting Coordination: The Integrated Model

It is not necessary to understand things in order to argue about them.
—Beaumarchais

Since the idea of parenting coordination (PC) was first introduced in the early 1990s, several approaches to this type of alternative dispute resolution process have emerged. For example, some areas have a "mediator/arbitrator" model where the parenting coordinator may have broad authority to arbitrate (or ultimately decide) disputes between parents. Another model is more of a pseudo-therapeutic model where "therapy" interventions are more a part of the process (AFCC Task Force Report, 2005; Kirkland, 2008). As parenting coordination becomes more prevalent across the globe, many other models are likely to emerge.

This book details a new "integrated model" of parenting coordination built upon research and decades of experience with other models of alternative dispute resolution. The integrated model incorporates professional training and experience in the areas of mental health, evaluation, mediation, education, and family law. This model integrates specific professional skills from each of these areas and applies the integrated skill set to the parenting coordination role. In this chapter, the skills needed from each of the professional areas will be described along with an outline for how to apply the integrated skill set to varying responsibilities of parenting coordinators. This chapter will also highlight the similarities and differences of the parenting coordinator role and other professional roles, emphasize potential pitfalls when role definition and boundaries become blurred, and provide case examples of the integrated model of parenting coordination at work. In subsequent chapters, the roles and skills of parenting coordination will be described in more depth to provide the necessary guidelines and implications for parenting coordinator practice.

1

The parenting coordinator must have skills and experience in mental health, mediation, evaluation, education, case management, and family law and learn how to professionally blend these skills within the parenting coordinator role in order to help parents build the necessary framework to help families get out of the crucible of conflict and stay out. The process of parenting coordination offers parents an opportunity to learn and practice the skills and "tools" they need to resolve their conflicts and avoid perpetuating polarizing, embittered battles. Some of the tools parents need include legal and mental health knowledge, an appraisal of possible outcomes of their parenting dispute were it to go to court, a dose of hope that they can disengage from positions of entrenched hostility, and encouragement to move beyond their destructive patterns of behavior.

In current family law systems, high-conflict families do not have ready access to the "tools" they need to resolve their parenting disputes efficiently and effectively. High-conflict parents often feel misunderstood, victimized, unfairly treated, and/or helpless in resolving conflicts with their co-parent. The often polarizing impact of an adversarial family court system (Stolz & Ney, 2002) also leaves parents feeling more entrenched in bitterness, resentment, and hostility.

While all individuals live within systems and are influenced by other individuals and other factors within the same system, individuals caught in high conflict are often operating simultaneously within several dysfunctional systems. Examples of these systems include family systems, employment systems, legal systems, education systems, and a myriad of others. Not only do they feel "trapped" within a dysfunctional relationship with the other parent, but they may also feel "caught" in a court system and legal process that may be viewed as adding to the problem rather than being a source of help. What often comes as a surprise to the parent who is engaged in a high-conflict relationship with their co-parent is the realization that the professionals they count on to assist and work with them, such as attorneys, mediators, judges, mental health professionals, and guardians ad litem, have limits on the scope of their authority, knowledge, experience, and ability.

Table 1.1 below delineates the role of professionals who are commonly involved in family law cases and compares their level of authority, accessibility, and knowledge. Parenting coordination often provides more authority, access, and knowledge in areas most helpful in resolving high-conflict parenting disputes.

TABLE 1.1   Professionals in Family Law Cases

	Authority	Accessibility	Mental Health Knowledge	Legal Knowledge
Judge	Yes	Some	No	Yes
Attorney	No	Yes	No	Yes
Mediator	No	Yes	Maybe	Yes, if Atty. Some, if other professional
Guardian ad Litem	Some	Yes	Maybe	Maybe
Therapist	No	Yes	Yes	No
Parenting Coordinator	Yes	Yes	Yes	Yes

PROFESSIONAL SKILLS FOR THE PARENTING COORDINATOR

The parenting coordinator must acquire and integrate skills from different professional areas and utilize the skills within the defined role of parenting coordination in order to help parents develop and practice the "tools" they need for constructive co-parenting. The integrated skill set for the parenting coordinator comes primarily from the following professional fields:

- Mental Health
- Evaluation
- Mediation
- Education
- Case Management
- Domestic Relations (Family) Law

Psychologists and other mental health providers are trained to understand human beings, their interactions, and how best to respond in both "normal" and "abnormal" circumstances. This knowledge, along with the knowledge of how individuals function within systems, provides the basis for the *mental health skills* needed and allows for interventions not typically afforded by the family court system. Mental health training helps the parenting coordinator to understand behaviors and reactions of adults and children when the family system is in flux and under stress. Additionally, psychology provides a foundation for understanding: normal and abnormal development, normal and abnormal behavior and thought patterns, traits or symptoms that may indicate a mental illness, and/or needs for specialized services. Many parenting coordinators will have mental health knowledge and training by virtue of their degree or license, but others may not. If a parenting coordinator does not have the requisite knowledge in child development, human behaviors, family systems, and emotional functioning, additional training in these areas must be acquired in order to integrate the basic mental health skills necessary for parenting coordination.

In addition to mental health skills, *evaluation skills* are needed. Evaluation skills include identification of relevant factors within each individual and the family, articulation of desired outcome or goals, and assessment of available resources. The parenting coordinator may find it helpful to borrow a business model to acquire the information they need to develop an effective intervention strategy. For example, parenting coordinators could start with a SWOT analysis. SWOT is an acronym for strengths, weaknesses, opportunities, and threats. Applied to parenting coordination work, a parenting coordinator needs to identify the parents' or families' strengths, weaknesses, opportunities, and threats. This type of analysis will allow the parenting coordinator to evaluate strengths in parents and the family system, individual and family needs for professional assistance (parent surrogates, education programs, mental health providers, etc.), the resources that are available to the family, and risk factors for parents and children. Risk factors for parents and children might include threats of physical harm, imbalance of power and control between the parents, a parent's mental illness, or a parent's substance abuse and dependence. Evaluating all of these variables, along with economic and social factors, will help the parenting coordinator develop a strategy for intervention that will allow the parenting coordination process to work effectively and efficiently and help parents build a sound framework to resolve disputes.

Mediation skills are needed to assist the parenting coordinator in helping parents who may have divergent positions and interests. Family law mediation has traditionally been a process by which two adults, with the assistance of a neutral professional, attempt to reach a consensual settlement of issues relating to their marriage, separation, or divorce. Children have largely been absent from mediation processes in postseparation parenting disputes (Moloney & McIntosh, 2004), although there are some professionals who advocate for including children in the process (McIntosh, Long, & Moloney, 2004) and others who combine therapy with mediation (Jacobs & Jaffe, 2010). Regardless of the model, mediation skills are needed and are often referred to as "facilitation" or "conciliation" tools in parenting coordination. These skills are invaluable in helping parents identify and build upon common interests between them, fostering consensus building strategies, and developing a parenting plan that takes into account everyone's (particularly the children's) needs.

As an *educator*, the parenting coordinator provides parents with the knowledge, "tools," and strategies they need to understand and assess their own personal needs and their children's social, emotional, intellectual, and physical needs. Parenting is generally perceived as a continuous process starting before parenthood and continuing through birth and school to grandparenthood. Children's needs change as they grow and mature and it is important for parents to understand a child's current and future needs. Parents often need education and information about child development, the effects of separation and divorce on children and families, the "realities" of the legal system, their role in continuing the conflict, viable alternatives to resolving entrenched conflict without litigation, and more effective means of communicating with their co-parent and with their children. Parenting coordination may provide this education and information directly or through other appropriate resources. It is often helpful to direct parents to books relevant to the children's growth and developmental needs, as well as books on moving beyond entrenched conflict. There may also be community programs, available at low cost, which offer an alternative method for parents to obtain information and education regarding parenting and co-parenting.

There are also essential *management skills* which need to be integrated into the parenting coordination skill set. They include time management skills, writing skills, planning skills, coaching, communication, and conflict management. Parenting coordinators work to help parents resolve problems as they arise. While this is a critical function in the parenting coordinator role, it may be even more important to prevent problems if at all possible. There is a difference between reactive management, which solves problems as they occur, and predictive management, which tries to prevent many problems from arising in the first place. A parenting coordinator needs both reactive and predictive management skills. Reactive management skills enable the parenting coordinator to take decisive and quick action, identify the root cause of problems, be creative and innovative in finding solutions to problems, and stay calm and in control in the midst of a "crisis."

Predictive management focuses on reducing the number of problems that require reactive management. A parenting coordinator needs to have skills that allow them to be thoughtful and analytic; not go chasing after the current panic; be more aware of the important than the merely urgent issues; be able to identify patterns in data and patterns of failures; focus on "why" something went wrong, in addition to "what" can be done to fix it; and be able to keep the big picture in mind when working through the details. The parenting coordinator must remain objective and neutral in order to identify the conditions that lead to ongoing parental conflict and to implement procedures that reduce or eliminate the sources of conflict. Rather than getting lost in the immediate problem, they are able to relate current conditions to earlier information and predict when problems might arise. The more problems that can be prevented through predictive management, the fewer resources will need to be spent on reacting to problems that have arisen. Predictive management does not replace reactive management, but it reduces the need for it.

Domestic relations (or family law) skills include basic knowledge about applicable laws and rules which apply to parents who are separated, divorced, or never married who are involved in parenting disputes. This knowledge encompasses when and how to communicate with the court, limits on confidentiality, ethical obligations of legal professionals, financial impact when time-sharing arrangements change, meaning of court orders and pleadings, and the legal obligations required in the parenting coordination role.

The *Integrated Model of Parenting Coordination* incorporates mental health, mediation, education, evaluation, management, and family law skills within the framework of a court-ordered appointment.

NAVIGATING A NEW PARENTING JOURNEY

The prospect of change presents emotional risks and frightening feelings, particularly when something as valued and precious as one's children are concerned. Most individuals are reluctant to embark on a journey fraught with change without knowledge of where they are going, how to get there, or the perils they are likely to encounter along the way. Learning to co-parent after separation and divorce or after a period of single parenting is a new journey for most people, and it is one which most individuals are ill-prepared to take. Parenting coordination gives parents, children, and families a GPS (Guidance for Parenting System) for this journey. Parents are offered the opportunity to develop and maintain a new system for interactions and behaviors that take into account the myriad of changes that occur within families, whether through separation or divorce, re-entry of a parent into a child's life, or change in romantic partner relationship. Parenting coordination offers a chance for all family members to find security, stability, and predictability in new patterns of thought, emotion, and behavior.

INTEGRATED SKILL SET FOR PARENTING COORDINATION

For the reasons previously outlined, it is clear that parenting coordinators need a broad knowledge base, refined skills, and the ability to apply their knowledge and skills in an adaptive and creative fashion in order to be most effective in working with the complexities of families characterized by high conflict. Therefore, the integrated skill set includes:

Knowledge

- Knowledge of human beings and their reactions in both "normal" and "abnormal" circumstances
- Knowledge of family systems and typical responses when those systems are in flux or under stress
- Knowledge of child development needs
- Knowledge of parenting styles and the impact on children
- Knowledge of the impact of separation/divorce on children and families
- Knowledge of intervention strategies to be most effective with people who are locked in conflict and under stress
- Knowledge of community resources available to assist the family
- Knowledge and recognition of behaviors or symptoms that indicate mental illness, substance abuse or dependence
- Knowledge of applicable laws and rules for domestic relations cases or civil cases involving parenting disputes
- Knowledge of applicable court procedures and rules of professional conduct
- Knowledge of domestic violence and the impact on children and families

Ability

- Ability to evaluate the parents' or families' strengths, weaknesses, opportunities, and threats
- Ability to evaluate risk factors for parents or children including risk for physical harm or imbalance of power and control
- Ability to evaluate the parents' and family resources

▪ Ability to foster consensus between parents
▪ Ability to teach parents the "tools" and strategies they need to understand and assess their own and their children's changing needs
▪ Ability to teach effective listening and communication skills
▪ Ability to remain calm in the midst of "crisis"
▪ Ability to anticipate where problems in the parenting system are likely to arise
▪ Ability to remain objective and neutral
▪ Ability to observe patterns of interactions and behaviors that predict successful versus unsuccessful resolution of parenting disputes
▪ Ability to be creative and innovative in finding solutions
▪ Ability to motivate individuals who are frightened and confused
▪ Ability to instill hope
▪ Ability to promote change and encourage parents to focus on the children
▪ Ability to maintain good boundaries within the professional role of parenting coordinator
▪ Ability to know when your services are doing more harm than good
▪ Ability to establish rapport and a trusting relationship

Skills

▪ Conflict resolution and negotiation skills to help parents identify and build upon common interests between them
▪ Time management skills
▪ Writing skills
▪ Planning skills
▪ Coaching skills

THE INTEGRATED SKILL SET APPLIED
TO PARENTING COORDINATION

Parenting coordination demands a comprehensive understanding of the complex nature of interpersonal variables for all families, the often polarizing impact of an adversarial legal system, and the unique characteristics of high-conflict parents and their children who are caught in a crucible of conflict. The broad range of knowledge and abilities outlined above plus experience working with individuals and families caught in conflict, both within and outside of the court system, lends an invaluable tool to the parenting coordinator and provides the foundation for parenting coordination work.

One of the primary roles for a parenting coordinator is to serve as a monitor for the children's best interests, which may be characterized as the "eyes and ears of the court" unless the process has been deemed confidential. The parenting coordinator serves to ensure that the children are able to maintain frequent, emotionally safe access to both parents (unless determined to be inappropriate) and to have a loving relationship with both parents without fear of reprisal or adverse consequences. The parenting coordinator also helps parents identify problematic patterns of thinking, reacting, and behaving and assists them in developing constructive strategies for resolving conflict. Ultimately, a parenting coordinator's role is to help parents and/or guardians learn the tools and skills necessary to co-parent independently and effectively without the need for oversight or intervention from the court.

The issues common to custody disputes are generally the focus of the parenting coordination work. It is important for the parenting coordinator to consider issues such as stability and predictability for children. This may include the type of parenting plan arrangements that will most likely foster a stable environment for the children and reduce disruption for the family. The parenting coordinator must recognize the parent–child connection and protect the opportunities for the child to maintain an uninterrupted and loving relationship with a parent and parent figures. The parenting coordinator is also responsible for assisting the family in setting realistic goals for their children and for their co-parenting relationship. A parenting coordinator may determine that working cooperatively as a parenting team is not viable or advisable and may suggest, as an alternative, a parallel or disengaged co-parenting model. These models, or types of co-parenting relationships, will be described in more detail in subsequent chapters.

The parenting coordinator must also be aware of a child's unique needs and address whether either or both parents are attuned sufficiently to the child's specific challenges. The parenting coordinator must be mindful of children's education, sibling relationships, parent's physical and emotional health, parents' work schedules, parent's finances, and styles of parenting and discipline. The parenting coordinator should not make value judgments about which parenting style is better, but focus on the "goodness of fit" between each parenting style and the child. The parenting coordinator must be aware of how each parent views the children's relationship with the other parent and each parent's willingness to foster a healthy emotional bond between their child and the other parent.

The parenting coordinator is not an advocate for either parent and must remain neutral and unbiased toward either parent. The parenting coordinator is not neutral when it comes to the children and strives to maintain awareness or anticipate when the children are at risk for physical or mental harm. Parenting coordinators must adhere to mandatory reporting laws in instances of abuse and neglect regardless of their professional discipline.

The parenting coordinator also attends to the social support systems for the children and the parents, such as grandparents, other relatives, or friends. These supports may have a bigger or smaller role in the child's life at one home versus another and supports may help enhance a parent's relationship with the child, particularly if a parent has a deficit or disability. If one or more family members need additional professional or social support to help build a more constructive framework for stabilizing the family unit, the parenting coordinator is expected to identify resources for these services and make appropriate referrals. Such services might include parenting classes; therapy for the children; therapy for the parent; legal consultation; or medical intervention. Understanding the individual and family needs helps the parenting coordinator make appropriate referrals at appropriate times.

Parenting coordinators should review information relevant to the family they are working with as part of collecting data and planning intervention strategies. Such information might include the parenting plan, school records, mental health records, legal pleadings, and investigative reports in an effort to inform the parenting coordination process. If a custody evaluation or parenting plan evaluation preceded the appointment of a parenting coordinator, these evaluations often provide very useful background information regarding a family and the history of their conflicts.

Religious background and beliefs also play a role in parenting and the parenting coordinator must be aware of each parent's belief system and practice of observance in order to assist the parties in resolving differences while maintaining a focus on the needs of the child. The parenting coordinator must guard against imposing his or her values onto the assessment of the parents' values or cultural beliefs. The parenting coordinator should see himself or herself as a facilitator for the parties in developing and maintaining a functional co-parenting relationship.

The parenting coordinator's advocacy for children is guided by the parenting plan, or custodial arrangement, as set forth by the court order or parents' agreement. In the *integrated model* of parenting coordination, the parenting coordinator works primarily with the parents, although there are some circumstances when it is desirable for the parenting coordinator to meet with the children and/or other members of the family unit. In other sections of the book, the rationale, concerns, advantages, and disadvantages of including children and other family members in the parenting coordination process will be discussed.

SIMILARITIES AND DIFFERENCES BETWEEN PARENTING COORDINATOR ROLE AND OTHER PROFESSIONAL ROLES

There are some basic similarities between mental health professionals, child custody (or parenting plan) evaluators, mediators, educators, and family law professionals. For example, all use skills to establish rapport and trust with the individuals with whom they are working. All of these professional roles involve data collection from which opinions are formulated, and each strives to communicate effectively when working toward a common goal or interest. In addition, each role has guidelines or standards which guide the professional in their work (see Table 1.2).

Some of the professional roles will be directed by a court order, such as parenting coordination, custody (parenting plan) evaluator, guardian ad litem, and mediation. Other professional roles will involve a private contractual arrangement between the professional and the person seeking services, such as mental health professionals, attorneys, and educators.

Some of these professional roles require an unbiased approach toward any individual or particular outcome where other roles specifically demand that the professional be an "advocate" for their client and their client's desired outcome. Some of the professional roles demand confidentiality and other roles prohibit it. The challenge for parenting coordinators usually does not come from the similarities between a parenting coordination role and other professional roles, but more with the differences between the roles and how and when those differences come into play.

Parenting coordinators should not establish more than one professional relationship with the parents or children. The role of a parenting coordinator is distinct from any other professional relationship, and parenting coordinators should not accept any other professional role, including mental health provider, custody (parenting plan) evaluator, mediator, attorney, guardian ad litem, or visitation supervisor with the

TABLE 1.2 Professional Role Comparison Chart

	Therapist	Mediator	Guardian ad Litem	Judge	PC	Educator	Attorney	Evaluator
Uses educational material	May	No	No	No	Yes	Yes	No	No
Monitors compliance to court order/settlement	No	No	May	No	Yes	No	No	No
Assesses veracity of parental allegations	May	No	Yes	Yes	Yes	No	May	Yes
Ensures parental access to the child, as appropriate	No	No	Yes	Yes	Yes	No	Yes	No
Requests outside services when needed	No	No	May	No	Yes	No	Yes	No
Meets with the child	Yes	No	Yes	No	May	Yes	May	Yes
Coordinates with all processionals involved in the case	No	No	Yes	No	Yes	No	Yes	No
Reports impasses and agreements to court/attorneys	No	Yes	No	No	Yes	No	Yes	No
May testify in the child's best interest	If court-ordered	No	Yes	No	If court-ordered	No	No	Yes
Temporarily arbitrates parental impasses	No	No	No	No	Yes	No	Yes	No
Writes court orders	No	No	No	Yes	Yes	No	Yes	No
Confidential process	Yes	Yes	No	No	No	No	Yes	No
Includes significant others as needed	Yes	No	Yes	No	May	May	No	Yes
Teaches conflict resolution skills	May	No	No	No	Yes	Yes	No	No
Requires a court order of appointment	No	May	Yes	Yes	Yes	No	No	Yes

parents or children. A parenting coordinator should not accept the role of parenting coordinator if there has been a prior professional relationship with either parent or the children.

In addition to avoiding a dual professional role with parents or children, it is important to understand where parenting coordination and other professional roles may overlap. For example, parenting coordination, like child custody (parenting plan) evaluations and mediation, generally operate under a court order which specifies the service to be provided and the expectations of the professional who is appointed to provide the service. However, the expectations and professional guidelines for each of these "court-appointed" roles differ greatly. For example, parenting coordination services occur over an extended period of time (i.e., 1 to 2 years), whereas mediation and custody evaluations are generally limited to days or months. Parenting coordination and custody (parenting plan) evaluations are usually not confidential, with some notable exceptions (e.g., Florida Statute 61.125). Mediation is almost always confidential (unless the parties agree otherwise) and parties have a right to have their attorneys present during the mediation process. Attorneys are generally not present during parenting coordination or child custody (parenting plan) evaluations.

Even within court-appointed roles, there is potential for confusion. A parenting coordinator and a custody (parenting plan) evaluator are expected to provide information to the court, but the extent and type of information to be provided is very different. For example, within the professional role of parenting coordination, a parenting coordinator may "evaluate" the strengths and weaknesses of a parent or family system, but the scope and process of this "evaluation" is not the same as that of a "custody" or parenting plan evaluator. A child custody evaluator is often appointed by the court when parents have filed for dissolution of marriage and are unable to reach an agreement regarding the specific time-sharing or decision-making issues involved in parenting their children. The process for a court-appointed custody (parenting plan) evaluation is defined by industry standards or guidelines (i.e., APA Guidelines for Child Custody Evaluations in Family Law Proceedings, 2009; AFCC Model Standards of Practice for Child Custody Evaluations, 2006; American Academy of Child & Adolescent Psychiatry Practice Parameters for Child Custody Evaluation, 1997; American Psychology-Law Society Specialty Guidelines for Forensic Psychologist, 1991) which set forth the type of information to be collected and the manner in which it is collected and reported. A custody evaluator is generally expected to provide specific recommendations regarding custody, time-sharing, and parental responsibility arrangements that best suit a particular family's needs, whereas in most jurisdictions, parenting coordinators are specifically prohibited from rendering such an opinion to the court. While both the parenting coordinator and the child custody evaluator are essentially unbiased data collectors and both may be court-appointed roles, there are substantial differences between the two professional roles.

Another area of potential confusion lies in understanding where the roles of parenting coordinator and mental health professional may intersect. Psychologists and other mental health professionals are trained to "diagnose" symptoms or conditions and to determine an appropriate course of treatment for their patient. Most psychologists are also trained to administer and interpret psychological tests or instruments to aid in identifying the presence or absence of a mental illness or to assess parenting strengths/weaknesses. While this type of information may be quite useful for the parenting coordinator, it is not appropriate for the parenting coordinator to provide "diagnostic" services or psychotherapy to their parenting coordination client even if they are trained to do so. This would constitute a "dual professional role" (e.g., APA Ethical Principles of Psychologists and Code of Conduct, 2002) for the parenting coordinator, which is ethically prohibited by most professional guidelines. A psychologist or mental health professional providing diagnostic testing or evaluation and/or psychotherapy is serving in a clinical or therapeutic role which carries with it certain expectations, such as confidentiality and privileged communication between the client and professional as well as an expectation of advocacy from the professional. Even if not expressly prohibited by statute or guideline, it is generally not a good idea for parenting coordinators to blur the boundaries between a clinical role as therapist or counselor and a court-ordered or forensic role as parenting coordinator.

The parenting coordinator, parenting educator, and mediator all provide information to parents to help them arrive at a resolution to their disagreements. However, the type of information provided differs in each of these professional roles. For example, a parenting coordinator and an educator may provide parents with knowledge about child development, children's changing needs, adult's needs, and what to expect as families evolve over time. Mediators do not typically provide this type of information (American Arbitration Association, American Bar Association's Section of Dispute Resolution, & Association for Conflict Resolution et al., 2005), but do offer creative solutions for areas of concern and parenting disputes just as parenting coordinators and parenting educators would do. All of these roles require an unbiased professional stance, but a mediator is neutral and impartial toward the parties and the outcome of the process. A parenting coordinator must be neutral and unbiased toward either parent, but not impartial regarding children's best interests since the parenting coordinator generally serves as an advocate for the children's best interests.

PRIMARY RESPONSIBILITIES OF A PARENTING COORDINATOR IN THE INTEGRATED MODEL

- Start with perceived needs of the parent
- Identify common interests between parents
- Find strategies of intervention that are likely to be effective
- Increase parents' competence in parenting skills and capacity
- Remind parents of children's rights
- Do follow-up to determine adjustment and well-being of all family members
- Prepare parents for possibility that interventions will not work all the time
- Prepare parents for difficulty in implementing plan and tools for handling challenges
- Provide strong primary prevention opportunities
- Build trust over time
- Model constructive communication and conflict resolution techniques
- Maintain clear boundaries with parents and all professionals

Table 1.3 illustrates how parenting coordination responsibilities differ from other professional roles in the integrated model.

When the parenting coordination process is clearly defined and practiced in accordance with national guidelines, such as the *Guidelines for Parenting Coordination* (AFCC Task Force on Parenting Coordination, 2005), and with applicable laws and rules of procedure which vary depending on the state, province, or jurisdiction, practitioners can facilitate resolution of child-focused issues out of court while maintaining parents' rights. However, when the parenting coordination process is practiced without clear parameters, the results can be confusing, inconsistent, and potentially dangerous. It is essential for parenting coordinators to set and maintain clear boundaries of role, responsibility, and intervention. While parenting coordination may be fraught with ethical challenges and potential abuse of power without clear ethical guidelines and standards of practice, the potential benefits far outweigh the risks for families caught in the crucible of conflict. Statutes, rules, and research are needed to guide this new and exciting alternative dispute resolution process.

TABLE 1.3 Comparison of Professional Roles and Responsibilities

	Parenting Coordination	Mediation	Psychotherapy or Counseling	Custody or Parenting Plan Evaluation
Objective or unbiased Prof.	Yes	Yes	Yes	Yes
Neutral Prof.	No	Yes	No	No
Communication admissible	Yes	No*	No, party consent required	Yes
Party confidentiality	No*	Yes*	Yes	No
Standards of practice	Yes	Yes	Yes	Yes
Decision-making	Parties or PC	Parties decide	Yes	No
Prof. recommendations	Yes	No*	Yes	Yes
Prof. provides information	Yes	Yes	Yes	Yes
Prof. facilitates negotiation	Yes	Yes	Yes	No
Prof. recommendation to court	Yes	No	No	Yes
Prof. is advocate for	Children	Mediation process	Health	Children
Insurance reimbursement	No	No	Yes	No
Mental health treatment	No	No	Yes	No
Records retention obligation	Yes	No	Yes	Yes
Types of parties	High conflict	All	All	All
Nature of issues to be addressed	Parenting issues	Any	Any	Time-sharing, parenting
Timing for referral	Pre/post divorce	Pre/post divorce	Pre/post divorce	Pre/post divorce
Participation of attorneys	Not directly	Parties have right	No	No
Prof. recommendations to party	Yes	No, may offer options	Yes	Yes

	Parenting Coordination	Mediation	Psychotherapy or Counseling	Custody or Parenting Plan Evaluation
Immunity-statutory protection	No	Yes, if court-ordered	No	Limited
Malpractice insurance available	Yes	Yes	Yes	Yes
Voluntary or court-ordered	Yes	Yes	Yes	Yes
Prof. consults with others	Yes	Rarely, except attorneys	Maybe	Yes

KEY: Prof., Professional; Psy, Psychology.

*If court-ordered or under agreement.

2

Parenting Coordination Procedures

I dwell in Possibility—
A fairer House than Prose—
More numerous of Windows—
Superior—for Doors
—Emily Dickinson (No. 657)

The procedures utilized in parenting coordination vary widely depending on the laws and structure of the laws in different geographic regions. In the previous chapter, the *Integrated Model of Parenting Coordination* was described. This model primarily refers to use of a parenting coordinator after the court has entered either a temporary or permanent time-sharing plan or custody arrangement for parents and their children.

WHEN DOES A PARENTING COORDINATOR GET INVOLVED WITH A FAMILY?

Identification of High-Conflict Cases

It is not essential that families be engaged in "high-conflict" behaviors in order to use parenting coordination services, but, generally, families that are able to resolve conflict constructively on their own utilize other forms of dispute resolution. A parenting coordinator often becomes involved when parents have been unable to successfully implement their parenting plan or previously agreed upon time-sharing and custody arrangement. Parents may recognize their need for help or they may be referred to parenting coordination by their attorneys, the court, mental-health professionals, mediators, or others who are familiar with parenting coordination. Parenting coordination, an alternative dispute resolution process, is designed to help families who are identified as high conflict because their pattern of interaction is characterized by chronic hostility and acrimony.

19

Janet Johnston (1994) identified three dimensions of high-conflict divorce: domain, tactics, and attitude. Disagreements over a series of divorce issues such as financial support, property division, custody, access to the children, and values and methods of child rearing are what she called the "domain" dimension. Divorcing couples often try to resolve disagreements, formally or informally, using the following "tactics": avoiding each other and the issues, verbal reasoning, verbal aggression, physical coercion and physical aggression or through the use of an attorney, mediation, or litigation. Attitude is the degree of negative emotional feeling or hostility directed by divorcing parties toward each other that may be overtly or covertly expressed.

Johnston's research suggests that the duration and developing pattern of each dimension helps identify conflict as either normal or pathological. The important factors to consider are the extent to which post-separation or post-marital hostility decreases the capacity for co-parental cooperation regarding the needs of the children. Factors associated with high-conflict co-parenting patterns include frequent arguments, undermining and sabotage of the other parent's role as a parent, and the absence of frequent attempts to communicate and co-ordinate with the other parent with respect to the children.

Characteristics of high-conflict families may include the following:

- Anger and distrust which results in difficulty communicating about the children
- Extreme distortion in the reporting of past events by each parent
- Children are denied emotional and/or physical access to a parent, or severely limited parental contact
- Children are denied access to extended family members
- Allegations that children are refusing to see other parent
- Constant disputes about unmeasurable or unprovable items
- Interference or refusal of access to information about children's health, education and welfare
- A parent withholds support payments
- High rate of re-litigation, especially concerning nonlegal issues
- Physical threats and assaults made by either or both parents
- Frequent change in lawyers
- Unsuccessful mediation

The characteristics of high-conflict families used by professionals who refer parents to this process are not necessarily the same as characteristics seen through the eyes of children who are being impacted by their parent's conflict (Stewart, 2001). Children characterize high conflict as:

- a parent refusing to speak with the other when children are picked up or dropped off
- a parent refusing to open the door to the other parent
- parents arguing violently in the presence of the children
- parents insisting that they (the children) carry verbal or written communications between homes about late support payments or missed visits
- parents' physically assaulting each other in the child's presence

The impact of exposure to these behaviors and interactions by parents warrant intervention for children as early on in the separation and divorce process as possible, because of the potential for long-term emotional damage.

Early Intervention

Many jurisdictions and court systems have developed early intervention programs to help families going through traumatic transitions in an effort to minimize conflict, promote the well-being of children, conserve family resources, encourage alternate dispute resolution, and reduce the significant burden on trial courts. The goal of early intervention programs is to allow for identification of issues in a timely fashion so that referrals for appropriate services may be made. Providing support to parents and families throughout the process of divorce or parenting dispute resolution makes more efficient use of court resources through docket control and case management thereby conserving the use of the court for those issues and cases that are not otherwise resolvable. Early identification and intervention programs allow for coordination with other dockets involving related family matters, such as Unified Family Court, and for the court to enter orders on procedural matters, and consensual orders on substantive matters.

Parenting coordinators may become involved with a family prior to a final dissolution of marriage or, in circumstances where parents never married, at the outset of a parenting dispute. For most families, the court will establish a "temporary" time-sharing or custody arrangement relatively early in the process of separation. Parenting coordinators can become involved without court intervention, although there are some potential pitfalls when parenting coordination is not court ordered, which will be considered in a later chapter. In situations where the court is not involved, parents may have developed a time-sharing arrangement or parenting plan on their own or they may have achieved an agreement through mediation but still may be having difficulty consistently implementing the plan.

In the initial stage of the divorce process, the court may not have entered an order, either temporary or permanent, setting out the nature and extent of the contact between the parents and children and/or division of parental responsibilities. Until the court has entered such an order, the parenting coordinator may be asked to help the parents devise a contact plan that will reduce the conflict to which the children are exposed and assist the court in finding a workable, temporary time-sharing and decision-making parenting plan that accommodates the needs and abilities of the parents and children.

If the parenting coordinator is asked to help parents develop a time-sharing arrangement and to craft a parenting plan, they are in a role more akin to a mediator or parenting plan (custody) evaluator. Using parenting coordinators in this manner is controversial in many professional arenas because of the potential for the parenting coordinator to be in a dual professional role with unclear parameters for the scope of their work. A "dual role," as mentioned in Chapter 1, is prohibited by most professional ethics (e.g., American Psychological Association, 2002; American Bar Association, 2002) and standards of practice. Another concern arises when parenting coordinators are asked to develop parenting plans with little or no guidance from the courts. This involves parent's rights. For example, individuals who are divorcing or have a parenting dispute are entitled to have their issues heard by the court and decided by a judge. The expectation is that the court would hear the issue and make a decision based on the evidence presented. The court's deferring the issue or decision to another person may be considered an inappropriate delegation of judicial authority and a potential violation of a parent's rights.

Proponents of early involvement of parenting coordinators suggest that a parenting coordinator may be the professional best suited to help parents create a parenting plan. This may be due to their more detailed familiarity with the parents, the children and their needs, and the ability to take more time to work with parents to create a parenting plan unique to their family and their children's needs. When courts, attorneys, or parents involve a parenting coordinator early in the process, the goal is to prevent parents from becoming bitterly entrenched in polarized positions. The aim is to help parents focus on developing a parenting plan that serves their children's best interests without the need to "prove" that they are the "best" parent as they might be expected to do in court. Although the emotional sting of the separation or divorce is still fresh and vulnerabilities are high, a parenting coordinator works to develop a trusting relationship with both parents and offers assistance in prioritizing their goals regarding their children. During the initial phases of divorce, parents and children are in a state of emotional upheaval and uncertainty about the future. Without objective and informed guidance, parents may become increasingly frightened and defensive as they attempt to deal with the family law system, mend the hurts of their own unrealized and broken dreams, and watch their children suffer.

Regardless of when a parenting coordinator becomes involved, most agree that any intervention that helps prevent or lessen the development of more hostility and bitterness between parents to which their children may be exposed is a desirable goal. As family law courts develop procedures to accomplish this goal, there is increasing interest in providing services and support early in the divorce process.

The parenting coordinator's role is always active and specifically focused on helping parents work together for the benefit of the children. When a parenting plan or custody arrangement has been agreed upon by the parents and/or ordered by the court, the parenting coordinator's role is to help parents *implement* their plan and to *minimize the conflict* to which the children are exposed because of unresolved differences and hostilities between the parties.

The goals of parenting coordination are as follows:

- Establish trust and rapport with parents
- Assist parents in making temporary, and sometimes permanent, decisions regarding their children
- Monitor parenting time
- Teach parents communication skills, principles of child development, and children's issues
- Maintain communication between parents by serving, if necessary, as a conduit for information
- Facilitate the ability of both parents to maintain ongoing relationships with the children
- Make recommendations to parents and to the Court, unless otherwise prohibited by law or court order, regarding modification of the parenting plan to reduce inter-parental conflict
- Facilitate dispute resolution between the parties concerning parenting issues
- Identify parenting issues over which there is an impasse and notify the Court if the parenting coordinator is unable to help parents resolve the impasse
- Refer parents to an appropriate parent education course or program as needed
- Refer the parents and/or children for therapeutic intervention as needed

HOW DOES A PARENTING COORDINATOR GET INVOLVED?

In many instances, the initial notification that a family is requesting (or ordered to) parenting coordination services occurs when the parenting coordinator receives a copy of the order of referral directly from the court. Prior to the order of referral, the parenting coordinator may receive an inquiry from parents, attorneys, or the court to determine if the parenting coordinator is available and willing to serve the family being referred and the parenting coordinator's fees. The appropriate time for each parent or their attorney to make sure the parenting coordinator does not have a professional conflict of interest and that the parenting coordinator's fees are affordable for the parents is prior to appointment of the parenting coordinator. (See Chapter 10 for additional information on ethics for parenting coordinators.) In regions of the country that do not require court orders, there may be a stipulated agreement between the parents to use a parenting coordinator. This agreement may be drafted by the parents or their attorneys. Regions that have established parenting coordination programs or court administered programs may maintain a list of qualified or trained parenting coordinators from which the court, attorneys, or parties may select. Notification of appointment may come from the Court, parents, or their attorneys.

Prior to commencement of the parenting coordinator process, it is important for the parenting coordinator to obtain a copy of the Court Order or Stipulated Agreement defining the scope of services to be rendered and the parameters or authority the parenting coordinator may utilize.

Court Order of Referral or Stipulated Agreement

For parenting coordination cases where services are court ordered, the court order of referral (COR) is the document that defines the authority and scope of the service from a legal perspective. There are several examples of court orders of referral in Appendix A which illustrate the vast differences in the parenting coordinator process depending upon the state, province, municipality, or jurisdiction in which it occurs. The COR identifies the parties, the minor children, counsel (if applicable), and the person who is to serve as the parenting coordinator along with contact information for all.

The COR also defines children's and a parent's rights as well as expectations for parents. For example, orders may indicate that the parenting coordinator is to assist the parties and their children in resolving any unresolved conflict by helping the parents learn strategies for problem solving and conflict reduction. The order may also authorize the parenting coordinator to act as a decision maker (arbitrator) with respect to parenting issues, particularly with respect to time-sharing and assurance that parenting time occurs. The expectation is that parents will employ the strategies learned in the parenting coordinator process to resolve their current and future parenting disputes.

Fees

The COR should address expenses associated with the parenting coordinator's service and how these expenses are to be divided between the parents. The order may direct the parenting coordinator not to proceed until he/she is satisfied with the terms and conditions of the payment for services and the procedure for notifying the court in the event of nonpayment.

Term of Appointment

The COR should specify the term of the parenting coordinator appointment. The length of time the parenting coordinator is to serve varies widely depending upon the parenting coordinator model, process, and laws or rules that authorize the court to order parents to parenting coordination. Many courts will limit the term to 1 or 2 years and may require a written "progress report" to determine whether the parenting coordinator should continue beyond this time frame. Other courts leave the parenting coordinator appointment term open and place the responsibility upon the parenting coordinator to notify the court if they determine that their services are no longer necessary or effective.

Jurisdictions handle the idea of limitations on the term of appointment differently. Some argue that there should not be an "open-ended" term because of the potential for perceived or actual abuse of families if the parenting coordinator uses their appointment as a continuous stream of income beyond the time of effective service. This is of particular concern if there is no predictable or regularly scheduled oversight, such as a periodic judicial review or requirement for a written update to the court. On the other hand, many courts recognize that the inherent nature of high-conflict families may require an objective facilitator in the form of a parenting coordinator for many years if the ultimate goal of "serving the best interests of children" is to be met. These courts would argue in favor of no limitation on the term of the parenting coordinator.

Time-Sharing Arrangement

The COR should also reference a "parenting plan" or the "custody" and time-sharing arrangement between the parents and the children. In most circumstances, the court will have entered either a temporary or a final order setting out the nature and extent of the contact between the children and each parent. This arrangement may have many different titles or names for the order. The arrangement may have been mediated and set forth as a marital settlement agreement or may be the result of an agreement by the parties (Stipulation) or the result of a litigated divorce. The detailed parenting arrangement including time-sharing and the rights and responsibilities of each parent is generally considered a "parenting plan," although many jurisdictions and states do not have a formal definition of a "parenting plan." Therefore, the actual document format, title, and specific arrangements regarding the children will vary widely.

Releases of Information

The COR generally directs parents to cooperate with the parenting coordinator, including signing any and all releases for the parenting coordinator to obtain privileged or confidential information as long as the information requested is reasonably related to the parenting issues presented for resolution. There are some jurisdictions where parents may sign releases for the parenting coordinator to obtain information about them but require a court directive for the parenting coordinator to obtain privileged or confidential information about the children. For example, the Florida Family Law Rules of Procedure (12.742) require the parenting coordinator to obtain "the express approval of the court" before they may have access to a child's confidential and privileged information.

The parenting coordinator will often need to receive information from other professionals involved with the family in order to facilitate resolution of disputes and monitor children's overall well-being. In circumstances where parents are not required by court order to sign releases for the parenting coordinator to obtain such information and the parents choose not to sign releases, the parenting coordinator is faced with the dilemma of having to work in a vacuum because they may not be able to get necessary information from other professionals, such as the child's therapist or school, the parent's therapist, the lab doing the drug screen for a substance dependent parent, and so on. In these circumstances, a parenting coordinator will likely need to ask the court to enter an order allowing them to have access to the information they need to perform their duties as a parenting coordinator.

Appointments

Both parents are usually directed to contact the parenting coordinator to schedule and arrange convenient times for meetings with the parenting coordinator within a specified time frame after the order of referral has been signed by the court. Appointments may be requested by either parent but are often scheduled when the parenting coordinator decides they are necessary.

Communication With the Court

The COR should set forth the manner in which the parenting coordinator is to interface with the court. It is likely to vary widely depending upon statutes, family law rules, and the culture of specific family law courts within a given area. Some courts may have mandatory reporting of progress in parenting coordinator cases, whereas others may not require any interface regarding progress. Some courts may require the parenting coordinator to notify the court if the family is not actively participating in the process, if they are unable to reach an agreement, or if they are no longer financially able to afford services. The parenting coordinator may be required to submit written reports to the Court describing any conflicts and recommended resolutions and/or report on parental compliance with the parenting plan or parenting schedule. Copies of all parenting coordinator's reports to the Court should be sent to the parties and their attorneys.

Parenting Coordinator as Expert Witness

The COR should address when and if a parenting coordinator is to appear in court and under what circumstances. If a parenting coordinator receives a subpoena and is directed to give an expert opinion to the court, the potential for compromise of their objective and unbiased stance rises considerably. It is for this reason that many courts only allow parenting coordinators to be called as expert witnesses after a hearing where a parent or their attorney has shown "good cause" or explained why the parenting coordinator needs to testify, and the

Court has ordered the parenting coordinator to provide expert testimony. Although many argue that parenting coordinators may be uniquely well qualified to offer expert opinion that may be of assistance to the court, a parent may perceive the parenting coordinator as "biased" toward one parent over the other based on the content of that professional opinion, and, therefore, the trust and rapport necessary for the parenting coordination process may be eroded.

Appearance and testimony in court as an expert witness is different than information provided to the court as a "status" or progress update. The former role requires testimony that is based on "expert opinion." If, instead, the parenting coordinator is called to give testimony as a "fact" witness, they may be more likely to sustain an unbiased and neutral stance because they are reporting "facts only" to the court. Such "factual" testimony might be whether the parties attend the sessions, pay for the expenses associated with parenting coordinator as ordered by the court, or follow directives issued by the court order (such as signing releases of information, etc.). There are times when it is necessary and appropriate for the parenting coordinator to give expert testimony to the court. In such cases, the court must carefully weigh the benefits versus the risk. If a parenting coordinator is no longer able to maintain an unbiased and objective role with the parents, then it is generally best to withdraw as the parenting coordinator and ask the court to appoint another professional.

Withdrawal From the Case

The COR should also specify when and how the parenting coordinator is to withdraw from a case and how parents may request such withdrawal. Since parenting coordination is used primarily with high-conflict families, it is not unusual that one parent may want the parenting coordinator to withdraw particularly if they do not feel the parenting coordinator is on their "side." It is for this reason that courts generally do not allow one parent to make a unilateral request that a parenting coordinator withdraw unless good cause has been shown. If both parents agree, the court will generally consider removal of a parenting coordinator from a case. With Court approval, the parenting coordinator may withdraw from the role of parenting coordinator for any reason. The court may also remove a parenting coordinator from a case if the parenting coordinator has had grievances filed against them by the parties or their attorneys or if the parenting coordinator is not qualified to provide parenting coordination services for any reason.

General Provisions and Directions for the Parenting Coordinator

The court, through the COR, gives direction to the parenting coordinator and specifies the expectations of the court. The COR may define the parenting coordinator's principal role and include general provisions such as the following:

- **In the event of an unresolved conflict,** the parenting coordinator shall assist the parties and the children *in the execution or implementation of the parenting plan* and to protect the children's rights to access to both parents and to protect the children's best interests in general. The parenting coordinator is entitled to communicate with the parties, children, health-care providers and any other person. The parties will cooperate with the parenting coordinator, including signing any and all releases of information requested by him/her.
- **In the event of an unresolved conflict,** the parenting coordinator shall assist the parties and their children in resolving the present high level of conflict by assisting the parents and their children to learn strategies for problem solving and conflict reduction and resolution, and act as a decision maker with respect to parenting issues, particularly with respect to scheduling and insuring that parenting time occurs. The expectation is that the parties will employ the learned strategies in solving all conflicts between them.

The scope of the parenting coordinator's work is defined in the COR and may include, but not be limited to, the following:

- Ensure implementation of the "parenting plan" or time-sharing arrangements specified in the Court's orders.
- Create approaches to the implementation of the parenting plan to reduce inter-parental conflict.
- Monitor parenting time and facilitate resolution of disputes between the parents.
- Facilitate the ability of both parents to maintain ongoing relationships with the children.
- Assist parents in improving communication skills, learn principles of child development, and understand issues facing children when their parents no longer live together. The parenting coordinator may devise detailed guidelines or rules for inter-parental communication and interaction and practice those rules with the parents. If parenting skills are lacking, the coordinator may work with one or both parents in learning those skills or refer them to an appropriate education course.

▪ Maintain communication between the parents by serving, if necessary, as a conduit for information.

▪ Reallocate parenting time but not reduce the quality or quantity of parenting time as a means of reducing conflict. (The court has the authority to make all permanent modifications to the parenting plan.)

▪ Make recommendations to the parents and to the court, unless otherwise prohibited by law or court order, regarding modification of the parenting plan to reduce inter-parental conflict.

▪ Work with both parents to update and fine tune their parenting schedule over time. Parenting schedules may need to be adjusted to children's changing developmental needs, new schools, new blended families, or evolving outside interests.

▪ Refer parents to an appropriate parent education course or program as needed.

▪ Meet with the parties or the children jointly or separately. The parenting coordinator shall determine whether appointments will be joint or separate, by telephone or in person.

▪ Act as the arbiter on any issue within the scope of the order of appointment when the parents reach an impasse.

▪ Modify the parenting plan when agreement or consensus cannot be reached, as a means of reducing conflict. The parenting coordinator may, under these circumstances, decide how a particular element of the parenting plan or parenting schedule will be implemented, including the frequency of contact between parent and children, temporary changes in the parenting schedule, holiday or vacation planning, logistics of pickups and drop-offs, suitability of accommodations, and issues dealing with stepparents and significant others.

▪ Translate the shared parenting plan and parenting schedule into a conflict-reduction plan tailored specifically to the dynamics of the family.

The primary aim of the parenting coordinator is to help parents develop strategies for parenting in a manner that minimizes conflict and allows the children to grow up free from the threat of being caught in the middle of their parents' disputes.

Scope of Authority

The COR delineates the scope of the parenting coordinator's authority over parents. In some jurisdictions, the parenting coordinator has broad authority to intervene and make changes. In other areas, the limits on intervention are very narrow. Many orders limit the parenting coordinator to one "role" or duty. For example, most orders specify that a parenting coordinator cannot combine services such as a custody evaluator or a therapist and a parenting coordinator. Generally, the parenting coordinator does not have the authority to change the primary residence of the children or to make substantial modifications to time-sharing arrangements or parental responsibilities.

The parenting coordinator may have the authority to arrange for an outside evaluation of either parent or child or direct the parents to arrange for psychotherapy for the child. This type of authority may become a critical parameter as the parenting coordinator is building a collaborative team as part of the framework needed to help the family stabilize. If the parenting coordinator does not have the authority to compel parents to seek professional or community support services that the parenting coordinator deems necessary, the parenting coordinator may need to request direction and support from the court to ensure that the integrity of the parenting coordinator process is not compromised and that the family has the support necessary to accomplish the stated goal of the parenting coordinator's work.

The parenting coordinator may be given the authority to act as an arbitrator to resolve disputes and direct both parents to abide by the parenting coordinator's decision. In some jurisdictions, this arbitration authority is intended to be temporary or until the court has time to review the decision and render a final opinion. In other jurisdictions, the arbitration authority is binding and is not intended to be a temporary decision. In these circumstances, the parenting coordinator may be directed to give both parents ample opportunity to present their side of the issue before making a decision and then present the decision in written form to parents to avoid miscommunication and misinterpretation.

In some jurisdictions, the parenting coordinator has the authority to decide whether supervised visitations shall be put in place. Generally, this is to protect the children and should not be used as a sanction. The decision to move from supervised to unsupervised visitations may also rest with the parenting coordinator in cases where the parenting coordinator originated or reestablished the supervised visitation or when supervised visitation was ordered for the purpose of reestablishing a parental bond. In other cases, the parenting coordinator may have the authority to discontinue supervised contact between a parent and child. Many areas do not allow the parenting coordinator this broad authority and require that all supervised contact or suspension of supervised contact be ordered by the Court.

Financial Matters Between Parents

Significant financial matters and child support are typically not addressed by the parenting coordinator. However, a parenting coordinator may facilitate resolution of disputes regarding financial matters that is not covered by the parent's dissolution of marriage or stipulated agreement.

CLARIFY THE REFERRAL—WHAT IS NEEDED?

Once the Order of Referral or Stipulated Agreement has been received, it is imperative for the parenting coordinator to clarify and define the scope of the service being requested. Many regions and jurisdictions have "standard" orders (see Appendix A for examples) that define the role and responsibilities of the parenting coordinator and the expectations of the parents involved. In regions of the country where parenting coordinator work is not done under court order or the orders are crafted on an individual, case-by-case basis, it is critical for the parenting coordinator to define the parameters of the service to be provided. These parameters may be spelled out in a professional services agreement between the parents and the parenting coordinator that parents must sign before beginning parenting coordination.

Because parenting coordination is a new and evolving process and there are vast differences in what defines parenting coordination across states, provinces, jurisdictions, and other municipalities, it is vital for the parenting coordinator to take responsibility for clarifying what is being asked of them. If the parenting coordinator does not make sure the boundaries of role and scope of authority are clear at the outset of the process, both the parenting coordinator and the parents may end up in a process that has the potential to do more harm than good and increases liability for all.

One of the most common "mis-steps" in the beginning of the parenting coordinator process is to proceed with all due speed in an effort to get relief for families who are being adversely affected by the hostility and chronic conflict that surrounds them and to "rescue" the children who are suffering the effects of this conflict. Even with very good intentions, parenting coordinators and parents can easily find themselves in conflict if they do not first make sure the expectations and operating parameters for all involved are clear and in writing. The court order and the contract for services are the best means of accomplishing this goal.

Many courts and legal professionals who are crafting an order appointing a parenting coordinator or a stipulated agreement to use a parenting coordinator may be unfamiliar with the details of the process and inadvertently create ethical mishaps before the process has begun. For example, courts may be aware that a mental-health professional has been involved with a family for some time either as a therapist or custody (parenting plan) evaluator or mediator and suggest or agree with a suggestion that this person should now serve as the family's parenting coordinator because they have a lot of history with the family and are already aware of the issues causing conflict. On the surface, this might sound like a good idea, particularly since the parties will not have to pay another professional to get up-to-speed on the history of the family, and the parenting coordinator may have already established a trusting relationship with one or both of the parents. However, potential disaster looms ahead if the parenting coordinator is unable to preserve and maintain an unbiased and objective role. For example, if a parenting coordinator has been a therapist for one of the parents in the past, potential for perception of bias either toward their former client or against the parent who was not their client is significant. The same potential for perception of bias exists if the parenting coordinator has been the custody evaluator or mediator for the parents.

Although there may be some merit to selecting a parenting coordinator with prior knowledge of the family and their circumstances, the potential damage to the objective, unbiased, professional, and trusted stance that the parenting coordinator must maintain at all times is significant, and, therefore, strongly discouraged. The parenting coordinator should not make the assumption that the court or attorneys "know best" if a COR or stipulated agreement clearly asks the parenting coordinator to take on dual roles or responsibilities. The parenting coordinator has the responsibility to educate any referring agent including the court, attorneys, or other programs about the scope of the work they can do that will not violate any professional standard (AFCC, 2005) or ethical guideline.

Ideally, the parenting coordinator will not have any current or prior relationship (personal or professional) with the parents, children, or other family members who may be involved in the parenting coordination process. This will serve to ensure all that the parenting coordinator does not have a bias or preconceived perception (positive or negative) of one parent or the other. Both personal and professional dual roles are fraught with conflict because of the potential for actual or perceived bias toward one party over another. Another example of a dual role that involves both a "personal" and a "professional" relationship with one or both parties is described in the following example. An individual owns a lawn maintenance service and provides this service to the parenting coordinator at their home and office (personal relationship) and the parenting coordinator is ordered to serve as the parenting coordinator to both the individual who owns the lawn maintenance company and their ex-spouse (professional relationship). Although the parenting coordinator may never actually see or communicate with the lawn maintenance person outside the office, it may create a perception of potential bias for the parent who does not have a personal relationship with the parenting coordinator. A parenting coordinator might also have treated one of the parent's family members in the past and have learned information about one of the parents that the other parent does not know. The professional parenting coordinator may not feel as though this would influence his or her judgment in their role as parenting coordinator, but should the information come to light at a later date, the parenting coordinator may be perceived as withholding information or "keeping secrets" that will only serve to undermine the trust with both parents involved in the parenting coordinator process.

The same potential for perceived bias holds true when parenting coordinators barter for services. An example of this occurred when the court ordered a second parenting coordinator for a family whose experience with their first parenting coordinator had not gone well. In this case, the first parenting coordinator had agreed not to charge a fee to the father in the parenting coordinator case in exchange for free food and beverage at a local restaurant that he owned. The original parenting coordinator had also previously served as the therapist for the father's children from his first marriage and had agreed to attend mediation of the father and his current ex-spouse (the mother of the current children who were the subject of dispute) and to help the attorneys craft the parenting plan that became part of the final marital settlement agreement. When the mother in the case later found out about these dual roles, she complained to the court who had appointed the first parenting coordinator about her perception that the original parenting coordinator was "biased" toward the father. Although the original parenting coordinator may have had good intentions, the very appearance of having a more favorable relationship with the father undermined the trust and eroded any possibility of success for the parenting coordinator process. Bartering for services in circumstances where individuals may not have adequate financial resources to pay for a parenting coordinator, but sorely need the service, creates a dilemma for many well-meaning professionals who may try to be creative to assist families, and particularly children, in need. Great caution is always warranted because of the potential for doing more harm than good.

PARENTING COORDINATOR CONTRACT OR PROFESSIONAL SERVICES AGREEMENT

A signed contract establishes the relationship rules between the parenting coordinator and the parents from the outset and is an essential protection in the parenting coordinator role. Although the court order defines the scope of authority, the expectations of the court, and the procedural necessities of the role, the parenting coordinator contract is a professional services agreement that defines the specific service to be provided. The role, responsibilities, and function of a parenting coordinator are detailed to ensure that all individuals who are entering into the agreement are clear about expectations and responsibilities.

The contract may also provide definitions of some functions that parents may not understand, such as facilitation, arbitration, or a decision-making process. The contract generally reiterates, in nonlegal language, the role, responsibilities, and authority of the parenting coordinator as set forth in the COR. The contract should define the term of appointment, if it is not specified in the COR, and the procedures for terminating parenting coordination services.

It is very important to clearly state the *role* in which the parenting coordinator will be engaged. For example, a parenting coordinator may be a licensed attorney, licensed psychologist, certified mediator, or other professional; but in their role as parenting coordinator, they do not offer legal advice, provide therapy or counseling to the parents or children, or provide mediation services. Since most parenting coordinators will have other professional roles, it is important to differentiate and clearly define the distinction between other professional roles and the role of parenting coordinator as it applies to the parents referred to parenting coordination.

The contract generally details how and when parenting coordination appointments will be made and the procedure for scheduling appointments. If the appointments are joint (both parents together), separate, in person, on the phone, or done in some other fashion, this should be detailed in the contract. The contract should spell out how and if appointments can be rescheduled or cancelled and the consequences of doing so. There should also be a provision for a parent who fails to attend or is unprepared to participate in an appointment. Often, the parenting coordinator will hold the nonattending or unprepared party responsible for both parents' fees.

The limits on confidentiality should be detailed along with clarification of each individual's right to privacy. The contract should identify when and how the parenting coordinator may collect information from collateral sources, such as mental-health providers, schools, employers, drug-testing laboratories, and so on. The contract should also specify how the information collected will be used and whether it will be shared with both parents.

If children are to be directly involved in the parenting coordinator process (e.g., interviewed alone or with parents), the contract should detail how and when this might occur and what protections, if any, may be in place to protect childrens' priviledged information or confidential records. If the parenting coordinator intends to share all information obtained about the children, either through direct interview or via report from others, the contract should detail how the information will be collected and if the information will be kept private.

The contract should detail how communication between the parents and the parenting coordinator will occur. For example, a parenting coordinator may allow either parent to provide them with information via mail, fax, or e-mail and indicate that all information received will be provided to the other parent also. Or, a parenting coordinator may allow telephone communication with one parent only. However, if a parenting coordinator is having "private" conversations with one parent and the other parent has no awareness of the conversation or the content of the conversation, the parenting coordinator may place themselves in the position of *appearing* to be biased toward one party over the other. However, the contract should delineate how and when communication will occur and whether the information received by the parenting coordinator will be shared with both parents.

The contract should detail how agreements or decisions are to be memorialized and the process for review of such documents. It is vital for the parenting coordinator to clearly document their work with a family, whether that work is in person, on the phone, or through other electronic means.

The contract should also address the issue of whether the parenting coordinator will be involved with litigation or called as an expert witness. The parameters of that involvement, including fees for travel, preparation for court, and testifying should be defined as well as whether the parenting coordinator will continue to provide parenting coordinator services after serving in an expert witness capacity. The same holds true with a request for records for litigation purposes.

Fees are a very critical part of the contract. Fees should be clearly detailed, including how monies are to be paid and the consequences for failure to pay. The parenting coordinator's hourly rate or fees should be identified as well as how charges will be accrued. For example, most parenting coordinator work will involve telephone calls, copying, faxing, reviewing records, or committing to writing any agreements or modifications to the parenting plan. It is also helpful to advise the parents, in advance, of any fees associated with "misuse" of the parenting coordinator's time. For example, one parent may be demanding more of the parenting coordinator's time than the other parent simply to create excess charges that the other parent is required to pay. The parenting coordinator contract should identify whether each parent pays for the individual time spent with the parenting coordinator, whether that is in person, on the phone, or in electronic communication.

Some parenting coordinators require a retainer. If so, the amount of the initial retainer and how the retainer is to be replenished should be specified. The consequences for nonpayment of fees in a timely manner should be detailed as well as how statements or bills will be used. A parenting coordinator may want to consider a provision for a fee increase since some parenting coordination cases last for years, and the parenting coordinator's fees may change during the tenure of the appointment. The parenting coordination contract should identify how and when parents will be notified of any change in fees.

Every contract should define "Emergency Procedures." The parenting coordinator is generally neither a crisis counselor nor an after-hours, on-call arbitrator. The parenting coordinator should not be contacted outside of his or her normal business hours unless the parenting coordinator specifically authorizes parents to call after hours, and then only for the specific purposes allowed by the parenting coordinator.

The parenting coordinator is not serving in a "clinical" or health-care professional role and generally does not accept "emergency" phone calls having to do with the behavior of the other party. It is important for the parenting coordinator to let parties know, at the beginning of the process, how information is to be communicated to them. The parenting coordinator may want to consider only accepting information via fax or e-mail so that there is a written record, and the other parent will have an opportunity to respond to the information given to the parenting coordinator. This helps to reassure both parents that the parenting coordinator will maintain an unbiased stance by treating one parent the same as the other. As part of the contractual arrangement, a parenting coordinator may want to indicate, in writing, that any and all information received from one parent will be shared with the other. This gives the parenting coordinator the opportunity to hear both sides of an issue and to gather additional data, if necessary, before drawing a conclusion about an allegation made by one parent about the other. If parents are in disagreement over any matter arising after normal business hours, the complaining parent should refrain from contacting the parenting coordinator until the next business day following the incident.

The contract may detail how vacation coverage will be handled and if another parenting coordinator will be "on call" during the time the parenting coordinator is away. If a child is in imminent danger of harm, law enforcement or social services, not the parenting coordinator, is the proper agency to contact. If they cannot render assistance at that moment, neither can the parenting coordinator.

Finally, the contract should have a provision indicating that the contract has been carefully reviewed and that each parent is agreeing to all provisions of the contract, including consent to proceed. There should be a signature line for each parent with a space to date the signature and a signature and dateline for the parenting coordinator to sign to finalize the agreement. Each parent should have the opportunity to review the contract with their attorney if one is involved prior to signing.

Following the procedures outlined in this chapter will provide a structure for the parenting coordination process. Careful review and consideration of these procedures will allow the parenting coordinator to tailor the parenting coordination service they provide to meet jurisdictional and professional requirements and maintain the integrity of the parenting coordination process.

3

Getting Started

Still round the corner there may wait,
A new road, or a secret gate.
—J.R.R. Tolkien

In the previous chapter we identified the type of parents who are likely to benefit from parenting coordination, how these individuals may be referred by the court, and basic parenting coordination procedures. The next step after being appointed by the court to provide parenting coordination services is to gather some basic information about the parents and children before meeting with them for the first appointment and in the initial phase of the parenting coordination process. This is done through direct interviews, review of the court file and other relevant documents, and review of data provided by the parents through questionnaires or surveys. This chapter will also outline the screening procedures to assess for risk factors and parties' ability to meaningfully participate in the parenting coordination process.

THE BASICS—IDENTIFYING THE PARTIES INVOLVED

The COR will identify the parents and the minor children who are parties in the case. By now, one or both of the parents may have remarried, or have new significant others, and/or additional children residing in either home. It is important to identify all the household residents in both homes, since it is likely that these relationships may impact the children and the parents who are the identified parties in the case. Although the court may not have jurisdiction (or control) over anyone other than the parties to the case, stepparents and/or parent surrogates as well as step or half siblings are likely to be very involved in the interactions with the identified parties. It is for this reason that the parenting coordinator should ask for a complete list of all household residents and gather some basic information about them in terms of their role in the family and any issues or conflicts which have arisen or may arise involving other household members and the parents or children who are the parties in the case.

There may also be nonhousehold residents who are in surrogate parenting roles with the children (i.e., non–live-in paramours, grandparents, childcare workers, etc.). It is important to identify individuals who are in parenting roles and their relationship with the parents and children. Some of these cases involve multiple marriages or sequential partnerships and may require a detailed diagram or chart to keep track of who is currently involved directly or indirectly with the family referred to parenting coordination.

It is also helpful to identify the primary sources of conflict in the family system both as a planning tool for the parenting coordination work, as well as a learning tool for the parents. For example, the primary conflict may be between a new stepmother and the biological mother or between very involved paternal grandparents and the children's mother. It is also not uncommon for conflicts to arise between "non-parties" to a case such as a stepfather and his wife's daughter from a previous marriage. As you can see in these brief examples, there are often multiple "players" who contribute to the conflict within a family crucible. It is particularly helpful to differentiate between adult–adult conflict or parent–child conflict or child–child conflict in order to determine the additional professional or community supports that may be needed to build the family framework.

HISTORY OF PARENTING PARTNERSHIP

An important part of data collecting is to determine the history of the parenting partnership. Not only will this data be used to help identify parental conflict or impasse styles, but it is also useful when looking for "underlying" causes of the ongoing hostility or conflict that may date back to one or both of the parents' families of origin, or it may be reflective of mental-health impairments or other co-parenting impediments.

Generally, the parenting coordinator should gather summary data about how the couple met, their impressions of one another at the onset of the relationship, their courtship, their decision to become a committed couple, and how they made the decision to have children. This should form a predicate for the next phase of data gathering, which is to identify when the conflicts in the partnership or marriage first arose, how the parents attempted to resolve these conflicts, their level of success or failure with these attempts, and ultimately, how the partnership ended. Some parents may not know each other very well or not at all as in the case of a "one night stand" or fleeting sexual relationship, which produced a child.

This data may be collected via questionnaires or forms prior to meeting with the couple or via interview. There are several tools available to help assess a parent's areas of conflict and to offer insight into the origin of a particular pattern of behavior. Some of the useful conflict identification tools include:

Acrimony Scale (Emery, 1987)
Best Interests of Children (Carter, D.*)
Conflict Scale (McIntosh, 2003, unpublished**)
Divorce Assessment Survey II (Silver, R., 2007, unpublished**)
Families Apart Questionnaire (Blau, 1993)

*(see Appendix) **contact author directly for copy.*

It is often helpful to ask parents to complete one or more screening questionnaires prior to the first appointment in order to help the parenting coordinator begin to develop an intervention strategy.

Since the interactional conflicts and issues are likely to change over time, it is helpful to gather this information in written form for comparison data gathered later in the process. If parenting partners are able to improve the quality of their co-parenting or collaboration, they often find it useful to reflect on their progress via a comparison of initial and intermediate or "final" questionnaires. This is also a way to help the parenting coordinator measure their effectiveness.

HISTORY OF FAMILY TO DATE

In addition to the identified parents who are the legal "parties," there may be several parent surrogates who have been involved in the children's lives since the time of the initial separation or divorce or before. There may also be a number of step- or half-siblings who have been in the children's lives. These siblings and parent surrogates may or may not still be a part of the family unit. The number and makeup of family reformulations is likely to give the parenting coordinator some history of the stability (or lack thereof) in the family's structure and may also indicate repetitive patterns of choices or judgments that may have proven to be predictive of current and future conflicts and hostilities. The history of the family will also highlight the number of logistical changes (i.e., multiple homes, schools, jobs, babysitters, etc.) to which the children have been exposed and may highlight multiple emotional and relationship losses the children have experienced. All of this data is helpful to the parenting coordinator when assessing the scope of the parenting coordination work with a family. In Chapter 5, we will later discuss how the parenting coordinator may anticipate future conflicts and how to prioritize issues to achieve and maintain family stabilization.

PARENTING DYNAMICS—PRESENT

In the initial data collection about the history of the parent's relationship, it is important to look for a chronology of events and map out a timeline of the coming together and breaking apart of a relationship. The temporal sequence of families uniting and unraveling and the resultant sequelae may help the parenting coordinator better appreciate how entrenched parents may be in their conflicts and seemingly "locked positions." This phase of data collection is focused on how parents are functioning in day-to-day life now. How is their life structured? Are they physically well? Are they enjoying social supports? Are they taking care of themselves emotionally and physically? What are the major stressors? Do they have childcare support? Is their work environment supportive? Do they have a balance between work and play? Where are they in the transition of family change? Are they locked in bitterness and resentment? Are they still feeling victimized by their ex-spouse or partner? Are they feeling victimized by the legal system? Are they moving on with new relationships? Are they retreating into a "rebound" relationship? Are they abusing alcohol or drugs?

One of my colleagues often refers to parental separation and divorce as a three-legged stool where one of the legs has been broken or removed. This leaves a stool that cannot stand without support. Unless that third, stabilizing, leg is repaired or replaced, the stool will continue to fall over no matter how many times it is set upright. This analogy describes many families who feel as though divorce has shattered the stability and predictability of their world. Often parents are able to rely upon family, friends, or other supports to provide a "temporary" third leg until more permanent repairs or replacements can be made. These are the parents who are able to manage through the crucible of conflicted divorce with relatively little damage done to themselves or their children. Long-term damaging effects are mitigated. However, many parents do not have readily available resources to stabilize the "stool" and, therefore, falter in their functioning both as an adult in day-to-day life and most certainly as a parent.

Research tells us that even the most stable and reliable of parents do not function well during and immediately after separation and divorce

(Amato, 2000; Emery, 2004; Hetherington, 1999). Therefore, gathering information about each parent's level of functioning as an individual versus part of a dyad helps the parenting coordinator make appropriate referrals to begin to build an infrastructure of support for the family or to stabilize the stool with the broken leg. If parents are not mentally or physically healthy, aside from any unhealthy interactions with their parenting partner, they are not likely to be functioning well as parents.

As early as 1977, Kelly and Wallerstein showed a strong connection between children's psychological adjustment and the overall quality of life in the parent's post-divorce family construction or remarried family. When the parents appeared settled and when stable new partners were introduced, the children managed well. However, if the parents continued to show that they were upset, or if several difficult adult relationships were introduced into the child's life, the children continued to show distress at the same level as the first year after divorce. Other researchers looking at children's outcomes have highlighted the importance of parenting, quality of relationships, and psychosocial resources (Bauserman, 2002; Johnston, 1995; Pruett, Ebling, & Insabella, 2004; Pearson & Thoennes, 1990; Smyth, 2009).

Kline et al. (1989) found that the actual custody arrangement had little effect on children's adjustment, but the parents' emotional adjustment to divorce and the post-separation childcare arrangements had significant impact on the children. In families where a parent became anxious or depressed about the divorce, the children developed a high rate of psychological and social problems.

It is important to identify and use criteria that help differentiate long-term, bitterly entrenched high-conflict divorces from those divorces where parents are able to resolve the emotional issues of ending a marriage or relationship without high levels of hostility and bitterness. It will be helpful for the parenting coordinator to differentiate level or type of conflict as an initial organizing step. Garrity and Baris (1994) identified conflict along a continuum of minimal to severe:

- *minimal conflict:* cooperative parenting, ability to separate children's needs from own needs, can validate importance of other parent, conflict is resolved between the adults using only occasional expressions of anger, and negative emotions quickly brought under control
- *mild conflict:* occasionally berates other parent in front of the child, occasional verbal quarrelling in front of the child, questioning child about personal matters in life of other parent, and occasional attempts to form a coalition with child against other parent

▨ *moderate conflict:* verbal abuse with no threat or history of physical violence, loud quarrelling, denigration of the other parent, threats of litigation, and ongoing attempts to form a coalition with child against other parent around isolated issues

▨ *moderately severe conflict:* child is not directly endangered, but parents are endangering each other; threatening violence; slamming doors, throwing things; verbally threatening harm or kidnapping; attempts to form a permanent or standing coalition with child against other parent (alienation syndrome); and child is experiencing emotional endangerment

▨ *severe conflict:* endangerment by physical or sexual abuse, drug or alcohol abuse to point of impairment, and severe psychological pathology

In addition to identifying the level of conflict described above, it is helpful to identify all sources of conflict that may be fueling the ongoing conflict. Several models for differentiating origin and type of conflict are presented in subsequent chapters. It is important for the parenting coordinator to understand all aspects of conflict between parents in order to develop an intervention strategy that will help parents address the practical issues of custody, time-sharing, decision-making, and other parenting arrangements. The goal is to build in enough structure to manage conflict constructively and shield the children from exposure to conflict if conflicts cannot be resolved.

HOW ARE THE CHILDREN FARING?

Two of the most significant factors that influence children's adjustment post-divorce are exposure to inter-parental conflict and quality of parenting (Amato & Keith, 1991; Kelly & Emery, 2003). Understanding the impact of conflict and parenting on children's well-being can be complicated because they are interrelated and often difficult to disentangle.

Therefore, it becomes imperative for the parenting coordinator to gather information regarding the children's functioning in all areas of their life (social, psychological, physical, academic, etc.) and to assess the relationship each child has with each parent. This data may be gathered directly from each parent, through the review of relevant records (e.g., school, medical, dental, mental health, etc.) and through collateral contacts (i.e., teachers, coaches, babysitters, etc.). If the information cannot be gathered through these resources, the parenting coordinator may need to gather the information directly from the children.

INTAKE—FIRST APPOINTMENT

The first appointment is generally a longer appointment than subsequent appointments in order to allow the parenting coordinator time to review documents that define the process and establish the "rules" of engagement. The documents are likely to include the court order of appointment; the signed parenting coordinator contract; and any documents the parents have completed providing background information, including questionnaires that describe the nature of their relationship in the past and present. The parenting coordinator should describe the parenting coordinator process to parents and give them an opportunity to ask for clarification and have their questions answered before asking parents to consent to proceed. The parenting coordinator should document this procedure and parents' consent to the process and keep it as part of the file.

The first appointment is generally with both parents together in order to review the process, procedure, and expectations. This serves to assure parents that both of them are being provided the same information and offers the parenting coordinator an opportunity to establish and reinforce boundaries from the beginning. It is important for the parenting coordinator to structure the appointment in a manner that establishes the "rules" of the relationship and models appropriate communication and interactions. The parenting coordinator should consider seating arrangements, establishing rules for taking turns in terms of speaking, the format for communications, and so on. The parenting coordinator may need to position parents in a manner that has each parent look at the parenting coordinator and not the other parent during the initial phase of parenting coordination work to emphasize the goal of disengagement from the conflict.

The parenting coordinator sets the agenda for the first appointment and guides the process with firm direction and prompting of the parties. The seven goals of the first appointment are as follows:

1. Introduce the parenting coordination process
2. Clarify the parenting coordinator's role and responsibilities
3. Establish focus on the children
4. Establish rules of engagement
5. Identify co-parenting conflicts
6. Identify any specific needs of a parent or child
7. Establish priorities and set goals including time lines

Often, a parent will want to tell "their story" and may be unable or unwilling to follow basic rules of interactions. It is important that the parenting coordinator intervene in a very direct and firm manner to make it clear that the parenting coordinator is in charge of establishing the structure within which all will work and that the parenting coordinator will not allow either parent to engage in behaviors or communications which violate the integrity of the parenting coordinator process or sabotages the process.

High-conflict parents often display, in their interactions with one another, what John Gottman (1994b) labels as the "Four Horsemen of the Apocalypse": contempt, criticism, stonewalling, and defensiveness. When parents interact in this manner, they are unable to communicate or resolve issues constructively. Many parents may also violate basic rules of engagement, such as interrupting when the other is speaking, talking over the other person, attempting to monopolize all the time and attention of the parenting coordinator, and so on. In addition, parents may display behaviors that are provocative and destructive to the process, such as speaking in a loud voice, refusing to remain seated, or moving toward the other parent in a threatening manner. The parenting coordinator must be directive and firm in setting limits and redirecting destructive interactions and behaviors by either parent (see Table 3.1).

It is important for the parenting coordinator to establish "safety" measures beyond physical and environmental safety. For example, the parenting coordinator should establish the boundaries within the parenting coordinator sessions so that each person has the opportunity to express their parenting concerns without fear of threat or reprisal. It is not appropriate for either parent to act in a threatening manner toward the other or to destroy property. If these circumstances arise, the parenting coordinator must determine whether the case is appropriate for parenting coordinator services. The goal is to establish an environment of "emotional" safety in addition to one of physical safety.

TABLE 3.1   Parenting Coordinator Tools to Establish Boundaries and Set Limits

---

1. Use egg timer so parents have equal time
2. Offer paper/pen to parent who keeps interrupting to help them remember what they want to say
3. Ask parent for 8 × 10 of each child and put in frame in front of parents
4. Position chairs of parents so eye contact is with parenting coordinator and not the other parent
5. Establish hand signals to alert parents to boundary violations, e.g., "time out" and "stop" signals

---

In this initial appointment, the parenting coordinator should clarify the process for the parents, that is, will they meet with both parents, the children, with stepparents or significant others, as necessary. The parenting coordinator should specify whether the meetings will be joint or individual and whether the appointments will be by telephone or in person or a combination of these arrangements. The parenting coordinator may also suggest frequency for meetings in the initial phase of work.

SUBSEQUENT APPOINTMENTS

Subsequent appointments are usually 1 hour to 1½ hours in length, but may be for any length of time that the parenting coordinator determines to be appropriate and effective for the work. The parenting coordinator may decide to meet with each parent individually to determine whether there are issues that the parent has not raised in parenting coordinator appointments with both parents. The parenting coordinator must avoid any circumstance where they are asked or expected to keep "secrets" of one parent from the other parent. Doing so will potentially undermine the trust that is necessary to proceed and appear to compromise the neutrality of the parenting coordinator.

The parenting coordinator may also decide to gather information directly from the children to determine the child's level of adjustment and to make appropriate referrals for services, if necessary. It is important that the parenting coordinator have a clear plan and well-thought-out rationale for the process they follow. There is a tendency for parenting coordinators who are mental-health professionals to "stray" into areas that are more likely to be defined as a diagnostic interview or psychosocial assessment if they do not have a clear agenda when meeting with parents or children.

Some parenting coordinators find it useful to meet with new significant others or spouses in order to determine their role in the family and whether or not they will be a useful resource or a source of conflict to be managed. This information may be gathered from the parents directly or it may require a separate appointment with the new significant other or spouses who are in a parenting role with the children. This should only be done with both parents' permission and knowledge in order to avoid accusation that the parenting coordinator has information about which one parent is unaware. Again, even the appearance of bias or loss of neutrality can sabotage the parenting coordination process.

The frequency of meetings is usually determined by the level of need and the acuity of the conflict. It may be helpful to meet weekly in the beginning of the process in order to get a more complete picture of the issues and to develop an intervention strategy. There is generally no requirement to meet at a certain frequency or interval, but the parenting coordinator must use their judgment about the amount of time they will need to identify the needs and begin building the infrastructure needed for intervention.

During the initial meetings, it is important for the parenting coordinator to ensure that parenting coordination is an appropriate process for this family. This is done through a series of screening procedures.

SCREENING FOR RISK FACTORS

It is helpful for a parenting coordinator to screen for risk factors in advance of work with clients. This may be done through questionnaires for identifying areas of conflict and nature of the co-parenting relationship or information provided by attorneys prior to meeting with the parents. A parenting coordinator may have information based on legal pleadings, previous court orders, mental-health records, or prior custody evaluations. Parents may identify potential risk factors in the screening questionnaires, which can be reviewed in advance of the first appointment. This allows the parenting coordinator to formulate an initial intervention strategy to streamline the process.

The parenting coordinator is not responsible for "evaluating" or investigating allegations as might be done through child protective services, but the parenting coordinator is responsible for determining whether additional information is needed or whether safety parameters need to be in place for the parenting coordinator process to proceed. For example, if a parent makes allegations that the other parent is unable to safely parent the children, it may be necessary for the parent who is the subject of the allegations to undergo an evaluation: to either substantiate the claim and determine the precautions that are necessary to protect the children; or to invalidate the allegations.

At the outset of the work, the parenting coordinator must determine whether the parents are able to effectively participate in the parenting coordinator process. Ideally the courts will have screened individuals to ensure that they are able to pay for the services and that there are no domestic violence or safety issues that would put anyone involved at risk for harm. In addition, it is important to determine that each parent is sufficiently free from any serious mental-health issues that may impair their ability to process information accurately or meaningfully participate in the process. Examples might include a parent with a substance abuse or dependence problem whose functioning is chronically or seriously impaired, a parent with serious cognitive impairment (limited intellectual capacity, minimal brain damage, etc.), or a parent with serious mental illness that is not receiving proper care or fails to follow medical advice to stabilize severe symptoms.

DOMESTIC VIOLENCE SCREENING

If issues of physical or emotional safety are a factor for the parents, it is important for the parenting coordinator to notify the court of these safety issues and request that additional safety parameters be implemented before proceeding with parenting coordination. In circumstances where the court has ordered the parent to parenting coordination and is aware of prior issues of domestic violence, safety parameters may already be in place. However, there may be circumstances when the courts have not identified a family as one in need of extra safety precautions, or there may have been no history of violence to date. It is the parenting coordinator's responsibility to be knowledgeable about and screen parties to ensure safety for all. Training in identification and proper assessment of domestic violence indicators is essential parenting coordination training.

If there are allegations of domestic violence that have not been substantiated, it may be necessary for the parenting coordinator to request an investigation or evaluation by a qualified professional to determine whether extra safety precautions should be put into place prior to beginning the parenting coordinator work. The parenting coordinator should be aware of both the legal and nonlegal definitions of what constitutes domestic violence.

Domestic violence laws in most jurisdictions apply not only to physical attacks but also to other types of conduct. Some examples of conduct that may be considered domestic violence include creating disturbance at a spouse's place of work, harassing telephone calls, surveillance, and threats against a spouse or family member (even though the threat may not have been carried out).

An example of a **legal definition** of domestic violence (Florida Statute §741.28) is as follows:

"Domestic violence" means any assault, aggravated assault, battery, aggravated battery, sexual assault, sexual battery, stalking, aggravated stalking, kidnapping, false imprisonment, or any criminal offense resulting in physical injury or death of one family or household member by another family or household member.

> "Family or household member" means spouses, former spouses, person related by blood or marriage, persons who are presently residing together as if a family or who have resided together in the past as if a family, and persons who are parents of a child in common regardless of whether they have been married. With the exception of persons who have a child in common, the family or household members must be currently residing or have in the past resided together in the same single dwelling unit.

Many jurisdictions have elaborate laws designed to protect spouses from domestic violence by their spouses or other family members and may also apply to people in dating relationships that have become abusive. A common remedy is for a court to issue a "protective order" directing the alleged abuser to stop abusing or harassing someone else. In addition, the court often will order the abuser to stay away from the spouse, the spouse's home, or place of work. If the person continues to abuse his or her spouse (or another person protected by the order), the abuser may be charged with a criminal violation of the order in addition to being charged with other offenses, such as battery.

A **non-legal** definition of domestic violence is:

> Acts of physical and sexual abuse; psychological maltreatment; chronic situations in which one person controls or intends to control another person's behavior; and/or misuse of power that may result in injury or harm to the *psychological well-being* of family members. (American Psychological Association, 1996)

Domestic violence may include a pattern of assault and coercive behaviors, such as economic coercion that is used to establish power and control over an intimate partner. These behaviors generally constitute more than mere isolated incidents; rather, they demonstrate a pattern of abuse.

Common tactics used by batterers to instill and maintain power and control include the following:

- Physical violence
- Intimidation, including threats to the victim's children, family, and pets
- Emotional abuse (name-calling, put-downs, humiliation, shunning)
- Isolation (cutting victim off from family and friends)
- Complete control over finances and/or not allowing the victim to have a job
- Blaming the victim for the abuse

The definition of domestic violence in the U.S. federal Violence Against Women Act (VAWA) (Department of Justice Reauthorization Act of 2005, P.L. 109-162) states:

> The term "domestic violence" includes felony or misdemeanor crimes of violence committed by a current or former spouse of the victim, by a person with whom the victim shares a child in common, by a person who is cohabitating with or has cohabitated with the victim as a spouse, by a person similarly situated to a spouse of the victim under the domestic or family violence laws of the jurisdiction receiving grant monies, or by any other person against an adult or youth victim who is protected from that person's acts under the domestic or family violence laws of the jurisdiction.

The parenting coordinator should be alert to interactional dynamics between parents that may speak of direct or indirect threats of risk or harm and to identify issues of power and control imbalance. The parenting coordinator may ascertain this information by direct observation, review of substantiated allegations that may not have been reported to the court, and review of the court file. The parenting coordinator should review any terms of an injunction that was entered and be aware of indicators of domestic violence even if the parents do not have a reported history. In addition, the parenting coordinator may directly inquire about risk or fear of violence. Some examples of domestic violence screening questions include the following:

- Has your intimate partner ever physically hurt you?
- Has your intimate partner ever threatened to hurt you or your family members?
- Do you feel unsafe, afraid, worried, or nervous around your intimate partner?

If the parenting coordinator determines that domestic violence issues are present, they should:

- recognize and address safety issues as they arise
- recognize that the parenting coordination process may augment the power of the abuser if it encourages the victim to be flexible, cooperative, and willing to negotiate
- recognize that parenting autonomously and separately may be more appropriate than attempting to have parents work together and communicate with one another directly
- recognize that even if the violence has ended, the victim and the children may still be frightened and anxious when the parents are in the same place

SUBSTANCE ABUSE SCREENING

Another step in the screening process is to determine whether either parent has a substance abuse or dependence problem that may impair their ability to participate in the parenting coordination process and/or impair their ability to parent safely and effectively. In the case of high-conflict parents, allegations of substance use or abuse may arise frequently. The parenting coordinator has the responsibility to determine the veracity of these claims and determine whether they might place the children at risk when they are in the care of that parent. The parenting coordinator has several options available to determine whether substance abuse and dependence is an issue. They may refer the party to a qualified mental-health professional to obtain an evaluation and rely upon the results of that evaluation to make recommendations to the parents. They may also review the court file, which may provide ample evidence of the use/abuse of substances in the past (e.g., DUIs, loss of driver's license, inpatient rehabilitation or detoxification records, etc.). Another source of information may be the substance abusing parent's therapist or treating professional. This information is generally "privileged," and the parenting coordinator will need to obtain a parent's consent to have access to substance abuse treatment records.

If a parent has a substance abuse or dependence problem, then safety parameters must be instituted and monitored as an ongoing part of the parent's time-sharing arrangements. For example, the court may have ordered a known substance abuser to have a clean urine screen prior to each contact with the children to ensure that the parent is not under the influence of a substance that may impair their parenting ability. The parenting coordinator may get copies of these reports to verify a parent's compliance.

It is not unusual for parents who are engaged in conflict with the other parent to make false allegations regarding substance abuse or dependence. It becomes the parenting coordinator's responsibility to determine whether the children are at risk in that parent's care (for any reason) and to facilitate the parties' agreement for safety precautions. In the event that the parenting coordinator believes there is a serious likelihood of a parent having a substance abuse/dependence problem and that the parent refuses to agree to any safety precautions, then the parenting coordinator must notify the court of the potential risk and harm to the child(ren) so that the court may take appropriate action. If the child is in imminent danger, then the parenting coordinator must report the matter to Child Protection Services in addition to notifying the court.

It is sometimes difficult, in the beginning of work with a high-conflict family, to determine whether allegations about substance abuse/dependence are spurious or valid as many negative and inflammatory comments by one parent about the other are common. However, the parenting coordinator is responsible for determining whether third-party or Court intervention is necessary in order to protect the children and preserve the integrity of the parenting coordination process.

MENTAL-HEALTH SCREENING

An additional step in the screening process is to determine whether one or both parents may have serious mental-health symptoms that impair their ability to parent effectively and/or participate meaningfully in the parenting coordinator process. The parenting coordinator may inquire directly about a history of mental illness or request to review treatment records. If the mental illness and symptom pattern has the potential to interfere with a parent's ability to parent safely and effectively, the parenting coordinator will need to develop a structure to monitor the parent's functioning and compliance with any treatment that allows for stable emotional and behavioral functioning. Parents with a history of mental illness may be reluctant to give the parenting coordinator permission to obtain such records for fear that their rights to privacy and access to their children may be hindered. The parenting coordinator is obligated to maintain basic "privacy" rights for any party, but they may be able to gather circumscribed information from a treating professional regarding that parent's parenting capacity at any given time.

An example of this occurred in a parenting coordination case where the mother, diagnosed with paranoid schizophrenia, had been designated as the primary custodian of her three young children. The father was aware of the diagnosis which predated the birth of their children. When the mother was taking her medication as directed, she was able to function very effectively as a full-time parent with the intermittent assistance of her mother. During one parenting coordination session, several months into the process, the mother appeared to be confused and seemed to be processing information much more slowly than in previous appointments. Because the parenting coordinator had knowledge of the mother's mental illness diagnosis and history, she asked the mother whether she recently had any change in medication. The mother said yes and the parenting coordinator decided to suspend the parenting coordinator session for that day. The father was in agreement and offered to either take the children for a few days or to call the maternal grandmother to enlist her assistance with parenting. In this case, the mother agreed to have her mother monitor her and assist with childcare. During the next several parenting coordination sessions, the mother's processing was much slower than usual while adjusting to new medications, so an accommodation was introduced into the session. The mother was allowed to write down any issues being discussed and to wait until the next session before making a decision. Since the father was aware of the diagnosis and impact, he was willing to go along with this accommodation although he insisted on more time with the children in return.

IDENTIFYING PARENTING STRENGTHS

Another important screening procedure in the beginning of the parenting coordination work is to ascertain each parent's strengths and needs as they transition into new parenting roles. One or both parents may have limited parenting skills and may need parenting skills training. Other parents may have had more than adequate parenting skills prior to the separation or divorce but may not be functioning at their best either during a prolonged separation or litigation process or as a result of their own temporary decline in functioning. In addition, new parenting skills may be required to help the children cope with the changes they are undergoing during the time of separation or divorce. It is the parenting coordinator's responsibility to assess parenting strengths and weaknesses in order to assist the parties in acquiring the "tools" they need for successful parenting. If a custody evaluation was done prior to the appointment of a parenting coordinator, the parenting coordinator may be able to obtain information about each parent's parenting abilities in this report. The custody evaluation can be a valuable source of information, and the parenting coordinator should review the report, if available, prior to making any recommendations regarding parenting skill acquisition. Many times, however, a custody evaluation may not have taken place, and the parenting coordinator is left with each parent's self-assessment or the report of the other parent. There are several questionnaires available that may assist the parenting coordinator in obtaining this information in a timely and cost-effective manner (e.g., Parenting History Survey, Co-Parenting Questionnaire, Parenting Styles and Dimensions Questionnaire, and so on. See Appendix D for a screening questionnaire).

DOCUMENTATION OF CONTACT

All interventions and interactions with parents and others involved in the parenting coordination process should be documented. The documentation should include the date and time of service, persons involved in each appointment, the issues addressed, any resolution reached, and issues to be addressed in the future. Some practitioners have developed a structured format to assist with accuracy and efficiency of documentation, but there are no requirements that documentation follow a specific form or format. Certainly any agreements reached between the parents should be memorialized in writing and a copy provided to both parents.

COMMUNICATION TO THE COURT, ATTORNEYS, AND PARENTS

Some jurisdictions provide a form for parenting coordinators to use when providing a report to the court about a family referred to parenting coordination. This mechanism may be used to assure uniformity of service provision and for the courts to have an oversight of quality control. Many areas do not have a guide for reporting information or a uniform format. In these circumstances, the parenting coordinator must develop a format for their own use and should consider including the following information: the case name, case number, the jurisdiction (i.e., 12th Judicial Circuit, County of Manatee), the judge who appointed the parenting coordinator, the parenting coordinator's name, and the attorneys of record. The names and ages of the minor children at issue in the case should be included along with the date of the report, the number of hours spent on the case since the last report, and any issues/observations/and resolutions which have resulted from the parenting coordination sessions.

The report should indicate whether the issues have been resolved by consent and agreement of the parties or whether the issues were resolved by the decision of the parenting coordinator. If appropriate, the report should list any recommendations by the parenting coordinator and extant issues remaining. Finally, the report should list any issues that require intervention or resolution by the court and the date the next session is to be held. The report should also indicate how and when the parents and their counsel have been provided with a copy of the report sent to the court. In jurisdictions where parenting coordination is confidential, this information is generally not shared with the court unless the court orders the parenting coordinator to do so. See Appendix E for a sample report.

There are also times when the parenting coordination sessions should be memorialized and sent to the parties. For example, the parenting coordinator may draft a letter to parents after the first meeting, which lists the date of the meeting and the issues covered in that meeting. This process affords parents an opportunity to make any corrections to the document and express questions or concerns. This also allows the parenting coordinator to illustrate how communication and the process will take place, including options for modification once issues have been addressed and resolved or if a decision has been made by the parenting coordinator that the parties are expected to honor until further order of the court. The following is an example of information that might be included in a letter to parents:

During our last parenting coordination appointment, you agreed to the following which shall be in effect unless modified in a subsequent parenting coordination appointment or by further order of the court.

1. *Christmas holidays: You have worked out the schedule for the holidays. Dad will have contact with the children on December 26th and 27th.*

2. *Overnights for the child at dad's house: Dad will call the parenting coach and set up regular contact with her. Dad and mom will individually consult with the child's therapist for an update. I agreed to meet with the child's therapist after her meeting with mom and dad in an effort to increase collaboration among professionals working with you.*

3. *Mom gave us her new mailing address: 101 S. Main St., Sarasota, FL 34243.*

4. *We went over unreimbursed health-care expenses, and pursuant to the order dad will reimburse mom $842.50 for the child's mental-health treatment, $645.00 for Dr. Peirce (child's dentist), and $340.00 for the supervision of transitions. This brings us up to date for past shared costs that mom has already paid out. Dad agreed to pay this total amount of $1827.50 in 1 week's time. Mom agreed to provide on a quarterly basis any documentation of unreimbursed costs to dad.*

5. *We continued to discuss your past experience with each other, focusing on the damaging impact of ongoing litigation. Although mom stressed she was the "respondent" and therefore felt dad drove the legal conflict, clearly you both initiated actions and responded to actions and feel victimized by the other. I stressed the importance of ending the litigation and encouraged dad to consider withdrawing the current motion.*

6. *We agreed to meet on Thursday, 1/18 at 10:30 A.M. for 1 hour.*

   Respectfully submitted,

   Parenting Coordinator

   cc: Parenting Coordination Support Team

There are also circumstances when a parenting coordinator needs direction and assistance from the court because of an impasse or unresolved parenting issue. In some areas, the parenting coordinator must request a status conference or case management conference to have the matter heard. In other areas, the parenting coordinator must notify the court of the issue, state the urgency of the issue, and inform the court whether or not there is an imminent danger or risk to the children or any party. It is important when communicating to the court that the parenting coordinator not provide detailed "evidence" of the issue to be addressed in writing. It is also not permissible for the parenting coordinator to have a private or "ex parte" communication with the judge. The letter which follows provides an example of how a parenting coordinator may communicate to the court that action is needed without the parenting coordinator providing an "expert" opinion or compromising their neutral, unbiased stance.

Honorable John Doe   *Sent Via Facsimile 941-741-5959*
Twelfth Judicial Circuit
1115 Manatee Ave. West
Bradenton, FL 34205

>   *RE: Albright v. Albright*
>   *Case No. 200XXXXXXX*

Dear Judge Doe:

I am writing to request a Case Management Conference on the above-noted case as soon as possible.

As you may recall, I was appointed Parenting Coordinator for this family by the court. The parties continue to participate in Parenting Coordination efforts to date. Dr. Robin Blue and Dr. Denise Green see the parties' minor children, Robert and Rachel, for psychotherapy, respectively. Both Dr. Blue and Dr. Green are licensed psychologists.

An incident occurred in my office on the evening of January 7 involving the parties, one of the minor children, and the current husband of the minor child's mother. The incident resulted in the arrest of one of the parties for assault, which was witnessed by the parties' minor child. Information provided to me by Drs. Blue and Green, who have offices in the same location and were present at the time the incident occurred, raises concerns regarding the minor children.

Please advise if additional information is required prior to granting a Case Management Conference. Thank you.

With best wishes, I remain,

Sincerely,

Debra K. Carter, Ph.D.

cc: G. Albright (father)   F. Lee Bailey, Esq. (counsel for father)
*   M. Albright (mother)   R. Blue, Ph.D.*
*   E. Kagan, Esq. (counsel for mother)   D. Green, Ph.D.*

If the parenting coordinator plans to communicate with attorneys involved in the case, they should make sure that each parent is copied so that the parenting coordinator maintains full disclosure and preserves the trust established as an objective and neutral professional.

By following the procedures outlined in this chapter, the parenting coordinator can help families begin to build the infrastructure they need to disengage from destructive patterns and protect their children from harmful exposure to high conflict. In all parenting coordination work, it is imperative to maintain boundaries and to remember: the parenting coordinator's responsibility to the parents is to be unbiased, the parenting coordinator's responsibilities to the children is to advocate for their best interests, and the parenting coordinator's responsibilities to the court is to be a professional and objective third party. The parenting coordinator should make sure they understand and adhere to their role and responsibilities as defined in the COR, the parenting coordinator contract, and any applicable professional standards or guidelines.

4

Developing an Intervention Strategy

Now here, you see, it takes all the running you can do, to stay in the same place.
If you want to get somewhere else, you must run at least twice as fast as that!
—Lewis Carroll, *Through the Looking-Glass*

The process of parenting coordination should be approached in a systematic, organized manner in order to maximize efficiency in terms of time and money, but more importantly, to develop a strategic plan for interventions and supports that the parents and children will need throughout the parenting coordination process. The needs of parents and children will change during the course of parenting coordination and the interventions and supports required will also need to be re-evaluated as these changes occur. Parents may need fewer supports and less frequent intervention by the parenting coordinator as skills and tools for co-parenting after separation are acquired, as adjustments to major changes in their life are made, as they become emotionally disengaged through structure, and when the cost of continuing the conflict becomes a price they are unwilling to pay.

Parenting coordination work should be organized and planned from the outset with specific goals identified and intervention strategies implemented. It may be helpful to think about the process of parenting coordination as occurring in sequential steps. After the initial paperwork and logistical arrangements have been made, the parenting coordinator gathers information about the parents and their children. The parenting coordinator identifies historical parenting and family dynamics and follows screening procedures, as outlined in Chapter 3 (Getting Started) to identify any potential risk factors that may impact the safety of any individuals involved or which may negatively impact the parenting coordination process. Once these steps have been taken, the parenting coordinator should develop an intervention strategy based on the parents' skills and interaction style, the unique needs of the family, underlying sources of conflict, and resources available.

IDENTIFIED SOURCES OF CONFLICT

In conjunction with screening for parenting dynamics and risk factors, the parenting coordinator must gather information from parents about their primary sources of conflict. This information is usually readily apparent during the meetings with the parents. There may be many points of conflict between them and it is important for the parenting coordinator to listen to each parent's concerns in order to help prioritize the issues to be addressed. Parents may not have the same concerns about parenting but, generally, the stated issues of conflict revolve around time-sharing arrangements, disrespectful communication between the parents, parenting styles, lack of flexibility in parenting arrangements, unresolved financial matters, and allegations of poor parenting.

The stated areas of conflict may not be the *primary* source of conflict so it is important for the parenting coordinator to determine whether there is an underlying, unresolved issue that is fueling the conflict. Common areas of conflict and disagreement for parents who are intact couples often continue to exist in separated and divorced parents. Potential sources of conflict may include involvement of extended family members, issues around money, politics, religion, discipline, education, and unresolved issues of hurt and betrayal. For separated and divorced parents, they may have conflicts around new spouses or paramours and the children's exposure to these new surrogate parent figures.

Parents in intact relationships often disagree with each other about childrearing, and because most parents believe that their child is a reflection of how good a parent they have been, they are eager to defend their status as the "good" or "better" parent. Even minor decisions are seen as having major consequences, so they are ready to vigorously challenge their partner when they disagree about their partner's approach. These disagreements become intensified in circumstances where the parent's partnership has dissolved or never existed. Issues around discipline, where one parent may be perceived as being too "soft" and the other as being too "hard," are common and, rather than being identified as differences in style or approach, become a battleground for asserting who is the more nurturing, supportive, loving parent.

Another common source of conflict involves parents' expectations for their children and which of them is better suited to help their child reach their full potential in terms of academic, athletic, artistic, or spiritual achievement. There are endless sources of conflict around childrearing, but it is important for the parenting coordinator to determine whether the stated or overt issues are the *primary* source of conflict that warrants intervention or whether underlying issues should also be a high priority. It is not uncommon in parenting coordinator work that both the overt and covert sources of conflict need to be addressed simultaneously and the intervention strategy should be designed to reduce, if not resolve, all sources of conflict.

COVERT SOURCES OF CONFLICT

In addition to the stated sources of conflict between the parents, there are often underlying issues which fuel the conflict and serve to keep the parents "connected" in spite of their claims of wanting to disengage from one another. Potential sources of covert, or underlying, conflict include unresolved family of origin issues, unresolved grief, and personality dynamics. It is widely recognized in the mental health community that individuals are likely to repeat patterns of response and behavior even if the result is not constructive or desired (Bonnet, 2005). This is particularly true if the individual is not aware of the pattern they are repeating. For example, parents may be engaged in a pattern of conflict that reflects the lessons they learned as children from their parent's marriage.

Children are also affected by the emotional climate of the home and learn what happens to people who are married by what they observe. These conclusions become a permanent part of their belief system and expectations of marriage even if the exchanges between their parents are not remembered (Siegel, 2000). Therefore, a parent who learned to deal with conflict by watching one of their parents ignore the other and exchange hostile glances may respond to any conflict by engaging in the same pattern of behavior even though there is a part of him or her that knows this is not constructive and only leads to more conflict.

Helping parents recognize patterns of reaction and behavior that may be a reflection of what they learned in their family of origin about intimate relationships and means of resolving conflict often allows the "underlying" issue to emerge and be dealt with in a more constructive manner. Another example of a covert influence is a parent whose parent died in their childhood. These children experience a profound and unexpected loss that often leaves a life-long emotional scar. This "scar" may not appear until the child is a parent themselves and may manifest as a pervasive expectation that they will be left or abandoned in their intimate relationships even if there is no evidence to support this belief. When these fears and expectations are outside the parent's awareness and have not been resolved, they are likely to impact their interactions with their partners and can lead to feelings of mistrust and unfounded allegations of infidelity which becomes the identified source of the conflict rather than an unresolved issue from childhood. It is important to note that the parenting coordinator is not in the role of a parent's therapist and should not work to help parents resolve underlying or hidden conflicts. The parenting coordinator should recognize when there is a "hidden agenda" or covert influence that is fueling the conflict and refer that parent for appropriate treatment or intervention.

IDENTIFYING CHARACTERISTICS
OF HIGH-CONFLICT PARENTS

Many high-conflict parents have been identified as having personality disorders (Eddy, 2006). In high-conflict legal disputes, the conflict may be driven more by internal distress than external events. Eddy (2006) identified patterns to these high-conflict cases which suggest that level and cost of conflict is not based on issues or amount of money involved and that individuals with these personalities have a life-long, enduring pattern of behavior and blame.

It is not hard to recognize individuals with underlying personality dynamics that perpetuate chronic conflict. Their lives are characterized by drama and exaggerated emotions and behaviors. They repeatedly get into interpersonal conflicts and constantly see themselves as helpless victims. They are unable to reflect on their own behavior and deny responsibility for any part in causing conflicts. They are not able to benefit from feedback about behavior change and often seek out others to confirm that their behavior is appropriate. They focus intense energy on analyzing and blaming others. These individuals are often completely unaware of how self-sabotaging they are. From a psychological perspective, these individuals feel chronic internal distress and behave inappropriately to attempt to relieve the distress. The pattern of blame serves to prevent them from looking at themselves honestly and results in unchanged behavior and continued conflict. They receive negative feedback about their behavior, but this only serves to escalate the internal distress, which causes them to behave inappropriately and so the cycle goes on.

High-conflict individuals may display an enduring pattern of behavior which usually exists from early adulthood. They are rigid, unchanging, and unable to recognize that their patterns of reaction and behavior lead to significant distress or impairment. Because they see their difficulties as external to them and independent of their behavior or input, they look for something or someone to blame. They may have personality disorders or, at least, maladaptive personality traits. You do not need to be a mental health professional or diagnose a personality disorder to see a pattern of dysfunctional behavior.

Sometimes both parents have high-conflict personalities. In other cases, there is only one individual who is perpetuating the conflict. The other parent may be fairly reasonable and trying to avoid the conflict or re-establish peace. In either circumstance, the parenting coordinator must identify whether one or both of the parents have a high-conflict personality and develop intervention strategies to manage the pattern of interaction and behavior that sabotages their co-parenting relationship and exposes their children to chronic conflict and hostility. If a parent is displaying high-conflict personality traits, the parenting coordinator may want to refer the individual for a psychological assessment to get a diagnosis and recommendations for therapeutic intervention. In addition to the suggestions below, Chapter 9, Intervention Strategies for Families with Extra Challenges, also includes tips and strategies for working with parents who have personality disorders and other types of mental illness.

Not every parent who is referred for parenting coordination has a personality disorder and not everyone with a personality disorder engages in high conflict. Only those who are "persuasive blamers" as Eddy (2006) describes them seem to get caught in long-term, high-conflict situations. Regardless of whether a diagnosis has been applied, it is important to understand that personality disorder characteristics occur along a continuum, but they have some commonalities.

Personality disorders are defined as an enduring pattern of experiencing and interacting with the world that deviates significantly from the expectations of the individual's culture or social norms. Commonalities in these disorders include disturbances in several of the following areas:

1. Distortions in the pattern of thinking/perceiving (cognitions)
2. Emotions or feelings
3. Behavioral control
4. Relationship or interpersonal functioning

Cognition is how a person perceives and interprets information. All human beings have cognitive distortions or misperceive and misinterpret information some of the time in some circumstances. But, misperception and faulty interpretation of information is pervasive in high-conflict individuals and consistently affects their judgment. Therefore, cognitive distortions are likely to create conflict with a co-parent due to the parent's focus on themselves and faulty decision-making that impacts the children. For example, these parents may expect their children to focus attention on the parent's needs first and expect their children to be their emotional support or confidant. Parents who experience cognitive distortions may expect their children to be more mature than their chronological age and ignore or invalidate their child's needs and feelings. These parents are at risk of being emotionally abusive and neglectful of their children.

Parenting capacity is often impaired when parents have a disturbance in cognition that causes misperceptions, misinterpretation of information, and poor judgment. Examples include:

- The parent dismisses the child's feelings for other parent and punishes the child if they say anything positive or "supportive" of the other parent.
- The parent demands that the child "keep secrets" from the other parent about behavior that the parent is displaying, for example, drinking, allowing a new paramour to live-in, use of illegal drugs.
- The parent leaves the child alone or with strangers so they can date or go out with friends.
- The parent gets angry if the child makes any demands (i.e., feels sick or needs help with homework) that interfere with a new romantic relationship.

Another commonality in personality disorder traits is disturbance of emotions or feelings. These parents have difficulty controlling their emotions and often display hysterical outbursts or unpredictable, intense emotions. They model inappropriate expressions of emotion for their children and do not know how to help their children learn to modulate or regulate their own emotions. Parents who experience and display a disturbance of emotions are also at risk of being emotionally abusive and neglectful of their children. Examples of this type of parenting may include

- The parent becomes despondent over the breakup on a new relationship and blames the child for the breakup because the child was "such a brat."
- The parent imposes punishments that do not fit the crime (e.g., taking away the cell phone for a month for going over their time limit by 2 minutes; throws child's toys or clothes away because they were

left on the floor; refusing the child a day's meals because they didn't eat their vegetables the evening before).

- The parent sporadically blows up at the child for a minor infraction and breaks objects or physically hits the child or pulls their hair.
- The parent follows an unreasonable punishment of the child by buying the child an extravagant gift because the parent feels guilty.
- The parent explodes at the child's coach for not allowing the child to start the game but later demeans and verbally abuses the child for his laziness and poor athletic ability.

Another commonality for parents with personality disordered traits is in the area of behavior or impulse control. Impulse control refers to how a person regulates or manages their own behavior in response to their needs and desires. These parents often act without thinking about consequences. For example, they may speed excessively, drive after drinking, spend money beyond their means, and leave children unattended or inadequately supervised. Additional examples of parents who have poor impulse control are those who

- Leave their children unattended or with a stranger because of last minute planning
- Become financially unstable and stressed because of impulsive spending
- Drive dangerously and do not use safety equipment for their children (i.e., car seats or seat belts)
- Give children alcohol or adult sleeping medicine so they will go to sleep and stop bothering the parent

The last area of commonality for parents who have personality disorder characteristics is seen in the parent's relationships or interpersonal functioning. They may choose a series of unstable partners and expose their children to multiple, intense relationships which are short-lived and chaotic. These parents are also often estranged from extended family members and have few consistent adult relationships to which the children can turn for help and support. Parents who have a disturbed pattern of interpersonal relationships impact their children in a negative manner. Examples may include

- The parent does not allow the child to see or spend time with extended family members who previously had close and loving relationships with the children because the family member criticized the parent's choices

▪ The parent may become involved in a series of short-term relationships and neglect the children's needs to focus on developing a new partner
▪ The child may become attached to a parent's new partners only to lose these close relationships
▪ The parent displays poor coping skills and poor communication skills for the child

Any of the personality disordered traits or characteristics described here may place the children at risk for physical and/or psychological harm. Many of these individuals may meet the diagnostic criteria for a personality disorder (*DSM-TR*, 2000) such as Borderline, Narcissistic, Antisocial, or Histrionic. The traits and characteristics of parents with these types of personality disorders are explored further in Chapter 9.

Persons with these types of personality disorders have characteristics that draw them into intense, prolonged and escalating, legal and interpersonal disputes. Eddy (2006) divides these types of individuals into two categories: Those who are "nonpersuasive blamers" and those who are "persuasive blamers." He says that nonpersuasive blamers are not very effective in maintaining high-conflict disputes that expand and escalate because either no one believes them, people just avoid them, or they get "constructively redirected." But the individuals who are "persuasive blamers" (Eddy, 2006) are able to keep the focus off their own behavior and gets others to join them in the blaming. They hire attorneys or other professionals to be their advocates and to join them in their quest to prove that the other parent is monstrous or wrong and that they are innocent or right. They expect the parenting coordinator to become their advocate also, to join them in their beliefs, and engage in this blaming behavior also. When the parenting coordinator fails to do so, these individuals often work to get the parenting coordinator dismissed by any method necessary, including threats of civil litigation or licensing board complaints against the parenting coordinator, and other behaviors intended to intimidate and bully the parenting coordinator. It is because of work with these individuals that parenting coordination is often described as "not for the faint of heart" because these individuals are challenging and difficult under the best of circumstances.

Factual Distortions

These parents will generate emotional "facts" that are triggered by their cognitive distortions rather than having any real basis in reality. These emotional facts may take different forms and are designed to create a sense of urgency. The parent may exaggerate real facts–"he is always late in picking up the kids" or "she never attends any school conferences" when it may have happened once or twice. The parent may also take real facts out of context—"he never spent any time with the kids"—when in reality dad may have had to work two jobs to support the family.

There are times when a parent may assert nonexistent facts based on their own fears or what they know will hurt the other parent the most–"he started drinking the moment he walked in the door until he went to bed at night. He will deny that and he always hid the liquor bottles and put his drink in a coffee mug to make the kids think he was having coffee." These facts are intended to persuade advocates to feel the same sense of urgency that the alleging parent feels and to do things on behalf of the high-conflict parent.

IDENTIFYING PARENT INTERACTION PATTERNS

In addition to individual characteristics that contribute to parents remaining locked in high-conflict patterns, there are regularly occurring interaction patterns between parents. Social scientists have identified factors and styles which characterize different parent interaction patterns. Parent interaction patterns or type of partnership in the past can be used to guide interventions in parenting coordination to maximize opportunities for success and provide for more time and cost-effective work.

Hetherington (2003) identified five broad types of marriage and the characteristics associated with divorce rates:

1. Pursuer-distancer marriages – This type of partnership is often defined by hostile criticism and contempt on the part of one partner met by withdrawal and denial by the other partner. They engage in frequent, intense conflict and this type of partnership is most likely to end in divorce. These marriages tend to end with a great deal of acrimony.
2. Disengaged marriages – This type of marriage is defined by partners who essentially lead parallel lives. They have few common interests, activities, or friends. These partners rarely fight, but they also express very little extreme positive or negative emotions and withdraw from most disagreements.
3. Operatic marriages – These are partners who are emotionally volatile sensation seekers. They view a harmonious peaceful environment as boring and like to function at an intense emotional level. Conflict is often a trigger for sex. Operatic marriages are characterized by a cycle of repeated break up and reconciliation.

4. Cohesive-individuated marriages – These partnerships are characterized by warmth, respect, equity, mutual support, autonomy, and stability. They share interests and enjoy spending time together.
5. Traditional marriages – This group had the lowest rates of divorce and lowest rates of marital instability. In these partnerships, the father is the main income producer and the mother provides nurturance, support, home and childcare. These couples enjoy being together, are warm and mutually supportive, and tend to be satisfied in both their marriage and in their sex lives.

Understanding the type of marriage or partner interaction pattern the parents had prior to the time of separation or divorce may help the parenting coordinator identify covert sources of conflict and the type of interventions that are likely to be more effective in helping parents extricate themselves from their crucible of conflict. John Gottman asserts that divorce is a process that begins before the actual day of separation and that "transition diversified marital constellations" coincide with the life cycle (Gottman, 1994a, 1999; Gottman & Declaire, 2001; Gottman & Levenson, 1999).

Just as there are predictable patterns of divorce recovery and time frames for couples who do not get locked in conflict, there are patterns of interaction in which high-conflict parents engage that keep them stuck. Gottman and colleagues conducted years of research in efforts to identify characteristics of couples that would allow for accurate prediction of the likelihood that a couple would stay together and the characteristics of couples that are not likely to sustain a healthy happy relationship. The characteristics of couples who seem doomed to partnership downfall display specific interaction features. These features are labeled the "Four Horsemen of the Apocalypse": Contempt; Criticism; Stonewalling, and Defensiveness. These "horsemen" are commonly seen in high-conflict couples and generally characterize most interactions between the parents, which invariably leads to escalation of their conflict and a breakdown of communication.

Of the four horsemen, overt criticism is the most easily recognizable, and the parenting coordinator can confront and redirect interactions that contain criticisms. However, subtle expressions of criticism may come couched in more passive-aggressive ways and are more difficult to anticipate and prevent. An example of this type of interaction occurred with Sue who started her comments by expressing admiration for her former husband's hard work and success as the family's bread winner. She looked at Tim directly and with a quiet, even tone said: "You have always been a hard worker and a wonderful breadwinner...It's just a shame you have such a hard time parting with your hard earned money, unless it is for something you want." Both the parenting coordinator and the former husband were taken aback. When confronted by the parenting coordinator, Sue did not seem to recognize how she had invited Tim to open up to hear what she had to say, only to then blast him with a passive-aggressive, but intentional criticism.

Contempt is also prevalent in high-conflict couples and relatively easy to recognize. It often manifests in facial expressions and posturing as well as in words and other deeds. Charlie and Judy did not attempt to hide their contempt for one another. Charlie had learned of Judy's rather public affair and could find nothing positive to say about or think about her. In his mind, everything she did was wrong. In parenting coordination appointments, he talked down to her and invalidated virtually every effort she made to build bridges across which they could co-parent. When confronted, Charlie protested that it is "unreasonable of that Judge to expect me to negotiate with this woman. She has no ethics, no morals, and she is a bad influence on my children. Someone who could sink as low as she did has no business around children, let alone my children."

Stonewalling, on the other hand, can be subtle or blatant. Rob and Kathy are clear examples of this type of interaction. Rob, who did not want to be divorced from Kathy, seemed bent on doing whatever she asked and trying to please her. There was one exception. Whenever the topic of activities for the children that involved tuition, fees, or other expenses arose, Rob invariably insisted that there were other issues that would have to be resolved before he would even consider Kathy's proposals. In one such interchange he insisted that "I am not going to spend this session discussing summer camps when we can't even agree on weekend visits." When Kathy persisted in her quest to nail down summer camp plans Rob said, in the calm quiet voice of a man who knew he had the upper hand: "Why don't we talk about how you don't ever take no for an answer, 'cause I'm not going to talk about camps."

Defensiveness also comes in a wide range of forms. Often it is piggy-backed to an assault in which the defensive parent tries to turn the tables. In their very first parenting coordination appointment, Jim made it known that "I'm not perfect, but I do my level best. One reason I divorced Connie is because she never accepts responsibility...she wouldn't carry her weight...So, I'd end up carrying the whole load and, when there was too much to handle she didn't lift a finger to help me." From that point forth, even Connie's most concrete examples of problems that needed solving were met with defensiveness. For example, Connie asked that the system by which their twin boys were transferred between homes be re-examined. She explained, in a factual tone, that she was often late to work when the boys were dropped off at her home by their dad. She suggested that they either alter the time of the drop-off to allow her more time to get to work, or make it a point to have the boys at her home at the pre-agreed time, or go to a system of evening drop-offs. Jim was livid. He turned to the parenting coordinator insisting that she observe how Connie "is always blaming me for her problems." He went on to say: "Sure, I'm late sometimes. But who can predict traffic? If she were more responsible, she'd work things out with her boss instead of blaming me for her being late."

Protective and Risk Factors in Partnerships

Hetherington and Kelly (2002) provides a schema for identifying the protective and risk factors in partnerships and explains how these factors operate to determine why some people "succeed" in divorce, where others fail or simply muddle through. Protective factors are described as planfulness, self-regulation, adaptability, social responsibility, internal locus of control, religiosity, work, social support, and new intimate relationships. Risk factors are described as antisocial personality, neuroticism, attachment to a former spouse, cohabitation, promiscuity, socioeconomic status, and family history.

Together, protective and risk factors represent more than just a series of individual buffers and vulnerabilities. Taken together they also determine resiliency or the capacity to adapt to hardships and to rebound from setbacks and defeat. Once properly identified, the parenting coordinator can use both the "protective" and "risk" factors in each parent to formulate effective intervention strategies and determine what other resources a family may need and then help parents build these resources into their support system.

Identifying Impasse Style

Janet Johnston has been a pioneer in researching separating and divorcing couples and looking at the impact on the family, both individually and as a system. She identified couples in conflict who have arrived at an "impasse" stage (Johnston & Campbell, 1988) as falling into two distinct categories.

The two types of interactional impasse are as follows:

Type I Interactional Impasse

- Couples maintain highly positive, idealized views of each other.
- They are enormously ambivalent about the separation.
- They engage in a never-ending search for ways to recapture their dreams.
- They cycle through repeated, promising reconciliations that dissipate into bitter disappointment and period conflict.
- The need for plan for the care of their children is painful because it necessitates renewed contact and triggers re-engagement.
- For the children of these relationships, the divorce is never finality and their reconciliation fantasies are continually fueled.
- The children in these relationships are often neglected by their parents because the parents are absorbed with each other.
- Parents who maintain an idealized view tend to be socially isolated, either through choice or circumstance.
- The couples are deeply enmeshed, sexually, bonded, or ideologically committed to one another.
- They have particular problems separating the parental from the spousal role.

These couples have long-standing problems with shared parenting after divorce. Too much contact with each other intensifies the painful cycle. The cyclical post divorce disputes over the children are usually an extension of their ambivalent relationship and are energized by their smoldering passions for one another.

Type II Interactional Impasse

- Ex-spouses have developed extremely negative polarized view of each other that are sustained by little or no evidence in current reality.
- Ex-spouses view each other as "crazy and mentally disturbed" or as "morally reprehensible monsters."
- They act on these negative polarized views of each other.
- They resist their children's contact with the other parent.
- They fight, consciously and righteously, to protect their children from the "bad, immoral, or neglectful" caretaking of the other parent.
- They mirror each other in a victim stance, each viewing the other as the persecutor.

- These couples avoid contact.
- They refuse to communicate directly and use others (friends, attorneys, or children) as spokespersons in attempt to make plans.
- For the children of these relationships, the transitions between parental homes are lonely and frightening.

There are several factors which contribute to different types of impasse including forces from the wider social system, the couple or family system dynamics, and individual intrapsychic processes. Johnston and Campbell (1988) noted that negative views of the ex-spouse may help individuals restore their self-esteem or ward-off depression or guilt. An example is the wife whose marriage ended because of her husband's extramarital affair with a younger woman or the husband whose wife left him to enter into a lesbian relationship. These circumstances tend to cause a severe blow to the self-esteem of the individual left behind which may then perpetuate feelings of depression or questions about themselves in terms of attractiveness and worth.

Idealized views of the ex-spouse may be a defensive denial of the loss and disappointment they experienced as a result of their marriage ending. Sam and Mary illustrated this type of interaction pattern well. At the time of their first appointment, the parenting coordinator went to greet them in the office lobby and found the couple sitting next to one another, chatting and laughing in an animated fashion. The parenting coordinator's initial thought was that this couple must be at the office to see another provider since the majority of parenting coordination cases this parenting coordinator had seen in the past were generally sitting in stony silence as far apart as possible or actively engaged in yelling at one another. As Sam and Mary began to tell their story, the "idealization" of each other became apparent. Sam came to the marital home every Saturday to mow the lawn and do all the yard work after which Mary would prepare his favorite casserole and both of them would have dinner together with their son. The "source" of their conflict according to their report had to do with Sam's frustration with Mary's demand that he only use the land-based telephone line at his home to call their son. She insisted that he not use his cell phone because of her belief that Sam "could be anywhere" when he called and she remained certain that Sam was having a sexual relationship with two of his female coworkers and she did not want their son exposed to this type of "illicit" behavior. Sam's work required him to travel to multiple locations throughout the day and he was finding it very difficult to travel back and forth to his home to make contact with his son, although he had been doing so for 2 years since the divorce. Although

Sam had consistently denied having a relationship with the female coworkers, Mary would become enraged if he called her home from his cell phone and she would not allow him to speak to their son. They both reported that their son had recently started doing poorly in school and was getting in trouble for his behavior at home and at school, a significant change from the past. It became clear that the weekly Saturday activities were fueling reconciliation fantasies for their son and keeping Sam and Mary stuck in a "still married" behavior pattern that was not allowing any of the family to move on. While this type of impasse may occur with less frequency in parenting coordination, it is important to recognize and help the parents build a co-parenting relationship that is separate and distinct from their marital or couple relationship.

Both at the time of courtship and marriage (coming together) and at the time of separation and divorce (parting), couples tend to redefine themselves and each other. These constructions or reconstructions of self and their new "love" may occur gradually or precipitously and may involve distortions of reality. Couples often develop idealized views of each other during the courtship phase of the relationship promoting the adage that "love is blind." After the "honeymoon" phase of a relationship, those blind spots tend to become clearer and the unappealing and annoying traits and characteristics of a partner may seem more prominent and distressing. This process is magnified significantly when couples are divorcing and often causes a partner to view what had previously been a relatively mild annoying trait in their former spouse as a vile and evil characteristic. This extreme, negative view of the ex-spouse is an example of "blindness" on the other end of the spectrum. These individuals can be characterized as those who "once could see, but now are blind." An example is the parent who had a habit of running a few minutes late who is now described as irresponsible, untrustworthy, uncaring, and controlling.

Most "successful" divorces result from a gradual change in redefining oneself (from husband/wife or committed partner to single person/single parent) along with an emotional disengagement from the marital relationship. For those couples who get stuck in impasse, the parting may have been so dramatic or traumatic and/or so infused with emotion and meaning that the images of self and the ex-spouse created during these significant events become fixed, unyielding to counterevidence and a script for the couples' turbulent relationship throughout the post divorce years. For example, the partner who had an extramarital affair during the marriage may be seen by the other partner as forever untrustworthy and deceitful in all areas of functioning and may be accused of acting in ways that harm the children because the partner who was left felt harmed by the betrayal.

Another classification of divorcing couples comes from Constance Ahrons, author of *The Good Divorce*, who identified the following three types of couples:

Amicable Group

Cooperative Colleagues
> These are couples who cope with their anger in productive ways. They manage their conflicts well and the children do not get caught up in them. One of the major characteristics of this group is their ability to separate their parental responsibilities from their spousal discontents.

Perfect Pals
> These couples represent a smaller, but significant minority in Ahrons' study. These couples remain best friends after divorce. They continue to enjoy an intimate, although nonsexual, relationship. Although their relationships have some conflicts, and anger flares at times, they remain close and caring.

Arch-Enemy Group

Angry Associates
> These couples are not able to confine their anger to their marital differences; it infuses all the relationships in the family.

Fiery Foes
> Ahrons' calls this group the real prototypical examples of bad divorces. These couples' rage taints their families' lives, leaving continued pain and distress for years afterward. These are the ones who make headlines having custody battle after custody battle, resorting sometimes to violence in their pursuit for revenge.

Atypical Group

Dissolved Duos
> These ex-spouses totally discontinue contact with each other and one parent disappears completely from the children's lives.

Couples who experience particularly traumatic separations are prime candidates for generating negative views of each other. A perceived experience of being suddenly and unexpectedly abandoned; betrayed by secret plotting and planning; left after a secret love affair with another person; left after uncharacteristic, explosive violence are all separation modes that are typically traumatic and involve inordinate degrees of humiliation, anger, defeat, guilt, and fear, thus setting the stage for the postseparation or divorce relationship. The common feature of these experiences is a major, unexpected assault on one's stable and predictable world, together with an absence of open, intimate, and corrective communication. Avoidance of issues, mistrust and feelings of betrayal are marked features in those couples who tend to be classified as "Arch Enemies" or have an "Impasse II" interaction style.

Even in circumstances where the separation was less traumatic, there are significant changes that each parent must undergo, including changes in roles and self-identity, as they embark on a new phase of their life after marriage. Ahrons (1995) described "two distinct stages of role-changing after divorce: coping with role losses, and establishing new roles." Each role we play, such as mother, father, son, daughter, niece, professional, friend, and so on gives meaning to our lives and helps define who we are. Even though all individuals change "roles" throughout life (i.e., when we marry and are no longer in a single role; when our children leave home, we are no longer actively parenting; when we retire, we are no longer identified with our professional work-life role, etc.), role losses can be difficult. However, when the role changes occur at predictable times of life, we can prepare for them and they are easier to handle. It is when roles change suddenly and unexpectedly in life that makes them much more difficult to adjust to and integrate into a new self-identity.

IDENTIFYING ADJUSTMENT PHASE FOR PARENTS

It is not unusual for parents who are engaged in high-conflict interactions to display atypical behaviors, following the period of actual separation, which may seem quite irrational to the outsider and very atypical of how the person usually behaves. For these individuals, the experience of separation causes a severe psychological trauma. The loss of stability and predictability in their lives is overwhelming. The predominate feeling is a sense of injustice, unfairness, and loss of control. As a result, they may display extreme and uncharacteristic behaviors such as drinking to excess or flagrant promiscuity. They may get into physical altercations or threaten suicide or homicide. They may threaten to kidnap the children and steal possessions from their former spouse.

In addition to extreme, hysterical behaviors, some parents may also express rage and panic. The extreme behaviors and expressions of emotion are attempts to recapture a sense of stability and predictability in their lives. When couples display bizarre behaviors and express polarized views of each other, it is important to determine whether separation-related factors prompted this interaction pattern or whether the pattern existed prior to separation. In circumstances when the extreme negative views of each other and very disturbed behavior occurred around separation, the behaviors may be confined only to the sphere of the former intimate partner relationship. In other areas of their life and in other relationships, they may function in a very rational and effective manner. In these circumstances, the parenting coordinator must determine whether parents are stuck in a phase of *traumatic reactivity* or whether they have the type of personality that will cause them to perpetually act in a disorganized, unpredictable, and self-sabotaging manner. The intervention strategies used by the parenting coordinator will differ depending on whether the cause of the erratic behaviors and extreme emotions are reactions to the traumatic separation or whether the pattern is more long standing.

It is important to identify the interaction style and origin of conflict at the outset of the parenting coordination work. While this will guide the intervention strategies that the parenting coordinator employs in the initial phase of work, it also helps predict how a parent will likely behave as they move into the next phase of their life. Ahrons (1995) points out that "the style of interaction and communication a couple develops post divorce affects all their future intimate relationships" and that "amicable ex-spouses, when they find [*sic*] new partners, are happier in their remarriages than were hostile or unfriendly ex-spouses." Based on prevalence rates of divorce in the United States (CDC, 2009) and other Western cultures, a parent may remarry and divorce several times throughout a child's life. If a parent has multiple, sequential partners and consistently experiences traumatic separations, their children are likely to be exposed to the parent's traumatic reaction of extreme behaviors and expressions of emotion. Parenting coordination offers parents an opportunity to develop the structure and supports they need to stabilize their lives and break the destructive pattern to which their children may be consistently exposed.

IDENTIFY PARENT'S APPROACH TO CONFLICT RESOLUTION

An additional variable that is helpful in organizing the parenting coordination work is to identify the parents' approach to conflict resolution. Morton Deutsch (2000) classified approaches to conflict resolution in terms of a cooperative or competitive disputing style. He asserted that a couple's approach to conflict resolution helps predict the type of interactions that occur between them when they are trying to negotiate or resolve differences. He suggested that the reasons behind the dispute and the goals each person seeks to achieve are the most important factors in determining whether a person approaches a conflict cooperatively or competitively. Therefore, it is important for the parenting coordinator to understand both the reasons behind the conflict and the goals of each parent in order to develop an intervention strategy aimed at neutralizing the competitive approach to conflict resolution.

Most parents who are characterized as high conflict engage in a competitive approach to resolving disputes and are unable to utilize more cooperative approaches. If parents are capable of learning to resolve their disputes cooperatively, then parenting coordination interventions will focus on helping parents acquire the tools and skills necessary to change their approach to resolving disputes from competitive to cooperative. However, some couples are likely to persist in utilizing a competitive approach to resolve their disputes regardless of any interventions. In those cases, the parenting coordinator must structure interventions to mitigate the potential damage to the children and family stability.

A cooperative approach to resolving disputes is characterized by:

- Effective communication where ideas are shared, each person listens to the other, and each is willing to consider the other's ideas;
- Friendliness and helpfulness in conversations;
- Coordination of efforts and division of labor;
- Orientation to task achievement;
- Similarities in beliefs and values;
- A willingness to share power and control;
- Conflicting interests are seen as a mutual problem; and
- Solutions must acknowledge everyone's interests and be responsive to the needs of all.

A competitive approach to resolving disputes is characterized by:

- Misleading communication, including false promises and misinformation;
- Mutual negative attitudes and suspicion of one another's intentions;
- Inability to effectively divide parenting duties leading to duplication of effort and a constant need to check up on the other;
- Criticism and rejection of the other's ideas; and
- An unwillingness to share power or control with their partner.

The competitive approach to conflict resolution fosters the notion that solutions to conflict can only be imposed by one side on the other.

This orientation also encourages the use of coercive tactics such as psychological or physical threats and/or violence. This process tends to turn all disagreements into power struggles, with each side seeking to "win." Parents who are locked into a competitive process are often willing to accept a mutual disaster rather than a partial defeat or compromise.

Parents who are locked in a competitive dispute resolution approach are fairly easy to identify and may require a series of confrontations to bring this approach and the consequences of continued engagement in this approach to the surface. The goal of parenting coordination is to help parents transition to a cooperative approach to resolving disputes, if possible, and to help them see the value of adopting a new approach that is likely to require creative problem-solving. The parenting coordinator will need to do some creative thinking and teach parents how to think creatively also. In Chapter 5 (Conflict Analysis, Transformation, and Containment), interventions to inspire creativity in problem-solving are discussed.

Often, parents need a "support team" as they embark on new patterns of thinking, behaving and interacting. The parenting coordinator should help parents identify the "team members" they will need during the process of change and establishment of a new infrastructure that allows for reduced conflict and more constructive co-parenting.

BUILDING A SUPPORT TEAM FOR THE FAMILY

Parents and children often need a lot of support after separation and divorce to help them adjust to the many changes that family reconstruction brings about and there are many potential support team members. The parenting coordinator may identify the type of support services needed and make appropriate referrals. Parents and children often need both a professional and nonprofessional support team to be successful in making changes and stabilizing their family. Professional support services might include:

Psychotherapy
Anger Management
Psychiatric Evaluation
Parenting Classes
Parenting "Fitness" Evaluation
EMDR (Eye Movement Desensitization Reprocessing)
"Reunification" therapy
Preparation for step-parenting
Postdivorce check-ups for children

Parents and children also need nonprofessional supports, which may include:

Grandparents
Stepparents
Extended family members
Friends
Clergy
Religious organizations
Community groups
Child care services

The parenting coordinator should consider any other resources which may help the family rebuild an infrastructure that supports change and maintains a conflict-free environment for all.

Table 4.1 below will help guide the parenting coordinator in selecting appropriate services for a professional support team for parents and children.

TABLE 4.1   Referral Guidelines for Professional Support Team Members

Services	Refer When:
Psychotherapy - for adults	Mental illness is present
	One or both parents are still emotionally engaged
Psychotherapy - for child	Mental illness is present in child or adult
	Parents have exposed children to chronic conflict
	Children display regressive behaviors
	Children display signs of distress
Batterer's Intervention Program; Domestic Violence Center (victim services)	Domestic violence exists or is suspected
Anger management	Family member does not have constructive means of expressing anger
Medication evaluation	Mental illness
	Impulse-control intervention needed
Parenting classes	Parent(s) lack knowledge of child development
	Parent(s) lack knowledge of appropriate discipline techniques
	Parent(s) lack basic communication skills
	Parent(s) lack understanding of parental conflict on children
	Parent planning to remarry and blend family

(Continued)

TABLE 4.1 *Continued*

Services	Refer When:
Parent "fitness" evaluation	Neglect exists or is suspected
Post-divorce "check-up"	Parent concerned about child's adjustment
EMDR	Parent has past traumas which interfere with effective functioning
Reunification therapy	Parental alienation exists
	Child is estranged from parent
	Parent-child relationship is strained
Medical doctor	Health issue exists
Attorney	Unresolved legal issue exists
Dentist/orthodontist	Dental issue exists

5

Conflict Analysis, Transformation, and Containment

The keenest sorrow is to recognize ourselves as the sole cause of all our adversities.
—Sophocles

To state the obvious, parents who enter the parenting coordination process are in conflict. Alternative dispute resolution processes, such as parenting coordination, are often utilized to help resolve conflicts. Therefore, it would follow that the primary goal and purpose of parenting coordination is to assist parents in conflict to resolve their disputes successfully so that they are able to be effective co-parents, to create a stable life and home environment for themselves and their children, and to shield their children from exposure to chronic hostility and conflict. On the surface, this should be relatively easy—analyze the elements of the conflict, identify interests and needs of each party, eliminate perceived incompatibility between parties, facilitate negotiation and voilà—conflict resolved!

However, those who have worked with parents in conflict know that conflict resolution is anything but easy. The origins of conflict are complex and are usually an outgrowth of the diverse thoughts, attitudes, beliefs, and perceptions of individuals as well as the social system or structures in which we live. Conflict in relationships is inevitable. So, how do we explain the persistence of destructive conflict when it is generally unpleasant, involves negative emotion, tears apart families, and diverts attention and energy from more constructive pursuits? How do we explain the enormous trade-offs in costs and adverse consequences that individuals and families are willing to pay to maintain a protracted conflict?

This chapter will examine different types of conflict and propose options for transformation or containment of conflicts within the parenting coordination process. Transforming conflicts into a dynamic between parents that can be objectively perceived and explored increases opportunities for resolution of conflict. Parenting coordinators seek to identify the conflict between parents that is due to perceived incompatible interests. With assistance and creative problem-solving, these perceived incompatibilities may be challenged and reframed. Helping parents visualize the possibility that conflicts may be resolved without causing long-term damage to the children or the family is the central goal of parenting coordination.

Some parents get caught in conflicts that become protracted affairs with no end in sight. The literature on conflict calls this type of conflict *intractable* (Azar, 1990; Bennett, 1996; Coleman, 2003; Deutsch et al., 2006; Kriesberg, 2005; Marshall & Gurr, 2005). Intractable conflicts tend to be extremely damaging, become self-perpetuating, and are often very resistant to intervention or a reasoned approach to resolution.

The parenting coordinator may need to point out to parents that not all conflicts are bad. When conflicts are used as an opportunity to learn alternative ways of thinking and behaving, they can be a source of personal development and a source of energy to reconstruct a new shared reality, which parents must do following separation or divorce. However, conflicts can also escalate beyond a point that has any benefits, and instead, lead to protracted acrimonious interactions that are destructive to all and particularly harmful to children. It is important for the parenting coordinator to identify and analyze the source of a conflict as well as the variables that have caused the conflict sustained between the parents. This includes identifying each parent's stated disputes with their co-parent, and when they began, as well as identifying underlying sources of conflict which may be causing disputes to escalate and expand.

Each parent can usually readily describe their overt parenting disputes and the problems they encounter with their co-parent, but they may be unaware of underlying issues which are fueling the continued battle. Parents may identify the same parenting issues, but have different ideas about how the dispute should be resolved. Alternatively, the parenting disputes each parent describes may be quite different in origin and scope. The parenting coordinator needs to start with what the parents identify as their dispute and look for areas of agreement and divergence. The parenting coordinator may want to write down the stated disputes in a manner that allows parents to reference them as they proceed through the process (e.g., flip chart, dry erase marker board, chalk board).

Once the overt disputes have been identified, the parenting coordinator should then attempt to identify each parent's interests or goals. This step introduces the concept of constructive conflict resolution. Helping parents understand that conflicts can be used for constructive purposes involves planting the seeds of peace, or at least détente. These seeds are the introduction of concepts that may help transform the negative conflict into one which can be constructive. However, if we follow the agricultural analogy, we know that seeds will not take root without proper soil preparation (e.g., advising parents of negative impact on their children if conflict remains high), appropriate nurturance such as sunshine, fertilization, and hydration (e.g., parent education, support team members, encouragement by the parenting coordinator, etc.), and weed control (minimizing destructive input).

Before introducing concepts of conflict transformation (seeds of peace), the parenting coordinator needs to assess whether parents are ready to hear or receive this information (preparing the soil). The parenting coordinator may suggest that understanding each parent's disputes and goals opens up possibilities for improving the relationship. Most parents will acknowledge that they want to improve the relationship with their co-parent, but often believe it is impossible to do. The parenting coordinator should also be watching for behaviors and nonverbal communications from each parent to indicate whether their assertion of wanting to improve the relationships with their co-parent is genuine or stated because they believe that is what is expected of them. The parenting coordinator will need to use their judgment about timing the introduction of these new concepts to increase the likelihood that the seeds of peace may take root.

A tool to begin the process of conflict transformation is to identify each parent's interests and goals. This "seed" of peace includes introduction of the idea that conflicts are not always a battle between competing and incompatible interests or desires. Distinguishing interests from positions that tend to be absolutes, such as right-wrong or good-evil, often helps open up possibilities for conflict resolution that neither parent had been able to see. The parenting coordinator may also point out that *the conflict* has come to define the entire relationship with the other parent, rather than one element of the relationship that has become dominant. A far more useful concept of conflict is that it is often only one part of a complex and long-term relationship.

Following identification of the overt conflicts and each parent's interests and goals, the parenting coordinator must also identify the resources available to the parents and the family systems. These resources may include access to mental health treatment, a supportive social network, financial resources and security, access to reliable child care, and so on. Once these elements have been identified, the parenting coordinator can expand the intervention strategy to include interventions that will help parents learn how to respond more constructively to their family situation and their co-parent, and begin to build an infrastructure for the family that serves the children's best interests.

The intervention strategy should include a plan for parents to acquire the new tools and skills they need within the restructured family framework to increase the likelihood of transforming their conflicts into constructive changes. Most parents will need oversight, encouragement, and monitoring by the parenting coordinator as they practice the new skills and try to embrace new perceptions of themselves and their co-parent. Ideally, both parents will ultimately be able to move on with their lives and create a family environment that allows for the children to thrive.

However, there are some circumstances when the conflicts are so intractable and resistant to interventions that allow for constructive change, that the parenting coordinator's role is to create an infrastructure to *contain* the conflicts rather than transform them. If the parenting coordinator determines that the parents are unwilling or unable to work toward constructive conflict resolution, then one of the intervention strategies is to help parents "encapsulate" the conflict in an effort to insulate the children from exposure to these enduring and extremely damaging conflicts. The parenting coordinator will need to gather data from the parents about the history of the conflict, the elements that have caused the conflict to fester, and the course of the conflict before determining whether the intervention strategy should include concepts for transformation or containment of the conflict.

HISTORY AND EVOLUTION OF THE CONFLICT

As presented in Chapter 3, Getting Started, it is helpful to get information about each parent and their relationship prior to separation or divorce. Of primary importance is the parenting dynamics which existed prior to separation or divorce. Several examples of different partner interaction styles were also presented in Chapter 4 (Developing an Intervention Strategy). The parents may be continuing a previous pattern or may have established a new pattern of interaction that was triggered by the separation and divorce. This information may be collected in the form of questionnaires or surveys that the parenting coordinator asks parents to complete prior to the initial appointments or during the parenting coordinator process. The parenting coordinator may also gather this information directly from parents during appointments.

Understanding the history of a conflict also involves understanding what caused the conflict in the first place, that is, the environment (literal or emotional) in which the conflict occurred and how long it has been in existence. For example, are the issues giving rise to the conflicts situational or are there long-standing unresolved issues which have been brought to the surface by the change in family structure? How much is fear and insecurity fueling the conflicts? How much of the conflict is due to the financial impact the separation has had on the family? What impact has the adversarial environment of family court had on the family system? Has trust been completely eroded between the parents and is it possible to rebuild some level of trust between them? All of these are questions the parenting coordinator will want to understand fully in order to structure interventions that are likely to be more successful.

As discussed in Chapter 4, there are different approaches to conflict resolution and each parent's style of resolving disputes is important to identify. Each parent may have naturally adopted a competitive approach to resolving disputes or this approach may have resulted from their exposure and immersion in an adversarial family law process. An adversarial process tends to promote competition and the goal of being a "winner" versus a "loser." The parenting coordinator has an opportunity to help parents identify and label their approach to resolving conflicts and point out that a competitive approach, and the decision to remain adversaries, will likely result in conflict escalation rather than conflict resolution. The parenting coordinator should introduce the idea of a cooperative approach. In parenting coordination, parents have an opportunity to learn the techniques needed to modify their style of conflict resolution and the parenting coordinator can model a conflict resolution approach that is more cooperative in nature. Most parents who need parenting coordination are locked in a competitive approach to conflict resolution and may be unable or unwilling to modify their approach to a more cooperative style.

CHANGING APPROACH TO CONFLICT RESOLUTION

Fisher, Ury, and Patton (1992) assert that negotiations to resolve conflicts that take the form of *positional* bargaining do not produce good agreements. Positional bargaining is similar to a competitive approach to resolving disputes where each parent may take a position and attempt to influence their co-parent to adopt their position. The other parent may do the same which sets up a situation where the outcome or resolution means one parent "wins" and the other "loses." This form of bargaining is inefficient, neglects each person's interests, and tends to harm an already deteriorated relationship. The goal is to reach resolution to conflicts that satisfies both parents' interests, is seen as fair to all, and produces lasting results.

A more cooperative approach to resolving disputes involves the use of "principled negotiation." Fisher et al. (1992) described four *principles of negotiation*: (1) separate the individual from the problem; (2) focus on interests rather than positions; (3) generate a variety of options before settling on an agreement; and (4) insist that the agreement be based on objective criteria. Applying these concepts to parenting coordination will help each parent identify their *interests* and help them differentiate their interests from their positions. Both parents are presumably interested in having their children be law-abiding citizens, achieve their full potential, and be physically and mentally healthy, happy individuals. The parenting coordinator may need to help parents articulate the interests they have in common as a starting point in changing their approach to resolving disputes.

The parenting coordinator must also structure interventions to help each party generate a variety of options for conflict resolution that takes into account each parent's interests, needs, and goals. This is where creative thinking on the part of the parenting coordinator and parents is needed.

INSPIRING CREATIVITY

Creative thinking involves three key elements: (1) generating motivation to solve a problem; (2) establishing conditions that permit "reframing" the problem once an impasse has been reached; and (3) generating diverse ideas that can be combined into new solutions. Conflict, itself, can generate motivation to solve a problem if the consequence of the conflict is distressing enough. However, the need for maintaining the status quo can also create a rigid and defensive adherence to a previously held position. Therefore, the challenge for the parenting coordinator is to establish an environment that is structured enough to reduce threat and encourage motivation to change, while maintaining an optimal level of pressure to try new ways of thinking and behaving. Reminding parents of the primary goal of protecting the children from chronic exposure to hostility and reducing conflict for all can be a powerful motivating force.

There are times when each parent's goals are tied together in such a way that the chance of one parent attaining their goal is *increased* by the probability of the other parent successfully attaining their goal also. For example, let's say dad accepts a new job that requires more travel and involves more money, but makes his schedule less predictable. He doesn't want to lose a lot of time with the kids and mom wants to spend more time with the children than the current schedule allows. If mom agrees to work with the schedule in a more flexible manner, dad makes more money, child support may increase which may allow mom to work fewer hours to meet her financial needs. This is an example of how parents' goals may be linked in a way that creates an opportunity for both parents to get their interests and goals met by working together.

There are other circumstances when each parent's goals are tied together in such a way that the probability of one parent attaining their goal is *decreased* by the probability of their co-parent successfully attaining their goal. This forces a more competitive situation because the only way for one parent to achieve their goals is for the other side not to achieve their goal. The challenge for parenting coordination is to help parents redefine their goals and their approach to resolving conflicts so that parents are able to focus on common interests and reach agreements that are more "win–win" than "win–lose." An example of this occurred with Jack and Jessie. From the moment of Hayley's birth Jessie, herself an Olympic medal winner, dreamt of her daughter winning the Olympic gold medal in gymnastics. While they were still married, both Jack and Jessie supported their daughter's gymnastics training, paying for lessons and attending competitions. Hayley proved to be talented, not just in the gym, but in school as well. IQ testing showed that Hayley had an IQ in the Genius range. Jack had dreams of her following in his footsteps as a physician. At the time Jack and Jessie started parenting coordination, Hayley was an entering high school freshman and had the chance to enroll in a highly competitive academic program or continue on her gymnastics track. Both programs were demanding, and it was not possible for Hayley to do both. Jessie was adamant that Hayley keep her focus on gymnastics. Jack was equally adamant that school should be the focus. Neither parent has considered the implications of the two options. Both were stuck on the question of the moment, gymnastics or scholastics?

One helpful intervention by the PC involved simply asking the parents about Hayley's self-confidence and her ability to make independent decisions. This took the focus off the logistical issue and got the parents thinking about how important the process by which the issue got resolved could be in Hayley's development. From there it was a short leap to asking the parents to consider their hopes and aspirations for their daughter's future independence and sense of self-direction. Jack and Jessie then had the room they needed to collaborate both with each other, and with their daughter. The parenting coordinator was able to help the parents transform what had initially seemed like mutually incompatible goals into a circumstance where they could refocus on their daughter and her best interests.

EVOLUTION OF CONFLICT

It is helpful for the parenting coordinator and parents to understand that their conflicts may change over time and the intensity of conflicts may have more of an ebb and flow pattern. Characterizing stages of conflict may help the parenting coordinator and parents identify where they are in the process and can also be a useful guide to specific interventions for the parenting coordinator. Conflicts occur along a continuum of stages and were illustrated by Brahm (2003) in the diagram below (Figure 5.1).

Parents entering parenting coordination will usually enter and be caught in stages of conflict that are just emerging, continuing to escalate, or already at stalemate. By analyzing the course of the conflict, parenting coordinators can help parents begin to get a more objective perspective of their conflict and start to think about whether they are interested in getting over the hump and moving toward de-escalation of the conflict, resolving their disputes and possibly building a longer lasting peace between them. It is important to note that the progress from one stage to the next is not a linear progression and parents often repeat stages several times.

The potential for conflict exists whenever people have different needs, values, or interests; this is the "latent conflict stage." A conflict

FIGURE 5.1   Brahm, Eric. "Conflict Stages." Beyond Intractability. Eds. Guy Burgess and Heidi Burgess. Conflict Research Consortium, University of Colorado, Boulder. Posted: September 2003, http://www.beyondintractability.org/essay/conflict_stages/.

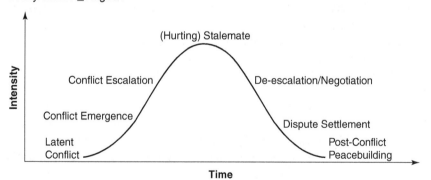

may not become apparent until a "triggering event" leads to the emergence (or beginning) of the overt conflict. An example of a "triggering event" might be filing for divorce or any event which led to the dissolution and deterioration of the parenting partnership. Emergence may be followed by settlement or resolution, or it may be followed by escalation. Parents who are able to resolve their disputes with minimal or temporary escalation of their conflict usually do not need parenting coordination services. De-escalation for these parents can be temporary or can be part of a broader trend toward settlement or resolution.

Parents caught in a prolonged conflict are often in the stage of escalation. Escalation, however, does not continue indefinitely and may lead to de-escalation or stalemate. Parents caught in an intractable conflict get stuck in the stalemate stage, a situation in which neither side can win. If the pain of continuing the conflict exceeds that of maintaining the confrontation, then parents are in what Zartman (1989) calls a "hurting stalemate," which often presents an ideal opportunity for negotiation and a potential settlement because the consequence of continuing the conflict is more painful or has greater likelihood of a negative outcome than trying to find a workable solution to the conflict. If the concept of any peace-building efforts seems impossible, then the parenting coordinator can help parents consider the possibility of at least resolving disputes to more effectively co-parent their children.

The parenting coordination process does not follow a linear path toward conflict resolution of warring parents. Parents should be prepared for the inevitable course of progress and setbacks toward resolution. The lack of linear progression toward sustained resolution of conflict often gives parents the sense that long-term resolution of their conflict is impossible. It is important for the parenting coordinator to distinguish between those parents who are experiencing normal ebbs and flows toward resolving conflict and those who are locked in an intractable conflict with no possibility of resolution.

Conflict may escalate even after parents have reached what they thought was a permanent resolution to their conflict. For example, when divorced parents want to remarry and introduce a new romantic partner or love interest into their children's lives, the former marital partner may see the new love interest as a threat to their role as parent (e.g., a new "step-parent" is now entering the picture) and/or feel angered by the loss of time and attention the former spouse may now be directing toward their new partner instead of the children.

Delineating different stages of a conflict can be useful in helping parents get a longitudinal view of their co-parenting relationship. By recognizing the different dynamics occurring at each stage of a conflict, the parenting coordinator can utilize different strategies and techniques depending on the phase of the conflict. Strategies for resolving conflicts and building consensus are covered in Chapters 6 and 7, respectively. Determining each parent's perception and assumptions regarding the "stage" of the conflict is important before the parenting coordinator can design an intervention strategy. It is important to note that each parent, and the parenting coordinator, may perceive the stage of a conflict differently. The utility of the tool is not necessarily to reach an agreement regarding a definitive stage, but to introduce the idea that conflicts ebb and flow. It is also to help parents see the possibility of resolving their disputes and to identify the consequences of staying in a "hurting" stalemate.

IDENTIFYING INTRACTABLE CONFLICTS

Questions yet to be answered by empirical research about the parenting coordination process and effective interventions abound. For example, can the parenting coordinator help parents transform their conflict into one where principled negotiation may occur? Can the parenting coordinator help parents transform an intractable conflict into one that is more benign? Can parents learn how to manage their conflicts so that harm to the children is mitigated? We can look to the research on divorce mediation as a potential source of information to answer some of these questions, but many questions about the process and outcome of parenting coordination remain. However, some of the concepts used as interventions in each of these alternative dispute resolution processes are similar. These concepts include an opportunity for parents to communicate with one another in a contained setting, and opportunity for each parent to express their point of view and to have their concerns taken seriously, and an opportunity to talk about their children and to learn helpful ideas about parenting issues and plans.

Drawing from studies on divorce or custody mediation, research indicates that most parents are satisfied with the mediation process and outcomes with ratings ranging from 60% to 85% (Bordow & Gibson, 1994; Depner, Cannata, & Ricci, 1994; Emery, 1994; Irving & Benjamin, 1992; Kelly & Duryee, 1992; Love, Moloney, Fisher, 1995). Several investigators (Emery, 1994; Irving & Benjamin, 1992; Kelly, 1996, 1990) have also reported higher rates of compliance with agreements that are mediated versus agreements that were reached through an adversarial process such as litigation. Given the overlap of concepts and skills used in mediation and parenting coordination, we have some indication that the interventions used to help reframe seemingly intractable conflicts and skills used to highlight interests versus positions will be useful in parenting coordination. However, much research is yet to be done to determine effectiveness of specific interventions used in the parenting coordination process. One study (Fieldstone, Carter, King, & McHale, in press) examined parenting coordination practices and identified some commonalities among parents involved, but did not focus specifically on outcome results.

Conflict transformation involves change. Many parents locked in conflict are unable to see how *they* need to change, but they can readily identify what their co-parent needs to change. The parenting coordinator has the opportunity to nurture the seeds of peace and prevent weeds (destructive interactions) from choking out budding growth by helping parents identify the causes of conflict that have allowed their disputes to fester and grow.

As mentioned at the beginning of this chapter, some of the more destructive conflicts are those that expand and escalate and often become independent of the initiating causes. These are the conflicts that are more likely to be intractable. The conflict becomes self-sustaining and often the original conflict has become irrelevant or forgotten. For parents caught in an intractable conflict, the costs (emotional and literal) they are willing to pay may reach enormous proportions.

Intractable conflicts are conflicts that remain unresolved for long periods of time and then become stuck at a high level of intensity and destructiveness. They typically involve more than just the parents themselves and often include other family and community members. There may have been attempts to resolve issues before, during and after separation without success. If parents have been involved in prolonged litigation, the court system itself may have, unwittingly, contributed to the intractability of the conflict. Attorneys may also be contributors to the intractability of the conflict, unless they can persuade their client to move to a more cooperative approach to resolving disputes.

Those locked in intractable conflicts often view the other parent as a threat to their very existence and everything they hold dear. These parents develop a mutual hatred of each other and a profound desire to inflict as much physical and psychological harm on each other as possible. This sense of threat and hostility often pervades the everyday lives of the parents involved and overrides their ability to recognize any shared concerns or interests they might have. The impact on their ability to shield their children from conflict and parent effectively is greatly compromised. The children will readily show signs of the strain from exposure to their parent's conflict. Parents locked in intractable conflicts pose serious and significant risks to the stability and well-being of their children (Featherstone, 2004; Jaffe, Johnston, Crooks, & Bala, 2008; Kelly, 2007; Kelly & Ward, 2002; Lamb et al., 1997; Pruett et al., 2004).

Parents caught in intractable conflicts may become so consumed with the conflict itself that they are unable to focus on their children's needs. They may be obsessed with the other parent's communications and behaviors and perceive all interactions as additional fuel to intensify the conflict. Vallacher et al. (2010) uses the metaphor of a "gravity well into which the surrounding mental, behavioral, and social–structural landscape begins to slide. Once parties are trapped in such a well, escape requires tremendous will and energy and thus feels impossible." The parenting coordinator has the challenge of determining whether parents who are caught in the gravity well can be helped out of the well with skillful intervention and support and whether the parent has the will and determination for such a daunting task.

Conflict theory and the concept of intractable conflict has been the subject of study for many years. In spite of considerable efforts to identify the fundamental processes underlying intractable conflict and efforts to generate effective strategies for transforming this type of conflict, there is no widespread consensus in the scientific and practitioner communities (http://www.beyondintractability.org; Azar, 1990; Burton, 1987; Coleman, 2003, 2004, 2006; Crocker et al., 2005; Valacher et al., 2010).

If intractable conflicts are so undesirable and destructive to all parties, why are they maintained for so long? Why are those locked in entrenched conflict often very resistant to interventions for resolution despite the self-destructive potential? Does this suggest that the conflict may have more to do with psychological needs than objective reality? Theory and research on self-concept (Baumeister, Smart, & Boden, 1996) suggests that individuals who have a high self-regard that is unrelated to accomplishments or other objective information tend to be very defensive in response to criticism and go to great lengths to eliminate the source of the threatening feedback (Vallacher et al., 2010). Stated another way, individuals who need to maintain a view of themselves as superior to others and need others to reinforce this view get easily locked into conflict with their co-parent who may provide unflattering appraisals and feedback that challenges their sense of self. It's a blow to their ego that feels unbearable and, therefore, they need to lash out at the "offender" to protect their sense of who they are.

As noted earlier, parents who are separated physically are not necessarily separated emotionally and many continue to experience ambivalent, unresolved feelings about their former partner. This is similar to what Johnston described as a "Type II Interactional Impasse" or ambivalent separating style of interaction which was described in greater detail in Chapter 4. Disputes about the children, money, or other points of conflict may take on a symbolic meaning, for example, fighting over money may be more about revenge or payback than any real financial needs. These underlying sources of conflict may not be conscious for parents and the original issues may have long been forgotten. There is a psychological investment in holding on to the view that the other parent is an enemy and must be guarded against at all times. This, of course, leaves many parents feeling as though there is no way out of the conflict.

Adding Fuel to the Fire

Intractability is more predictable when the dynamics between partners involve interactions that are particularly destructive. For example, disrespectful treatment and perceived injustice will usually deepen antagonism and may prompt determination to seek revenge. A common example of this in separating and divorcing parents is when one partner is unfaithful and openly flaunts the new relationship in front of the "left behind" and rejected partner. A popular expression to characterize the intensity of rage and reaction of an unfaithful spouse comes from a play by William Congreve (1697): "Heaven has no rage like love to hatred turned/ Nor hell a fury like a woman scorned."

Other factors that make some conflicts extremely difficult to resolve include the vast number of people who may see themselves as "stake holders" in the conflict, that is, extended family members, attorneys, mental health professionals, other expert witnesses, and the adversarial nature of the family court system itself. Other issues may be more personal in nature such as one's perception of self as a good/ bad parent, guilt about past behaviors or wrong-doing, sense of self as a good or valued partner/spouse, and a previous history of relationships. Regardless of the myriad factors that may contribute to the intractability of a conflict, there are common dynamics that underlie these destructive conflicts.

Commonalities of Intractable Conflicts

Common to all intractable conflicts is that they involve interests or values that an individual regards as critically important. Some of the central underlying causes of intractable conflict revolve around moral issues, issues of justice, human rights, human needs, and identity (Deutsch, 2000). For parents caught in an intractable conflict, efforts to resolve disputes by negotiation or compromise are generally unsuccessful because the conflict is perceived in a manner that seems unsolvable. If one value system is followed, another is threatened. If one person is perceived as "in control," then the other parent loses control. While sharing power and control is possible in theory, parents caught in intractable conflicts usually regard compromise as a loss. This is especially true when fear and hatred is so ingrained that parents cannot imagine working cooperatively with the other parent. Instead, they are often willing to take whatever means necessary to ensure personal and family "survival" and protect their way of life.

In general, conflicts over intolerable moral differences tend to be intractable and long-lasting. The substantive issues are often a matter of rigidly held moral beliefs, based in fundamental assumptions that cannot be proven wrong. These fundamental moral, religious, and personal values are not easily changed, and people who adhere to a particular ideology are often unwilling to compromise their world view. An example of this is manifest in individuals who have very different views about abortion. If a pro-choice individual tries to explain in detail to another individual why their pro-life position on abortion is wrong, the pro-life individual may tune the other person out, challenge the pro-choice belief, refuse to talk to this person, or avoid them. Attempts to directly challenge the validity or practicality of someone's fundamental belief is doomed to fail and is more likely to intensify the person's belief and their determination to defend their position at all costs.

The challenge for the parenting coordinator is to reframe such conflicts into a clash between differing views versus a conflict of absolute right and wrong. One person's most fundamental and cherished assumptions about the best way to live may differ radically from the values held by the other parent. This might include strongly held views about religious education and observation, private versus public school, exposure to same sex adult partnerships versus strict adherence to a heterosexual only definition of marriage, and so on. Parents may have different standards of "rightness" and "goodness" and give fundamentally different justifications for their beliefs. Parents often stress the importance of different aspects of child-rearing, and may develop radically different or incompatible goals. In some cases, one parent may regard the beliefs and actions of their co-parent as fundamentally evil, exceeding the bounds of tolerance, and requiring active, committed opposition.

If parents' disputes are deeply embedded in moral issues, the conflicts are likely to seem nonnegotiable and a parent may have great difficulty imagining a win–win resolution. Those involved in moral conflict may even regard perpetuation of the conflict as virtuous or necessary. They may identity themselves as morally superior and virtuous and as champions of their cause. This, in turn, reinforces the continuation of the conflict as legitimate and necessary. An example of this occurred with a father who was strongly opposed to his ex-wife exposing their children to her new, same sex romantic partner. He vehemently opposed the children having contact with his ex-wife and her lesbian lover insisting that his position was justified and sanctified by his religious beliefs. These types of conflict often come into play when one parent observes a particular religious practice and belief and becomes vehemently opposed to the children being raised in a faith which does not observe the same belief system.

An example of this occurred with Mary and Jake, a family who observed the Jewish faith while married. Mary had converted to Judaism shortly after she and Jake married and their two children were raised in the Jewish faith with plans for both boys to be called as a Bar Mitzvah. Following the divorce, Mary reverted to the religious faith of her family of origin which was Catholic. Both parents became locked in intractable conflict over the children's religious education and observance. Mary insisted that the children should attend catechism classes, weekly mass, and participate in Holy Communion. Jake insisted that the children continue to attend Hebrew school and was adamantly opposed to any observance of the Christian faith which he felt undermined the children's faith and heritage. On the weekends when the children were with Mary, she insisted that they attend Sunday school classes on Sunday morning which conflicted with their attendance of classes at Jake's synagogue. The parenting coordinator's challenge was to re-frame the issue about religious beliefs and observances to an issue of their children's best interests. Ultimately, the parenting coordinator was able to help Jake and Mary arrive at an agreement where the children would be exposed to both religions and work out a schedule where the religious observance at Mary's church and Jake's synagogue did not conflict.

Fundamental differences in religious beliefs and vastly different religious observances have led to wars between countries. A parenting coordinator should not attempt to challenge a firmly held religious belief of a parent and must at all times be respectful of differences, but the impact on children of exposure to conflict is an issue to address and presents very difficult challenges when fundamental beliefs are at stake.

In addition to religious differences, parents may view any compromise about their most cherished values as a threat to their basic human needs and their sense of identity. The continuation of a conflict may seem preferable to what would have to be given up in order to accommodate the other parent and parents may have a great stake in neutralizing, injuring, or eliminating their co-parent in the children's lives. Such was the case with Lou and Jennifer. Jennifer discovered that her husband had been cross-dressing for much of their marriage and had dissipated assets to support his lifestyle and that of his gay lover. She only discovered the history and extramarital relationship when she was served with documents indicating the marital home was to be foreclosed. Lou, a practicing attorney in a large firm, was threatened with "exposure" of his cross-dressing habits and gay relationship if he did not agree to his former wife's demands that contact with the children be under supervised circumstances at all times.

While there were no allegations that Lou had been inappropriate with the children or would place them at any risk, Jennifer's threat and Lou's fear of exposure and the damage he thought this might do to his career, was enough of a threat for him to defer to his ex-wife's wishes. In this circumstance, Jennifer felt so betrayed and emotionally wounded by her former husband's activities, that she was primarily invested in "injuring" Lou and his reputation. The children's relationship with their father was "irrelevant" to her and she was convinced that she had no choice but to protect the children from their father whom she now characterized as evil and dangerous. She defended her stance based upon religious and moral grounds, suggesting that exposing the children to their father's "sinful" and "perverted" behavior was tantamount to "losing their souls" forever, which in her belief system was intolerable.

Because the desire for justice is one that people tend to be unwilling to compromise, assertions of injustice often lead to intractable conflicts as well. An individual's sense of justice is connected to the norms, rights, and entitlements that are thought to underlie decent human treatment. If there is a discrepancy between a parent's expectations and the reality of their circumstance, they may feel as though they have been treated unfairly or that they have been denied justice. Issues of entitlement are often present in these intractable conflicts. Such was the case with Abby and Randy. Randy had started an entrepreneurial venture involving clean energy shortly after college and married Abby 3 years later. He was very successful financially and provided a lavish lifestyle which Abby very much enjoyed. Abby quit college and enjoyed the travel and unlimited expense budget Randy provided. When Randy filed for divorce, Abby insisted that she was entitled to the lifestyle to which she had become accustomed. Abby was devastated when the court did not agree with her that she was entitled to permanent financial support from Randy and 50% of the assets of his company which was now worth millions.

When people believe that they have been treated unfairly, they may try to "get even" or challenge those who have treated them unjustly. Such was the case with Bill and Joanne. Bill owned a very successful business and Joanne was a physician. She had stopped work after giving birth to their first child and continued to be a homemaker and stay-at-home mom for 5 years after the birth of their second child. At the time of the divorce, Bill alleged that Joanne was not entitled to alimony because she retained her license to practice medicine and could readily obtain employment that would provide her with a good income. Joanne argued that she had interrupted her career with Bill's support to raise their children and their children were still in need of a full-time parent at home. Ultimately, the court agreed with Bill and Joanne was forced to go back to work to support herself. This left her very bitter and it set in motion a pattern of thinking and behaving that fueled ongoing conflict between them and brought them into parenting coordination.

A sense of injustice or unfairness often motivates aggression or retaliation. Individuals may come to view vengeance or "payback" as the only way to address the injustice they have suffered. This is especially likely if no procedures are in place to correct the perception of injustice or to bring about restorative justice when unfair treatment did occur. The perception of injustice is where the parenting coordinator must begin. The parent perceived as the "perpetrator" of injustice may deny or minimize the other parent's perception and make allegations that the parent is crazy. There are circumstances where the only way to quell the anger and intent for retribution is to attempt to restore a sense of justice.

Bob and Alice represented this challenge. Bob and Alice had been married for 6 years when she first threatened divorce. Their daughter was 3 years at the time and Bob eventually convinced Alice to reconcile. He promised to go to counseling and quit drinking. His promises lasted about 2 months and he was back to his old behaviors. Approximately 18 months after Alice had originally asked for divorce, Bob filed for divorce. In the interim, he sold his company and allowed his employment contract to end. He also dissipated all of the marital assets prior to filing and ultimately left Alice in a circumstance where she had to go back to work. Once their divorce was final, Bob admitted to Alice that he had planned the reconciliation as a ruse so that he had time to get his financial circumstances in order so that she would have no access to any financial support. While Alice suspected this, Bob's admission enraged her and left her feeling stupid and set up. He took great pleasure in pointing out how stupid she was to believe him and how easily he had been able to manipulate her. The interventions for this couple centered around encapsulating the conflict so that Alice's rage did not impair her parenting, but rather, allowed her to preserve enough mental energy to take care of herself and her children. Bob had proven himself untrustworthy and therefore, there was no room for latitude or flexibility in the parenting arrangements.

Conflicts that center on issues of justice tend to be intractable in part because reaching an agreement about what qualifies as injustice is often exceedingly difficult. Justice is in the eye of the beholder and this subjectivity can serve to intensify rather than mitigate conflict. For example, when there is an unequal division of resources the potential for conflict may be enhanced if one parent perceives himself or herself as victimized and views the other parent as unfair, greedy, or bad. These perceptions may serve to justify aggressive actions in the service of restoring justice. For the parent who received the greater share of resources, they may justify the unequal asset distribution as a reflection of their superiority and greater deservingness. In this example, both parents frame the issue in terms of justice. Many parents in parenting coordination will make assertions of unjust treatment which essentially amounts to justification of their actions and attitudes.

The challenge for the parenting coordinator is how to approach conflict resolution when one or both parents advance their claim as a matter of justice. Parents who believe they have suffered injustice are typically unwilling to compromise or even enter into dialogue with those whose points of view differ from their own. Negotiation and creative problem-solving thus become more difficult, and actual interests are obscured as the conflict becomes framed as win–lose. Parents who believe that their cause is just are unlikely to back down or to begin the process of working toward cooperation or effective co-parenting, much less forgiveness and long-term peace. If there is no way to "restore" justice or the perception of a more fair outcome, parenting coordinator interventions will likely center around encapsulating the conflict, preventing further perceived injustice, and detailed parent arrangements that keep the focus on the children.

Some parents who feel they have been the victims of injustice or unfair treatment may grow extremely angry and feel justified in seeking revenge. They may blame members of the other parent's family or friends and denigrate them. They may also blame the court and attorneys for their plight and the injustice inflicted upon them. In extreme circumstances, these individuals can present a very real threat of harm to professionals who are involved with the family, even in a peripheral manner. If vengeance becomes the primary goal, attention may be shifted away from addressing the central justice issues that gave rise to conflict in the first place. The parenting coordinator must assess the danger or risk to not only the children and the other parent, but to others who may be a potential target of the wrath being sought and work toward de-escalation of the conflict, if possible.

Rights-based grievances likewise contribute to intractability. A dispute begins when one parent makes a demand on the other parent insisting that it is their "right" to have what they want and the other parent refuses to comply with their demand. One way to resolve disputes is to rely on some independent standard of perceived legitimacy or fairness which, in family law cases, is often the court. However, if both parents advance their claim as a right, it becomes difficult to compromise or reach consensus. An example of this was a parent who had been the primary caregiver for the children for many years prior to separation/divorce who believed she had the "right" to have "custody" of the children because she was the parent who gave birth. This mother felt she had superior parenting ability based on gender alone.

Social science tells us that a parent does not have superior abilities simply by virtue of gender (Whiteside, 1998), but some parents have no interest in the "facts" and assert their "rights" based upon their beliefs. Rights talk generally shuts down further communication with those whose points of view differ from our own. This is in part because people treat rights-based arguments as "trump cards" that neutralize all other positions. A tendency toward absolute formulations in a dialogue about rights promotes unrealistic expectations and increases the likelihood of conflict. It also ignores emotional and literal costs and the rights/needs of others (particularly the children). It inhibits dialogue that might lead to the discovery of common ground or compromise. For example, a parent who "gave up" their career to be a full-time parent and has been in this role for many years, may assert their "right" to remain in this role and cannot see "sharing custody" of the children or returning to the work place as an option. This sort of absolute, win–lose framing is typically not conducive to problem-solving.

Linked to justice issues, there is a strong interdependence between human rights violations and intractable conflict. Violations of personal rights to safety and security and economic rights are the root causes of many crisis situations. For example, when one parent fails to provide financial support to the other as ordered by the court or dissipates family financial assets, basic rights to adequate food, housing, employment, and so on are denied. Usually, the court will issue a temporary order wherein the family's assets are secure from squandering and/or issue a mandate ordering one parent to pay the other for child support. However, issuance of a court order does not ensure compliance as many parents can attest. This type of violation of basic economic rights tends to lead to fear and/or intent on revenge for the party whose rights have been violated. This is certainly true in circumstances where threat or physical harm to a parent or the children is at issue, such as in cases of domestic violence.

Many intractable conflicts between parties are caused by the perception that their fundamental human needs have not and will not be met following separation and divorce. These perceptions may be emotionally based, as in circumstances where one party has been so emotionally dependent upon the other that they cannot imagine living or functioning without the partnership. However, it arises most commonly in high-conflict families when "wishes and wants" are characterized as needs, such as when an individual's lifestyle is compromised or radically altered after equitable distribution of assets (or debts). These more complex needs center on the capacity to exercise choice in all aspects of one's life and to have one's identity and values accepted as legitimate. The need for and the ability to continue to maintain a lifestyle to which one has become accustomed is seen as crucial. Therefore, it becomes important for the parenting coordinator to help a parent differentiate "needs" from "wants" or preferences and to learn to accept the changes that are inherent in some family's lives after separation and divorce.

Identity is another one of the fundamental human needs that underlie many intractable conflicts. Conflicts over identity arise when a parent feels that their sense of self is threatened or is not respected. For example, if one parent may assert that the other is a "bad" parent and, therefore, unworthy, or unsuitable to care for the children. The accused parent's identity and sense of self is threatened and because identity is integral to one's self-esteem, any threat to identity is likely to produce a strong response. This response may be both aggressive and defensive, and can escalate quickly into an intractable conflict. Because threats to identity are not easily resolved or encapsulated, conflicts involving identity threats tend to persist.

Intractable conflicts are often maintained by the development of polarized identities among parents. For example, a parent may identify themselves as the "good" parent and try to organize supporters against the other "bad" parent and those with whom he/she associates. As the conflict escalates, parents become increasingly polarized and develop hostility toward the other parent. A high level of support for an individual who sees themselves as the "good" parent, together with a high degree of perceived threat from the other "bad" parent, leads to a basic impulse to preserve oneself and destroy the opponent.

Rigid collective identities (such as when a parent gets family members or others in the community to take "their side") often make it more difficult for a parent to compromise. Parents may view the other parent (their adversary) as evil or even nonhuman and regard their views and feelings as unworthy of attention. Because merely sitting down with the opponent can be seen as a threat to one's own identity, even beginning efforts at cooperation or collaboration can be extremely difficult. This is where the parenting coordinator often plays a crucial role. With the backing of the court, the parents may be strongly encouraged to participate in a process to begin to focus on the needs of the children and to work toward setting and maintaining parameters that meet the children's needs versus remaining stuck in their own rigidly held perspective of the other and the intractable conflict.

Conflicts surrounding who gets what and how much they get can also lead to intractable conflicts. The items to be distributed include tangible resources such as money, land, or other assets, as well as intangible resources such as social status or power. If there are plenty of resources available, then everyone simply takes what they need and no conflict develops. However, when there is not enough of a given resource to satisfy everyone's needs or wants, and no more can be found or created, the conflict becomes a "win–lose" situation. The more one party gets (wins), the less the other party gets (or loses). When the item in question is very important or valuable, these conflicts tend to become very intractable.

For example, one parenting coordination case involved a well-known and well-respected politician whose family business had appeared on the cover of prominent magazines and had won many awards. As a result of his profession, he had entrée into all prominent social and political affairs and was highly sought after as a social guest. After his divorce, his ex-wife received a generous financial settlement, but the money did not afford her entrée into the coveted social affairs or public prominence that she had enjoyed when married. This loss of "status" was so devastating to her sense of self-esteem that she continued to provoke conflict with her ex-husband, including dumping bags of garbage outside his office and barging into private social affairs when he was in attendance claiming her need to communicate with him about an "emergency" circumstance with one of their children.

CONFLICT TRANSFORMATION OPTIONS

The parenting coordinator should obtain information about the strategies and tactics that have been used by both parents in the past to resolve disputes and the effectiveness of each of the strategies. The consequences of the conflicts to each parent, the children, and others involved in their lives may be apparent to the parenting coordinator and others, but not explicitly recognized by the parents. Articulating consequences of the ongoing conflict, through the use of empirically based parent education, may help parents begin to consider making changes to avoid future painful and distressing consequences for themselves and their children.

However, most intractable conflicts are so deeply rooted that the parties need outside help to transform the conflict into something more constructive. There are many strategies the parenting coordinator can use to help transform intractable conflicts. In his book, *The Third Side*, Ury (2000) suggests that there are at least 10 intervention strategies that can be used to help transform conflicts. Most of these strategies need to be employed by third parties who may be a part of the

TABLE 5.1

Process	Role	What They Say:
Prevention	Provider	What is needed here?
	Teacher	Here's another way. (This information may be helpful)
	Bridge Builder	I'd like to introduce you to…(referral to therapist/etc.)
Resolution	Mediator	Let's find a way to work out your conflicts.
	Arbiter	What's fair here is …
	Equalizer	Let's level the playing field.
	Healer	Let's make amends and develop peace.
Containment	Witness	Hey! Look what they are doing!
	Referee	Rules of engagement must be maintained
	Peacekeeper	OK! Break it up!

family's "support" team. The strategies can be divided into three roles: prevention, resolution, or containment. Prevention strategies involve identifying what is needed to prevent an escalation of conflict and to introduce the idea of conflict resolution. Prevention also involves the use of individuals that may facilitate the process. Resolution strategies involve mediation or facilitating the resolution process, arbitrating decisions, creating an environment of fairness, and developing, if possible, an opportunity for creating long-standing peace. If conflicts cannot be prevented or resolved, then interventions are aimed at containment. Containment strategies include serving as an independent accountability monitor, establishing rules of engagement, and interrupting any conflict escalation process. The chart above summarizes intervention processes and roles within each process.

The parenting coordinator or support team members may use one or all of these strategies at any given point in time. Many families will need a support team, both professional and nonprofessional, to help them disengage from ongoing intractable conflicts. With each strategy the parenting coordinator may be working to prevent escalation or contain different levels of a conflict, even when the conflict is not ripe for resolution.

RIPENESS OF THE CONFLICT

Zartman (2000) suggests that there are two approaches to the successful resolution of conflicts—one involves the *substance*, or acceptability, of the proposals for resolution and the other involves *timing*. He argues that substance alone is insufficient to foster successful resolution of conflicts, and suggests that the *timing* of efforts for resolution, or what he calls "ripeness," is a critical factor. Ripeness theory (Zartman & Berman, 1982) is used to explain why and when individuals involved in conflict are susceptible to efforts to turn a conflict toward resolution through negotiation, with or without facilitation. They assert that the concept of a "ripe moment" centers around each parties' perception of a mutually hurting stalemate (Zartman, 1989). This stalemate is described as a circumstance when both parties find themselves locked in a no-win situation that is painful to both. Ripeness theory suggests that individuals will seek a way out of the conflict because failing to do so is likely to increase the pain. Expanding this concept includes different phases of the stalemate: that of the *plateau*, an unending painful conflict without relief, and that of a *precipice*, the point where things will suddenly and predictably get worse.

During the course of parenting coordination, there are circumstances when it may become clear to parents that failure to resolve or contain their conflict will lead to enormous pain and cost, both literal and emotional. This may occur with protracted litigation where the money and time involved reach proportions that will financially devastate both parents and their families. This may also occur when the emotional price that is evident in the children is such that failure to resolve the conflict may very well lead to catastrophic results. This occurred with the Reinhart family who had been in conflict over many issues for almost 5 years. Their 12-year-old son, Taylor, made a "mock" suicide video which he posted on MySpace, a social networking site. Several family members saw the video and showed it to Taylor's parents who were shocked and scared. This produced a turning point in their willingness to work toward resolving their conflicts more constructively. However, they still had no idea *how* to get out of the stalemate. The parenting coordinator seized the "ripeness" for resolution and introduced the other element necessary for resolution: creating the perception of *possibility* for resolution. Without a sense of a way out of the conflict, the impact of the *precipice* (or potentially catastrophic results of failure to find constructive solutions to conflict) would lead nowhere. Essentially, Taylor's parents were finally ready to consider the possibility that they could interact differently and resolve their conflicts, but they didn't know where to begin.

While there are times when it is clear to the parents caught in an intractable conflict that the moment of ripeness is upon them, there are also times when the parenting coordinator may be able to help cultivate the perception that they are on a pain-producing path based on a cost-benefit analysis. The idea of ripeness for resolution is not based in objective reality; rather, it is necessarily a perception. When a parent reaches the point where they recognize that, "It can't go on like this," then the circumstance becomes ripe to work toward resolution of conflict. The parenting coordinator must be alert to the notion of ripeness, since it can be a fleeting opportunity, and help parents in conflict feel and understand the pain of their mutual stalemate and turn it into negotiations and possible resolution. To summarize, ripeness for resolution of conflict exists when parties' experience of pain, impasse, and inability to bear the costs of continuing the conflict is combined with a sense of a way out (Zartman, 2000).

Pruitt (1997) extended the elements that ripeness theory seeks to explain (i.e., motivation to cooperate and a perception that there is a way out of the conflict) and describes them as the push/pull factors that drive negotiation to conclusion. He calls this "readiness theory," and suggests that motivational ripeness represents a push toward negotiation. Motivational ripeness is the parties' "willingness to give up a lot now in exchange for substantial concessions from the other rather than waiting until later in the hope that the other can be persuaded to make these concessions unilaterally." Others have also written about "readiness" referring to a negotiator's skill and resources as necessary components without which parties' are unlikely to be able to seize the ripe moment (Crocker, Hampson, & Aali, 1999; Maundi, Khadiagala, Nuemah, Touval, & Zartman, 2000).

Ripeness theory and its application have not been researched in terms of better understanding of successful techniques and strategies for parenting coordination. Ripeness theory has been applied to human interactions as well as group interactions and produced useful insight into how intractable conflicts might be challenged and transformed. There are certain problems raised by ripeness theory that are yet to be fully understood, for example, when a hurting stalemate and increased pain increase resistance rather than reducing it. Parenting coordination, and the techniques associated with it as an alternative dispute resolution process, have yet to undergo rigorous research. Conflict theory and ripeness theory are offered as suggestions for consideration for the parenting coordinator as a means of identifying tools and strategies to assist parents caught in conflict.

CONFLICT CONTAINMENT

Some parents are not able or willing to resolve their disputes. In cases where conflicts are either irresolvable or not ripe for resolution, the parenting coordinator has the challenge of helping parents learn how to *contain* their conflict. Such circumstances may arise when human needs are at stake. Although both interests and needs can be thought of as underlying desires, human needs are more fundamental than interests. There may be interests that are tangible things that can be traded or compromised, whereas needs such as identity, security, and recognition are not for trading or easily compromised. If the issues in contention are nonnegotiable (e.g., religious education/observance for the children or having the children reside with a parent and their same-sex romantic partner), any attempts to reconcile interests are likely to fail and may even make the conflict more entrenched and difficult to resolve. Thus, disputes rooted in human needs or fundamental value differences should not be handled in the same way as disputes rooted in parties' conflicting interests.

The concept of conflict containment or encapsulation is best represented by what is referred to as the Gandhian style (Wehr, 1979) of self-limiting conflict. This concept introduces the notion that parties waging conflict can learn to keep their conflict within bounds and limit its intensity. A corollary to this concept in group interactions is the notion of nonviolent social movements or resistance. The Gandhian style looks at conflict processes that are self-regulating in nature, that is, that have built-in devices to keep the conflict within acceptable bounds and to inhibit violent extremism and unrestrained escalation. In some societies, the process of socialization may provide this self-regulation. For example, a hostile action toward another person might produce feelings of regret or guilt or perhaps a reconsideration of the person's positive qualities. These thoughts and feelings may help control a reactive aggressive impulse and allow for a more restrained interaction with the offending party. However, for parents caught in an irresolvable conflict, the social inhibitions that might occur in other relationships or in society at large have often eroded to a point of nonexistence.

Wehr asserts that "self-encapsulation can also occur through both ideological restraints and tactical approach." Mahatma Gandhi's movement involved such techniques as have others in this century, for example, Martin Luther King Jr.'s civil rights movement. The ideological restraint would be the commitment to nonviolence. The tactical approach involves use of techniques to interfere with an escalating spiral of conflict, using a step-wise strategy which begins with negotiation and arbitration. The strategy includes (1) accumulation and analysis of facts involving participation of both parties; (2) identification of interests in common; (3) formulation of goals acceptable to all parties; and (4) a search for compromise without conceding on essentials (Naess, 1958).

In this approach, steps are taken to avoid further escalation. While not ideal and certainly not as desirable as resolution of conflict, the parenting coordinator may have the opportunity to prevent the escalation of conflicts and to establish a relationship between parents that is built on a mutual focus on the best interests of their children and, perhaps, respect. This, in turn, may later limit the spiraling hostile interactions that had characterized all previous interactions and prevent an escalation of more conflict. Entrenched conflicts are often a product of desperation, fear, and a sense of no control. Parenting coordinators must break into an escalating conflict cycle with a nonhostile and redirective response. Encapsulating the conflict is a strategy to help parents regulate their conflict until conflict resolution is achieved.

The concepts in this chapter introduce the concepts of conflict transformation and conflict containment within the parenting coordination process. Rather than describing a dispute in terms of parents' positions about what they want, conflict analysis helps redefine a conflict in terms of mutual interests. By focusing on underlying interests rather than absolute positions, resolution-resistant conflicts that had seemed intractable often become solvable. This creates the opportunity for parents to identify win–win solutions to problems. When parents are unable or unwilling to work toward resolution, intervention strategies should focus on conflict containment with the goal of mitigating the damaging effect on children of exposure to chronic acrimony and hostility.

6

Strategies to Disengage From Conflict

How many a dispute could have been deflated into a single paragraph if the disputants had dared to define their terms.
—Aristotle

REDEFINING THE CO-PARENT RELATIONSHIP

Along the dimensions of conflict and cooperation following divorce, parents generally divide into three types of co-parenting relationships. Approximately 25% to 30% of parents have a *cooperative* co-parenting relationship (Kelly, 2006), characterized by joint planning, flexibility of schedule, provision of some parenting support to each other, and co-ordination of children's activities and schedules. The majority, more than half, settle into *parallel* parenting in which emotional disengagement, low conflict, and minimal communication about their children predominate. While this is less optimal for children than cooperative co-parenting, children do adjust well in these arrangements, particularly when the quality of parenting in each home is nurturing and adequate. The remaining parents, about 20%, have a continuing *conflictual* parenting relationship, with poor communication and little, if any, cooperation (Hetherington & Kelly, 2002; Maccoby & Mnookin, 1992).

One of the earliest objectives and challenges for the parenting coordinator is to determine the type of co-parenting relationship that is likely to be most effective for the co-parents based on the history and source of their conflict, impasse and interaction style, and conflict management style. In Chapter 4 (Developing an Intervention Strategy), we learned to identify parenting interaction and impasse style. In Chapter 5 (Conflict Analysis, Transformation, and Containment), we learned to identify source and type of conflicts, conflicts which were intractable, and parents' conflict management style.

Identifying the level of conflict and the level of engagement or interaction is a helpful way to determine where to start in terms of directing parents to a more effective co-parenting relationship. The parenting coordinator should look at the interactive effects of conflict and engagement to help identify which type of co-parenting relationship may be most suitable for a family.

The co-parenting relationship, or parenting track, is modifiable and can be targeted to help parents disengage from a deteriorated marital or partnership relationship and impaired parenting to a more functional parenting relationship (Margolin, Gordis, & John, 2001). Parents can usually describe their co-parenting relationship in terms of the level of interaction and conflict, but they may not be aware that it is possible to shift from a dysfunctional relationship to a type of co-parenting relationship that is more effective. Parents who need parenting coordination will most likely be in a chronically conflicted co-parenting relationship. The parenting coordinator should help parents restructure their co-parenting relationship so that they are able to move away from a chronically conflicted relationship to a relationship that is more functional and serves to shield their children from exposure to chronic conflict. This often involves teaching parents how to redefine their relationship to accomplish this goal.

Redefining a co-parenting relationship starts with the parenting coordinator helping parents clarify and redefine the "boundaries" of their relationship. Most parents have been in a partnership relationship, whether that be a marriage or romantic arrangement. It is often difficult for parents to redefine their relationship from one that had been romantic and perhaps presumed to be permanent, to one that is not about the interaction and feelings between the adults, but rather about their need to work together cooperatively because of their common bond, that is, their children. Parenting coordinators often need to help parents recognize that they may be responding to their co-parent as though they were still emotionally engaged on a romantic partnership level. This is usually evident because of the intensity of emotions and behaviors that are triggered between the parents. Once parents have been able to emotionally and behaviorally disengage from their former relationship dynamic, they are in a better position to define boundaries that are commensurate with creating an effective and functional co-parenting relationship, whether it is defined as cooperative, parallel, or disengaged.

Ideally, parents will be able to eventually achieve a cooperative co-parenting relationship. A *cooperative* co-parenting relationship is one where parents are able to communicate effectively, share experiences with their children, provide practical and emotional support to one another in their parenting role, and generally shield their children from disagreements between them (Table 6.1). A cooperative co-parenting

TABLE 6.1 Cooperative Co-Parenting Relationship

1. Low levels of conflict between parents.
2. Similar parenting values.
3. Consistent parenting styles.
4. Good communication.
5. Willing to provide literal and emotional support to each other.
6. Enjoy shared experiences with their child, i.e., birthdays, holidays, school field trips, etc.
7. Resolve differences constructively.
8. Generally shield their children from disagreements.

relationship is possible when conflict is low and parents agree on most parenting values. These parents are usually relatively consistent in their parenting style and have few disagreements about how to raise their children. If differences do arise, parents are able to solve them peacefully. As may be obvious by the very definition of this type of co-parenting relationship, parents referred to parenting coordination have not been able to achieve a cooperative style. It is the goal of parenting coordination to assist parents in working toward a cooperative style, if possible, since research shows that children of divorce fare best when parents can be cooperative in their parenting. However, some parents are not able or willing to achieve a cooperative co-parenting relationship. When this occurs, the parenting coordinator should help parents structure either a parallel or disengaged style of co-parenting (Tables 6.2 and 6.3).

A *parallel* co-parenting relationship is a style where each parent learns how to effectively parent their child, when the child is with them, with little or no consultation with the other parent. Parallel parenting is similar to a concept in children's play where young children play next to one another, but do not have the skills to interact. Each child is engaged with their toy or activity and, essentially, ignores the other child. As they learn more skills, they are able to interact cooperatively and play together. Parents who are still emotionally engaged with one another, and maintain a high level of conflict as a result, are better suited to a parallel co-parenting track. The parenting coordinator should introduce the concepts of parallel parenting and help parents structure their interactions and parenting plan to accomplish the goals of emotional and behavioral disengagement as well as independent, effective parenting of their child.

In a parallel co-parenting relationship, parents do not communicate about minor issues involving their children or attempt to adhere to similar parenting styles. They may have different rules for the child in each home and do not generally share joint experiences with their child, that is, child's birthday celebration, holiday dinners, school field trips, parent-teacher conferences, and so on. They may attend functions involving the child (e.g., school award ceremonies, child's sporting events), but they do not generally sit together and may not even acknowledge the other parent's presence. While this type of co-parenting relationship is not ideal for the child, it may be a better alternative than exposure to hostility and acrimony, which occurs in a chronically conflicted co-parenting relationship.

In a parallel co-parenting arrangement, the parenting coordinator helps parents learn how to share important information about their child in a manner that is more business-like than social or friendly. A model of this type of communication is found in an old television program where the main character often repeated, "just the facts." By sharing only essential information and doing so in a factual, professional manner, parents are able to communicate, but avoid constantly refueling debates and maintaining intense, negative engagement with one another. Examples of important information may include facts about a child's illness and medication needed, school or social information (i.e., field trip or friend's birthday party) that may require the other parent's timely response, or follow-up medical/dental appointments.

A detailed parenting plan that identifies parameters of the parallel co-parenting arrangements is an essential tool. The parenting coordinator may need to help parents specify who goes on which field trip, who takes the child to the doctor/dentist, who accompanies the child to extracurricular activities, and so on. Generally, each parent is responsible for obtaining information directly from the child's school and health care providers, as well as any schedules including extracurricular functions. Nonemergency information should only be shared via email, fax, or postal service with a copy to the parenting coordinator until each parent is able to consistently stick to the rules of communication. There are some inexpensive software programs available for parents to share nonemergency information electronically. The parenting coordinator may need to monitor the information posted by parents to ensure that the rules of engagement are being followed. The rules of communication include factual information about the child without sarcasm or unsolicited inflammatory comments. By communicating in writing, each parent is able to take some time before they respond to avoid reactive, impulsive communication that may be provocative or argumentative (Table 6.2).

In the early phases of parenting coordination, it may be helpful for parents to use the parenting coordinator as a conduit of information or a "go between." This intervention directs each parent to send any communication to the parenting coordinator directly. The

TABLE 6.2 Parallel Co-Parenting Relationship

1. Moderate to high conflict between parents.
2. Non-emergency communication through fax, U.S. mail, e-mail, or other electronic means.
3. Communication restricted to factual exchange about the children.
4. Little or no consultation between parents.
5. No attempt to adhere to similar parenting styles.
6. Rules for children may differ in each home.
7. Parents obtain school, health care, or other relevant information about their child independent of the other parent.
8. Parents avoid direct contact with one another except when essential.
9. Do not share joint experiences with the child, i.e., birthday parties, holidays, etc.

parenting coordinator then determines whether the communication should be forwarded without edits or whether it is necessary to redact nonfactual, provocative, and inflammatory comments from the communication. If the parent initiating communication is able to stick to the communication rules, then the parenting coordinator can simply forward the communication as originally drafted. If the parent initiating communication has not learned, or is not consistently able, to limit their communication to "facts only," then the parenting coordinator can edit out the sarcasm and inflammatory comments before the other parent receives the communiqué. The parenting coordinator may use this opportunity to highlight the parts of the communication that were provocative and not helpful and ask the offending parent to try again. This intervention strategy helps teach the parent who is continuing to engage in inflammatory comments to edit or restrict their interactions to more effectively avoid further conflict. It also allows communication between the parents to occur but shields the receiving parent from communications which may lead to increased negative engagement between the parents. Using the parenting coordinator as a conduit of information also helps assure both parents that they have a "buffer" that will shield them from verbal assaults they may have experienced in the past and help each of them learn to communicate more effectively without escalating conflicts. By reducing the need for contact and sharing of nonessential information, parents have an opportunity to work toward emotional and behavioral disengagement in order to get out of the crucible of conflict.

Some parents who are extremely high conflict will not be able to effectively parent and shield their child from conflict in a parallel co-parenting track. They may need a *disengaged* co-parenting arrangement in order to do so (Table 6.3). A disengaged co-parenting relationship should not be confused with a disengaged parenting style which is explored more fully in Chapter 8 (Parenting Plans). A disengaged

TABLE 6.3 Disengaged Co-Parenting Relationship

1. Extreme high conflict between parents.
2. No direct communication between parents.
3. No shared experiences with their child.
4. Contact with one another is avoided.
5. One parent may become disengaged and limit contact with the child to avoid conflict with the other parent.

co-parenting relationship is one where parents have little or no contact with the other parent. They avoid contact with the other parent so that conflict cannot develop. They use a third party for all communications and generally refuse to speak to the other parent. They do not consult with one another about anything other than emergencies involving the child and often, they do not attend functions involving the child if the other parent is present. In circumstances where a disengaged co-parenting relationship is the best or only option available, one parent may function much more like a single parent with the other parent becoming increasingly less involved and sharing little time with their children. An example of this occurred with John and Ellie.

After a prolonged and bitter divorce, John and Ellie were referred to parenting coordination. They hated one another and could not interact without making hostile, sarcastic comments to the other in front of the children. Ellie referred to John as the "sperm donor" and John looked for every opportunity to state his longing to "dance on her [Ellie's] grave." Early in the process, the parenting coordinator learned that Ellie had been in the habit of abruptly leaving any public setting if John appeared. This included their youngest son's soccer games. John had contact with his son every other weekend and on the weekends when John was parenting, he took Patrick to his soccer games and Ellie did not attend. On Ellie's weekends, she did not want John anywhere near the soccer field and would pull Patrick off the field, in the middle of a game if necessary, and abruptly leave the area if John appeared. John insisted that it was a public setting and he had a right to be there whether it was his weekend or not.

The parenting coordinator tried valiantly to help John and Ellie work out a plan that would limit their son's exposure to their hostile interactions and consistently pointed out the adverse effect this was having on their son. All efforts fell on deaf ears as each of them remained defiant and locked into their positions. The parenting coordinator decided it was essential to help John and Ellie develop a structure to disengage. Ultimately, by introducing the concepts of a disengaged co-parenting relationship and developing a structure that completely eliminated all contact and exposure to one another, John and Ellie were able to begin the process of de-escalating their destructive interactions to which their son had been exposed. The parenting coordinator was actively involved in setting up and monitoring their disengaged co-parenting relationship for several years before they were finally willing to work toward a parallel path. For John and Ellie, the goal of developing and maintaining a parallel parenting arrangement was a lofty goal. During the years when they were on a disengaged track, John spent much less time with their son and Ellie essentially assumed the role of a single parent. The damaging impact on their son was obvious, but the alternative was exposure to prolonged hostility and vitriolic communication between the parents. The parenting coordinator was in a position of trying to determine what the "least worst alternative" was since no good options were available (Table 6.3).

The parenting coordinator must teach parents how to set and maintain boundaries for their new co-parenting relationship whether it is a cooperative, parallel, disengaged, or mixed model. A mixed model of a co-parenting relationship is one that may contain elements of each type described in this chapter and generally depends on the needs of the children and abilities of the parents. Regardless of the type of co-parenting arrangements that are achieved, the goal is to help parents disengage from a conflicted, ineffective, and damaging pattern of parenting. Within an emotionally disengaged context, parents may be able to eventually discuss issues about their children effectively and resolve differences without outside intervention. Strategies for maintaining and reinforcing boundaries in a new co-parenting partnership are discussed in Chapter 7 (Strategies to Build Consensus).

Constructing a Detailed Parenting Plan

Regardless of the type of new co-parenting relationship parents are able to achieve, a detailed parenting plan is a vital tool to help parents maintain more effective co-parenting. The parenting plan should indicate which child-related decisions will be jointly made, if any; what type of child-related information will be shared between parents and how this is to be accomplished; how parents will resolve parenting disputes as they arise (i.e., mediation, parenting coordination, counseling, etc); and specific time-sharing arrangements. If parents do not have such a plan, the parenting coordinator may help parents develop such a document within the bounds of jurisdictional restrictions for the parenting coordinator. Information regarding types of parenting plans and specific components are addressed in Chapter 8 (The Parenting Plan).

The specific time-sharing arrangement may be set forth by the court, but even a well thought out, detailed parenting plan which takes the form of a court order does not resolve the emotional issues that may have developed and may interfere with the implementation of the parenting plan. If parents have been engaged in significant conflict and exposed their children to hostile interactions they are likely to need a detailed parenting plan and a support team. Together, these tools and the help of the parenting coordinator may assist the parents and children until new family constellations can be stabilized, parents can achieve a functional co-parenting relationship, and any damage done by exposure to chronic conflict has been repaired.

Uncovering Hidden Issues

By the time most parents get to parenting coordination, many strong negative feelings and rigid postures may have developed between them. The animosity, resentment, hurt, and fear may have been building for years prior to the dissolution of the marriage and involvement of a parenting coordinator. Many issues of conflict may not be based on disagreements or perspectives about parenting that cannot be resolved, but may be a symbolic representation of a hidden or undisclosed issue that prompts parents to "act out" their feelings. It is helpful for the parenting coordinator to identify the areas of conflict that are fueled by long-standing personal and/or relationship issues that may impair a parent's ability to address parenting issues from a more objective or realistic position.

Sometimes parents are very well aware of why they act and feel toward their child's other parent the way that they do. But, often, parents are not objective enough about themselves to see their pattern of feeling and behavior that might help them identify the origin of the conflict and the "reasons" for behaving as they do when it comes to parenting with their child's other parent.

When parents cannot identify the underlying reasons for maintaining conflict, they are destined to repeat patterns of behavior that are destructive. However, identification of underlying reasons, or "insight," offers parents an opportunity to make changes in their reactions and in their behaviors. Referral to a therapist is appropriate when a parent is repeating destructive patterns of behavior and interaction that is causing chronic parenting disputes.

In addition to identifying unresolved areas of individual conflict, it is helpful to determine the way in which unresolved individual issues may be contributing to relationship or co-parenting conflict. Unresolved issues from the past can guide and direct a parent's perceptions and behaviors of themselves and others. If they remain unresolved, they are likely to interfere with a parent's willingness to work toward resolving parenting issues in a reasonable and effective manner. Therefore, unresolved individual issues may intensify the relationship conflict and prevent both parents from being able to identify options for consensus building or options for resolution. For example, a mother may perceive herself as having been wronged, embarrassed, humiliated, and victimized by a father who left the marriage after having an affair. This "marital or relationship issue" may interfere with one or both parents' ability to identify and seek solutions for issues related to parenting their children. In this circumstance, a parent may "act out" the unresolved personal feelings by withholding or interfering with the other parent's access to the children without good cause, although an excuse may be offered. This occurred with the McNamara family.

Sean and Maureen met while he was at college, married shortly after his graduation, and their union produced four children. After 18 years of marriage, when their youngest child was three, Sean announced that he wanted a divorce. He had always been the primary breadwinner and had always been very active in parenting the children when he was not traveling for work. Maureen had been a stay-at-home mom since the birth of their first child. She was stunned by Sean's announcement and even more shocked when Sean married his long-time assistant one month after their divorce was final. Shortly after Sean's marriage, he also announced that he and his new wife were expecting their first child together. In spite of Maureen's hurt and embarrassment, she worked very hard to keep civility in her co-parenting relationship since she realized that exposing the children to ongoing conflict would hurt them. Sean and Maureen worked out a time-sharing arrangement where they each saw the children approximately 50% of the time and were both able to participate in the children's school and extra curricular activities.

Sean's new daughter was born and his four older children delighted in having a new baby in their life. About 18 months later, Sean lost his job due to an economic down turn. Since Sean was the primary breadwinner now for two families, he earnestly searched for work in the same geographic region for 4 months. Fortunately, he was able to locate a position as CFO of another company, but the job would require him to move 3,000 miles away. The parenting plan and time-sharing arrangement he had worked out with Maureen needed to be changed and Sean wanted to mediate. Maureen, however, steadfastly refused to discuss any changes or to mediate which left Sean no choice but to pursue litigation. Sean was very surprised that Maureen was being "so difficult" since she knew he had to work or no one would have money to live on. Maureen could not explain her refusal other than to say that she had already negotiated a parenting plan and that's the one she was using.

Ultimately, the family was referred to parenting coordination to assist them in modifying their parenting plan to take into account the changes in geographic distance between the parties. Both Sean and Maureen presented as bright, pleasant, reasonable, loving parents. It wasn't until the parenting coordinator suggested that perhaps Maureen's refusal to discuss any options might be connected to some past hurt or injustice she felt she may have suffered at Sean's hands, that Maureen burst into tears and began to unleash her pent up feelings of hurt, humiliation, and anger at Sean for leaving the marriage without warning (by her perception) and "replacing" her with another wife and family. The parenting coordinator suggested Maureen address these very valid feelings with her therapist. Sean was able to tell Maureen that he felt like she had not cared about him for years before the marriage ended so he was completely surprised by her response. This family represents a common example of "underlying" issues that parents may not realize are affecting their ability to work out disputes that will be best for their children. When the parenting coordinator recognizes that hidden issues may be interfering, it is helpful to bring the issues into the open so the parents can move forward and the parenting coordinator can make appropriate referrals for services, if needed.

IDENTIFY INGREDIENTS OF THE CONFLICT

Often parents enter parenting coordination convinced that the other parent is the problem and are shocked to realize that, actually, there may be a number of ingredients in the conflict that a parent has not considered or is aware that they exist. The parenting coordinator must embark on a mission to help identify all ingredients of the conflicts and one way to do so is by questioning each parent's certainty that their definition of the problem is the whole story. The aim of such questioning is to challenge each parent's sense of certainty that they know all that can be known about themselves and their own underlying issues, or even more dangerously, that they know all that can be known about their co-parent and what that parent's hidden issues or concerns may be.

Parenting coordinators may need to do a bit of education to help parents begin to think about all possible ingredients in their conflicts. For example, diversity and differences in culture/belief are common ingredients in conflicts and, often, parents in conflict are unable to differentiate between their *position* on an issue and their interest. However, conflicts are not always limited to battles between interests and desires. Needs, perceptions, power, values and principles, feelings or emotions, and internal conflicts are critical ingredients of all relationships. Understanding the ingredients involved in conflicts and understanding how those ingredients punctuate a relationship is essential to resolving the conflict effectively.

Needs-based conflicts may involve needs being ignored, needs and desires being confused, or when needs seem incompatible. Perception-based conflicts may involve distortion in self-perception, distortion in the perception of the other person, distortion in the perception of situations, or perceptions of threat. How we understand conflict influences how we approach conflict resolution. Introducing the notion that conflict is not always negative is a useful strategy for parenting coordinators to use. Armed with knowledge and greater understanding of the ingredients of conflict and strategies for resolution creates the opportunity for conflicts to be used to clarify relationships, open up alternative possibilities, and provide opportunities for growth.

In addition to individual ingredients such as needs, values, perceptions, goals, feelings, and/or interests, there are also relationship ingredients. The relationship between parents will have conflicts, commonalities, differences, and shared needs and interests. Most parents who enter parenting coordination are focused on the conflicts between them and may have great difficulty identifying commonalities and things they share. There are times when interests are directly opposed. When this occurs, a helpful strategy is to help parents develop objective criteria by which options and solutions may be judged. Usually there are a number of different criteria which could be used. The parenting coordinator may need to help parents reach agreement about the best criteria to use for their situation. Scientific findings, professional standards, or legal precedent are possible sources of objective criteria. Even if parents are unable to agree on specific criteria, they may be willing to agree to a fair procedure for resolving their dispute.

An example of this strategy occurred with the Hudson family. The parents were unable to agree on the need for their son to have medication for ADHD. The father did not want his son on medication and labeled the child's behavior as "normal guy stuff." The mother was concerned about the child's poor grades in school and increasing problems managing his behavior. The parenting coordinator suggested that the parties agree to gather independent information from a number of different professionals to assist them in making this decision. They ultimately agreed to consult a child psychiatrist, a psychologist who specialized in the assessment and treatment of Attention Disorders, and an educator. Gathering additional data helped reframe the conflict from one that was positional (i.e., it's either right or wrong to medicate the child) to a framework where the options and consequences of options are outlined without the "valence" of good/bad or right/wrong. The parents agreed to meet with each professional separately to make sure their underlying interests were expressed before having the professional meet with their son. They also agreed to assemble a list of their interests for the other parent to review and comment on. Once the data from the objective third parties was collected, the parenting coordinator reviewed the opinions and potential outcomes with the parents. The parents were able to reach an agreement to have the child medicated for 6 weeks with specific behavioral criteria that each would judge. They also agreed to not medicate the child for the 6 weeks after and use the same criteria to judge effectiveness or difference in behavior and academic performance of the child. The parenting coordinator memorialized the agreement and the parents were able to move on.

Allowing parents to get drawn into power struggles will only serve to destroy any tenuous goodwill that may have developed and serve to further erode the co-parenting relationship. The parenting coordinator may need to help parents avoid falling into a win-lose mentality by reminding them to focus on shared interests. When each parent's interests differ, the strategy is to seek options in which those differences can be made compatible or even complementary.

Another common ingredient in relationship conflicts is blame. Winsdale and Monk (2000) suggest the use of a technique they call externalizing rhetoric and point out that "Blame and its counterpart, guilt, are burdens that can best be thought of as hindrances to the task of finding a constructive way forward in conflict situations." The parenting coordinator should highlight when one or both parents are using blame and show them how it is keeping them stuck in the conflict. Posing questions to help objective the conflict invites parents to see the conflict as separate from themselves as individuals. To do so, the parenting coordinator might say: "So the conflict has gotten you to feel a very intense feeling like hatred. How did it manage to take over your feelings in such a strong way?" Or, "How did this argument catch you both in its clutches?" This approach reduces the sense of blame and invites parents to observe the conflict as an objective entity. Therefore, the *problem* is not the other person, but rather, the *problem* is the problem. The conflict has been turned into a noun and objectified which can open possibilities for new ways of thinking.

Separate Individual Conflicts From the Relationship Conflict

A principle strategy in parenting coordinator is to help parents separate the *issues* in conflict from the *individual* with whom they are in conflict. Judgment and accusation are typically woven so tightly around the participants in a conflict that there is little opportunity to shift the negative emotions that the conflicted parties have about each other. Just as a parent who disciplines a child may focus on the unacceptable behavior of a child, they do not label the child himself as unacceptable. It is important for parents to learn how to identify their parenting disputes in behavioral terms rather than character assassinations of the other parent. For example, a parent who identifies their co-parent as a selfish jerk is not identifying a parenting dispute. However, if the parent identifies a pattern of behavior where the children's wishes or needs are considered only after the parent's needs have been met, then specific behavior patterns can be identified as an area of concern.

It is not uncommon for parents in conflict to have strong feelings about the other parent and many try to build allies for their "side" of an issue. This may come in the form of trying to get other family members or professionals involved with the family to declare that they are "right" and justified in their position. When the other parent disagrees, a parent may take responses to those issues and positions as personal attacks and respond in an emotional manner. Separating the individual from the issues allows parents to focus on problem-solving rather than contributing to further damage of their relationship. The parenting coordinator can create an objective framework to accomplish this goal which creates the opportunity for relationship repair, even if the repair is tenuous. It also helps parents get a clearer view of the substantive problem.

How does the parenting coordinator create such an objective framework? The parenting coordinator is the objective third party who can reframe issues and rephrase complaints or allegations so that each parent, as an individual, is separated from any pattern of behavior or reaction that is at the source of the parenting dispute. The parenting coordinator may serve as the "translator" between the parents until such time as they learn to express their concerns in a manner that articulates an issue rather than a diatribe that amounts to character assassination.

Using Parenting Education as Intervention

Another strategy is to highlight the effects the conflicts have had on each parent and their children. The use of clarifying questions, some of which may be rhetorical, is helpful in accomplishing this goal. For example, the parenting coordinator may ask: "What impact has this conflict had on your personal life, your business, your relationships, your performance at work, your rest and relaxation, your confidence, your attitudes, your beliefs, your bank balance, your future?" Or, "What effects would you say distrust has had on your ability to co-parent?" "What has this ongoing conflict cost you?" "Are there ways in which this conflict has gotten you to act out of character?" "Has the conflict improved or lessened your effectiveness as a parent?"

It can also be helpful to highlight effects of conflict by asking parents to speculate about the future. An example of this would be: "What will happen if the conflicts between you are continued over the next 3 months, 6 months, 1 year, 2 years, 5 years, 10 years?" Often parents are caught up in the moment and have difficulty looking at the long-term impact of maintaining the conflict. Even if parents are unwilling to let go of the conflict for their own well-being, they may be persuaded to consider letting go or resolving the conflict because of the impact it has on their children.

There is a large body of empirical research that highlights the negative impact on children when they are exposed to prolonged hostility and conflict between their parents including behaviors that put children in the middle of a conflict (Buchanan, Maccoby, & Dornbusch, 1991; Hetherington & Kelly, 2002). For example, asking children to carry hostile messages to the other parent, demeaning the other parent in an open and contemptuous manner, asking intrusive questions about the other parent, or creating a need for the child to hide information from or their feelings about the other parent are all ways of putting the child squarely in the middle of the conflict. The parenting coordinator may need to help parents identify ways in which they are damaging their child by putting them in the middle. It may seem obvious to the parenting coordinator or to an outside observer, but it may not be obvious to the parent who is caught up in their own unresolved feelings of anger, hurt, or betrayal.

Research on risk factors for children and adolescents who experience separation and divorce in their families tells us that the risk of problems is double that of children, in comparison groups, who remain in intact families (Amato, 2000; Clark-Stewart & Brentano, 2006; Emery, 1999, 2004; Hetherington & Kelly, 2000; Kelly, 2002; Kelly & Emery, 2003; Simons et al., 1996). Children who experience separation and divorce are at greater risk of developing academic and achievement problems and may develop psychological symptoms, including depression, anxiety, and excessive fears. Some children also develop physical symptoms (e.g., stomachaches, headaches) and some act out in an aggressive or defiant manner.

There is also a wealth of empirical evidence about the adjustment of parents after divorce and the impact this has on their children (Carlson, Marcia, & Corcoran, 2001; Dickstein, 1998; Emery et al., 1999; Kelly, 2000; Kelly & Emery, 2003; Kline et al., 1989; Mezulis, Hyde, & Clark, 2004; Pruett et al., 2003). Investigators found a strong link between parent adjustment and adjustment of children and adolescents. If the parent with the most parenting time was depressed or anxious or had a personality disorder or mental illness, the children were at much greater risk of developing problems as well.

The parenting coordinator should also educate parents about the importance of building in buffers that protect their children from the damaging impact of parental conflict. These buffers include a good relationship with at least one parent or primary caregiver, parental warmth, a good relationship with siblings, and encapsulating parental conflict (Emery & Forehand, 1994; Hetherington & Kelly, 2002; Sandler, Miles, Cookston, & Braver, 2008; Neighbors, Forhand, Rex, McVicar, & Dave, 1993; Vandewater & Lansford, 1998). In addition, the parenting coordinator should also educate parents about research on the protective factors that reduce risks for their children (Amato & Gilbreth, 1999; Emery, 1999; Hetherington & Kelly, 2002; Kelly & Emery, 2003; Kelly, 2005; Kelly, 2007; Maccoby & Mnookin, 1992). These include good adjustment of the primary parent, competent parenting by mother and father, active involvement of an effective nonresidential father, reduced or encapsulated conflict between parents, parallel or cooperative co-parenting relationship, economic stability, and a limited number of family transitions.

Empirical research on effective parenting after divorce tells us that the *quality* of parenting is just as important as exposure to conflict in assessing risks to children (Amato, 2000; Amato & Fowler, 2002; Amato & Gilbreth, 1999; Buchanan, 1996; Finley & Schwartz, 2007; Hetherington, 1999; Hetherington & Kelly, 2002; Maccoby & Mnookin, 1992; Martinez & Forgatch, 2002; Simons et al., 1996; Stewart, Copeland, Chester, & Malley, 1997) Effective parenting has been demonstrated to diminish the impact of multiple family transitions and to moderate the impact of separation and divorce.

Using empirical research about the impact of separation and divorce on children and parents, how to build in protective factors and minimize risk factors, as well as what we know about effective parenting after divorce is an essential tool for the parenting coordinator. The parenting coordination should be familiar with the relevant social science literature and incorporate this knowledge into their intervention strategy.

Articulating Parenting Disputes and Developing a Plan to Address Them

Before long-standing and effective conflict resolution can be achieved, the parenting coordinator needs to help parents articulate and prioritize their parenting disputes. Parents often come into parenting coordination with complaints about the other parent and dissatisfaction with the time-sharing or parental responsibility arrangements. These are the "stated" or overt issues expressed by each parent. These issues can be relatively minor in nature, such as wanting to change the location to transfer the child, or the issues can be substantive. It is not unusual for parents who come into parenting coordination to make serious allegations about the other parent which may or may not be substantiated.

Allegations about substance abuse and dependence, allegations about physical threats or harm, and/or allegations about neglect or abuse to the children are all serious in nature and could place the children at risk. In Chapter 3, we discussed screening procedures to help the parenting coordinator discern the veracity and severity of the "risk" factors for the children and parent and determine an appropriate course of action. Generally, issues of physical safety have been addressed by the court and any safety parameters are included in the order of referral. However, this does not absolve the parenting coordinator from the need to assess any domestic violence concerns throughout the process. Assessing safety and risk factors is an ongoing process in parenting coordination.

There are other complaints that high-conflict parents may assert that do not appear to place the children or either parent at serious risk for harm. They may include disagreements over parenting style, the other parent's lifestyle, reliability and consistency of the other parent to adhere specifically to the parenting plan, and so on. Parents may have tried to resolve their parenting disputes without success or they have may no idea how to begin to address the disputes in a constructive manner. Usually, by virtue of the fact that a parenting coordinator is needed, the lack of creativity in problem-solving is apparent. There may be many reasons for a parent failing to engage in creative problem-solving. Parents may have decided on an option ahead of time and be unwilling to consider alternatives. A parent may be intent on narrowing options to find a single answer. Parents may define the problem in win-lose terms, assuming that the only options are for one side to win and the other to lose. Or a parent may decide that it is up to the other side to come up with a solution to the problem and insist that it's the other parent's problem, so why should they help with resolution.

An example of this strategy in action occurred with Tim and Ruth. When they were ordered to parenting coordination, Tim and Ruth had been divorced for 9 years and had one child who was adopted at birth shortly after their marriage. The child's birth mother had been involved in selecting the adoptive parents and prepared a beautiful book that included photos of her and her family as well a letter to the unborn child explaining why she had chosen adoption. The book was beautifully illustrated with details about the mother including her likes/dislikes, talents, dreams, and so on. She had included all of her family medical history and that of the child's biological father. The birth mother had presented this to Tim and Ruth at the court hearing when the adoption was finalized. Within 2 years after the adoption, Tim and Ruth filed for divorce and were granted joint legal custody and equal time-sharing by the court. However, many years of conflict ensued including an incident where Ruth filed for a restraining order after Tim showed up at her home, pushed his way into the house and began searching Ruth's bedroom and closet for the book the birth mother had given them. Tim had requested a copy of the book many times and Ruth refused to provide Tim a copy.

The dispute had to do with Tim insisting that he should have a copy of this book and Ruth insisting that Tim would show the book to the child "prematurely" and without her consent. Tim asserted that the child had been told when she was 5 that she had been adopted and now, at age 9, had started asking questions. Tim wanted to show the book to their daughter and go through it with her to show her how much she was wanted and loved even before her birth. Ruth's position was that the child should not have access to the book until she was 18 because they (Tim and Ruth) weren't "babysitters" for the child, but rather were the true and legitimate parents. Ruth believed that Tim was unwilling to share in important decisions about their child and would do whatever he wanted and would not respect her concerns. Tim asserted that Ruth was controlling and overreacting.

To the objective observer, the *parenting* issue had to do with when it was appropriate to share this information with the child and the parents disagreed. The parenting coordinator's role was to separate the "issue" from the individual and then to "reframe" the issue in terms that illustrated the concerns behind each parent's position. That is, articulate the *parenting* dispute so that the parents could focus on possible solutions rather than continue their negative, inflammatory comments about the other. Ruth needed help to see that she had an *individual* conflict which was her fear that showing the book to their daughter would somehow cause the child not to see Ruth as her "real" mom and would negatively impact the close, loving relationship that she cherished. Tim needed help to see that beyond Ruth's individual needs, she also held a valid and legitimate position in terms of when it was appropriate to share this information with their child.

The goal was to help Tim understand and empathize with Ruth's concerns and position even if he disagreed with her. Only after they were able to disengage from the emotional conflict were they able to identify possible solutions for resolving their dispute. The parenting coordinator then helped them identify four options: (1) identify an expert in adoption and ask that person to offer a professional opinion about the timing of presenting this information; (2) tell their daughter together (with the parenting coordinator present) that the book existed and that they would give it to her as she got older; (3) make a duplicate copy of the book and agree to a time-frame for sharing the book with their daughter; or (4) ask the parenting coordinator to arbitrate the issue.

The parenting coordinator has the responsibility to help parents learn how to generate creative options. This often begins with the parenting coordinator helping parents articulate the relationship problem or dispute. The next step is to analyze the problem and reframe ingredients such as interests, needs, goals, values, and so on. Then, the creative problem-solving can begin. The parenting coordinator can help parents generate a number of creative options, including those that might seem "wild" or "crazy" or "out of the box." Each parent may have an idea that is a partial solution. Each parent should have the opportunity for input without fear of criticism. The parenting coordinator can help parents visualize options by writing them down and asking each parent to rank order their preference. By doing so, the parents have started the creative problem-solving process.

Some high-conflict parents have adopted the habit, in the midst of their conflict, of dismissing the other parent's feelings by labeling them as "unreasonable" or "stupid." This is likely to provoke an even more intense emotional response and the parenting coordinator can point this out. For example, "I know you may not think Sally's feelings are important or reasonable, but everyone is entitled to their own feelings.

Feelings aren't right or wrong. Let's see whether we can understand what's behind Sally's feelings, so we can move forward in resolving the conflicts between you that are affecting your children."

Helping parents articulate their parenting conflicts as opposed to individual conflicts is very important. The parenting coordinator needs to help parents develop a plan to address the parenting disputes, which includes a priority list since it is difficult to address many major issues at once. The plan should include goals and time frames. It should also include objective steps for each parent to take in working toward resolution.

Confront and Avoid Flooding

The parenting coordinator may allow each parent to express their emotions, but the parenting coordinator should structure the interaction in such a manner that reduces the likelihood that the other parent will react to emotional outbursts. Gottman (1999) refers to intense emotional responses as flooding, where an individual feels overwhelmed and disorganized by the way their partner expresses negativity or complaints. When a person experiences emotional flooding, they often become hypervigilant and their body is a confused jumble of signals. Their muscles tense and stay tensed and they may find it hard to breathe. The heart beats fast and once the heart rate reaches 95 to 100 beats per minute, the adrenal glands go into action delivering adrenalin. This excited state interferes with listening and other understanding skills needed to do constructive work in a relationship.

The parenting coordinator should identify when flooding is occurring and disrupt the negative interaction. This often involves talking about how the parents are communicating. A parenting coordinator may make statements such as, "I think we are off the subject." "I think we have lost our focus on the children and the goal." "Your comment was aggressive and will not help us move forward." "I don't think listening is occurring between the two of you." Pointing out how parents are communicating is what Gottman refers to as repair attempts. In high-conflict relationships, teaching parents to accept and use the repair attempts versus ignoring them is critical. Even when repair attempts are presented in a heated emotional conflict, parents can learn to respond without reverting to criticism, defensiveness, and stonewalling with their co-parent. This repair work is in an effort to prevent a downward spiral of blame and defensive reactivity. It's a form of transition from mostly negative interactions to a healthier way of resolving conflict.

Confront Entitlement

Another likely and destructive element in the parenting coordinator process is entitlement. What is entitlement? What effect does it have on the creation of conflict? What implications does entitlement have for managing the parenting coordinator process? It is not uncommon for one person to believe that he or she deserves to be treated in a favored manner, that is, "entitled," even though that person may have done nothing to deserve any special favors. When one parent experiences a discrepancy between what he or she believes is deserved (based on a notion of entitlement), and what is actually received, a strong negative response may emerge.

An example of entitlement occurred with a nonmarried couple where the mother had raised the child alone for many years before the father became aware of the child's existence and, after many years, demanded his parental rights for access to the child. The mother felt she was entitled to "have" the child without interference from the father because she had been the sole care giver and provider for the child for 4 years. In exchange, she was willing to "give up" child support and she wanted the father to go away and not be a part of the child's life. A single parent who receives no financial, emotional, or literal support from the other parent may feel resentful of the previously uninvolved parent if that parent suddenly wants to assert their right to an "equal" time-sharing arrangement with a child.

Conflict can often be understood as a clash of entitlements. Rather than judging or blaming a parent for what appears to be inappropriate behavior or demands, it is more helpful to focus on how their sense of entitlement restrains them from demonstrating fairness and equity in dealing with their co-parent. When one parent has an exaggerated sense of entitlement, they tend to blame the other person for their own abusive behavior. Winsdale and Monk (2000) suggest that one "approach to dealing with exaggerated versions of entitlement invites the parties to engage in discussion about the issues without becoming overly defensive or losing face."

Examples of questions a parenting coordinator might pose include

- Do you want a relationship within which you can respect each other?
- How important is it for you to have a relationship with your child's other parent that is based on genuine respect and trust?

Confront Cycle of Blame–Defense (Anger Cycle)

Another common occurrence that can sabotage the parenting coordinator process is when parents revert to a cycle of blame–defense–anger. Both parents may be caught up in an intensive defense of their positions. One parent drags up an incident that proves what is wrong with the other person and why they can't be trusted, so the other parent is prompted to do the same. Each move in the cycle of blame and resentment focuses attention on the characteristics of the other parent and seeks to pin responsibility for the "problem" on these characteristics. Such exchanges lead to rapid escalation of conflict, and whatever goodwill may have been built is gone. And the cycle of blame–defense–anger starts all over again. So, how does the parenting coordinator help parents understand the concept of goodwill and of making goodwill "deposits" versus goodwill "withdrawals"? For most high-conflict parents, their goodwill bank account is seriously in the red when they begin the parenting coordination process.

One strategy to accomplish this goal is to pose questions that invite reflection and, sometimes, response. Examples of these questions are "How did this vicious cycle start to take over? How did it catch you both in its patterns against your better judgment? How did you get swept along the wake of this conflict? What would be your guess about how much blame is in charge of your views of each other? To what extent is blame stopping you from resolving your difference? How much are you in charge rather than letting blame have things its own way?"

It is important for the parenting coordinator to help parents detach blame from either party and lay the groundwork for building consensus, if possible. To that end, it is helpful for the parenting coordinator to ask parents directly whether they would like for the cycle of anger and hostility to continue. Most parents will prefer that it stop, but generally sees the "problem" as the other parent. Asking parents to reflect on the toll the cycle has taken is useful. "Has this conflict escalated as far as it can get or could things still get worse?" "Has the conflict pushed you as far as you are willing to go?" "Are you planning to allow the conflict to continue to speak for you and direct your behavior?"

Use of the strategies outlined in this chapter will give the parenting coordinator an indication of whether parents are ready to start building consensus. Some parents will get there relatively quickly and others will need interventions to keep the hostility at bay for many years. Maintaining a dose of hope and encouraging parents to think of possibilities of peace should be a recurrent theme for the parenting coordination process.

7

Strategies to Build Consensus

Never does the human soul appear so strong as when it forgoes revenge,
and dares forgive an injury.
—E. H. Chapin

High-conflict parents are often unable to identify any areas of agreement between them. Pointing out areas of agreement to the parents which may seem like stating the obvious is a helpful tool to create opportunities to build consensus. For example, most parents will admit that they want their children to be physically healthy and law-abiding citizens. Creating any working alliance or relationship good-will between warring parents may seem like an impossible task to the parents and a daunting task for the parenting coordinator. However, with some education, modeling, encouragement, and skillful intervention, it is possible to help parents learn to work as allies toward the goal of raising healthy, happy, well-adjusted children and parenting without outside intervention or oversight. But, as the old adage about leading a horse to water implies, parenting coordinators have no magic—the horse may be thirsty, in front of water, and still choose not to drink.

WHEN MOTIVATION TO PARTICIPATE IS LACKING

Many parents will be ordered to participate in the parenting coordination process. Some may have asked for the service and others may feel as though they have been "forced" into the process. If a parent feels as though they were coerced or pressured to participate, they may lack motivation to actively participate in a meaningful manner. If this occurs, the parenting coordinator should attempt to motivate parents and understand their reasons for not wanting to participate. One strategy for accomplishing this goal is to determine whether the parent has considered that their participation may produce better results than could be obtained if they did not try to resolve parenting conflicts. The parenting coordinator may also point out the likely consequences of failure to resolve conflicts on the children and parents. The parenting coordinator may highlight for both parties the pros and cons of participation which may help clarify the process and also highlight any concerns the parent may have regarding perceived risks of participation. The parenting coordinator should also point out that there is no reason to work toward an agreement that would be worse than the status quo and ask parents to consider the alternatives of failure to negotiate and resolve conflicts. The challenge for the parenting coordinator is to structure the parenting coordination process in a way that invites parties to participate. How is this achieved?

The parent coordinator should affirm a parent's right to choose whether or not to participate. However, most of the time the process will be court ordered and the parent coordinator may remind the unmotivated parent that the court thought it was a good idea. In addition, the parent coordinator may ask the unmotivated parent what they think the next step will be if they do not choose to participate. In most jurisdictions, the parent coordinator is required to notify the court if a party does not comply with the court order of referral to parent coordination and it may be helpful to remind an unmotivated parent of this requirement in as unthreatening a manner as possible.

A parent coordinator should avoid attempts to pressure a parent to participate. Instead, it may be helpful to understand why a parent does not want to participate. If the parent is fearful or ambivalent, the parent coordinator can acknowledge and validate their feelings. The parent coordinator can also invite the parent to present their reasoning and rationale. If parents can clearly outline their reasons, the parent coordinator may be able to help them overcome obstacles or correct misperceptions. For example, some parents are fearful that is they participate they will have to "give up" something that is valuable whether that be time with their children or decision-making authority. The parent coordinator can reassure a parent who may have a distorted perception of what the parenting coordination process is about. Another strategy is to ask parents to think ahead and wonder aloud what is likely to be the result in 3 months, 6 months, 1 year, and so on, if they choose to participate in the process and if they choose not to participate in the process.

BUILD TRUST IN THE PARENT COORDINATOR AND PARENT COORDINATION PROCESS

One of the first requirements for a successful working relationship in parenting coordination is to establish a relationship of trust and respect with the parties. Typically, trust is one of the casualties of conflict. The parties' willingness to trust one another has usually been badly damaged by the experiences they have suffered in their conflict. The parenting coordinator must earn the trust of the parties by adopting and maintaining a stance that proves trustworthy.

The parent coordinator can capitalize on a number of advantages including the professional role that the parents explicitly expect the parent coordinator to play. In this professional role, the parent coordinator should treat the parties as individuals from whom a great deal can be learned. An attitude of wonder or curiosity is a helpful stance for the parent coordinator to take and models a respectful desire to better understand the individuals and the conflicts that have captured them. The parent coordinator has clear roles and responsibilities as was outlined in previous chapters and must not deviate from their court-ordered obligations, but the approach used is important and can be a subtle, but invaluable tool. The parent coordinator may ask to collect data or verify information. Data collection is useful, but it is also useful to understand how a parent thinks. In psychological terms, this technique is often referred to as objective curiosity. Examples of these type of questions include:

- Can you help me understand how you came to consider this issue so important?
- So what exactly do you mean by reliable?
- What does it look like to you on a day-to-day basis?
- What has caused this to be such a strong value for you?

IDENTIFY COMMON GOALS FOR THE CHILDREN

Another strategy to help parents build consensus is to focus on the children. As noted earlier in this chapter, high-conflict parents often see no areas of agreement. However, the parent coordinator can help point out what may seem obvious to the outside observer, but may not be readily identifiable for the parent embroiled in a co-parenting dispute. For example, in addition to wanting their children to be physically healthy and law-abiding, most parents will agree that they also want their children to have a good education, to have enough financial resources to meet their needs, to be well-adjusted mentally, to have good friends, and to have a future that is filled with happiness and joy. If parents will admit that they agree on these things, they have already begun to begin consensus even if they intended not to do so with their co-parent.

Pointing out areas of agreement can be helpful when parents are caught up in the areas of disagreement. It is easy to get lost in the conflicts with emotions running high and "forget" that there are basic agreements between the parents. The parent coordinator has the responsibility of helping parents focus on the areas of agreement and common goals for their children in the midst of resolving conflicts. This can be done by having photos of the children present during the parent coordination process or using a "reminder" list on an easel or flip chart or both. The parenting coordinator may ask the parents to articulate their goals or use the following examples (see Table 7.1) as a start.

TABLE 7.1   Focus on the Goals

1. Healthy/happy children
2. A workable family system
3. Enhanced parenting skills
4. Re-building trust and respect, if possible
5. Resolving "real" parenting disputes quickly
6. Letting go of anger/hurt/resentment
7. Moving on

MAINTAIN/REINFORCE BOUNDARIES IN NEW CO-PARENT RELATIONSHIP

In Chapter 6 (Strategies to Disengage from Conflict), we reviewed how to help parents create a new type of relationship that is focused on their children. Regardless of the type of co-parenting partnership (i.e., conflicted, parallel, disengaged, etc.), it is important for parents to also learn how to maintain new boundaries or rules of engagement in this partnership. One strategic intervention to accomplish this goal is to highlight the difference between perceptions and facts. Since most conflicts are based in differing interpretations of the facts or perceptions, it is crucial for both sides to understand the other's viewpoint even if those viewpoints are diametrically opposed. The parenting coordinator may try to help each parent put themselves in the other's place, but this is no small feat. High-conflict parents have invested a great deal in reinforcing their position and are usually unwilling or unable to disengage, even momentarily, from their defensive position without assistance.

Many parents in conflict make assumptions about the actions of the other parent based on their own fears. The parenting coordinator must point out the illogic of this type of thinking without invalidating either parent's perspective. The parenting coordinator may also help parents disengage by pointing out blaming behaviors or words.

When parents are stuck in the "blame game," they are still emotionally engaged and lacking objectivity. The parenting coordinator can reframe demands into proposals or requests which may be more appealing to the other parent. As Kelly (1996) pointed out, the more the parents are involved in the process, the more likely they are to be involved in and supportive of the outcome.

Parenting coordinators often need to help parents identify the emotions that they are bringing into the conflict. Parenting coordination can be a frustrating process and parents often react with fear or anger when they feel that their interests and needs are threatened. The first step in dealing with emotions is to acknowledge them. If a parent or the parent coordinator understands the source of the emotion, then the parent can be directed to a resource to help resolve the emotional reactivity which is interfering with resolving conflicts in a constructive manner. This strategy should not be confused with the techniques used by therapists to help a patient identify and resolve underlying sources of conflict. The parenting coordinator may acknowledge the fact that certain emotions are present, even if a parent doesn't see those emotions or feelings as reasonable. For example, a parenting coordinator may say, "It is clear you are very angry and frustrated. It is also clear that you feel unheard. Let's work on trying to get your message across in a way that your co-parent can hear it better."

Reinforcing boundaries requires constant effort and monitoring by the parenting coordinator and parents until they are more accustomed to their new co-parenting relationship. Asking parents to articulate what they see as appropriate boundaries in the new relationship is a good beginning. It is also helpful to teach parents how to identify and communicate what they perceive to be boundary violations. For example, over what boundaries should someone not go if they want to maintain a feeling of trust? Continue co-parenting with minimal conflict? The reason for posing questions and wondering about boundaries is to help parents understand that the familiar taken-for-granted aspects of their former relationship no longer exist and need to be redefined.

Another important strategy for parenting coordinators in helping parents learn to maintain and reinforce boundaries in their new co-parenting relationship is to learn how to communicate with one another more effectively. Parents caught in high conflict are often not speaking to communicate, but may simply be grandstanding for their respective positions. The parents may not be listening to each other, but may instead be planning their retort. Even when the parents are speaking to each other and are listening, misunderstandings may occur. To combat these problems, the parent coordinator can teach parents some simple communication tools, such a using "I" statements and how to employ active listening.

The parent coordinator can model this technique and coach parents in their communication with each other by pointing out that a listener gives the speaker their full attention, occasionally summarizing the speaker's points to confirm their understanding. It is important to remember that understanding the other's perspective does not mean agreeing with it. Parents may need help in knowing how to direct their speech toward the other parent and keep focused on what they are trying to communicate. The parenting coordinator may model this technique and teach parents about using first person pronouns, for example, "I" statements, when they are speaking about themselves and their experience. This helps parents learn to avoid using blaming words such as: "You did...." " or "You never..." or "You always.... " It also helps parents learn to communicate *their* thoughts, *their* feelings, or *their* experience more effectively.

In addition to identifying negative emotions and blaming words, the parent coordinator may also need to reinforce the boundary of no name calling. For example, calling a parent "the sperm donor" is likely to be provocative and inflammatory. Redirecting parents when they use insulting and ridiculing language is necessary to reinforce the boundaries for a new, constructive co-parenting relationship.

TEACH PARENTS DIFFERENT APPROACHES TO RESOLVE CONFLICT

Most parents do not know that there are different approaches to resolving conflict. By posing questions to each parent such as "How do you usually go about resolving conflicts?" the parenting coordinator gathers valuable information about each parent's approach and resources for conflict resolution. The parenting coordinator needs to have several conflict resolution approach strategies in their tool kit when working with high-conflict parents. Using different approaches at different times is part of the "art" of the process.

Conventional approaches to conflict resolution focus on how people have unmet needs that must be satisfied if a conflict is to be settled. Interest-based or problem-solving conflict resolution models address the issues that conflicting parties feel are unfair or unjust by seeking out possible compatible interests and needs in an attempt to help defuse the conflict. This is a technique used often in mediation.

Use of this technique in the parenting coordination process allows the parenting coordinator to help parents recognize their interests, rather than their positions. As Fisher, Ury, and Ury (1992) explain, "Your position is something you have decided upon. Your interests are what caused you to so decide." Defining a problem in terms of positions places the dispute in a win–lose framework. When a problem is defined in terms of the parents' underlying interests, it is often possible to find a solution which satisfies both parties' interests.

The first step for the parent coordinator is to educate parents about the concept of a win–win framework. This often involves explaining the difference between an interest and a position and then helping parents identify their interests. This can be done by asking a parent why they hold the positions they do, and by considering why they don't hold some other possible position. Each parent usually has a number of different interests underlying their positions and interests may differ between the parents. However, all people will share certain basic interests or needs, such as the need for security, economic well-being, health and good education for the children.

Once the parenting coordinator has helped parents identify their interests, the interests must be discussed. If a parent wants the other parent to take their interests into account, that parent must explain their interests clearly. A parent may be more motivated to take the other parent's interests into account if they are both paying attention to the other parent's interests. The parenting coordinator should focus discussions on possible solutions by keeping parents forward-oriented, rather than focusing on past events. Parents can learn to keep a clear focus on their interests, but remain open to different proposals and positions. The parenting coordinator will often have to remind parents of this strategy and model examples of listening, generating options, validating perspectives, reframing a request, and pointing out the possible consequences if parents do not attempt to negotiate and resolve disputes.

Winsdale and Monk (2000) challenge the traditional problem-solving, interest-based model of conflict resolution. They believe that "entitlement has merit in helping us to appreciate how conflict is produced. It points to conflict as a contest over entitlements rather than over interests or needs." They introduced the idea of "narrative mediation" which has as its goal the creation of a relationship that is incompatible with conflict. They suggest that conflict can be transformed through "stories of understanding, respect, and collaboration."

Weeks (1992) describes several other approaches to resolving conflict, many of which are common but ineffective. He labels one such approach as the Conquest Approach.

The goals of this approach are to score a victory, defeat the opponent, and prove how right you are and how wrong the other person is. A conflict becomes a battle to win, a struggle to gain advantage in the relationship or to attain dominance in the relationship. Persons using this approach try to weaken the other party, assuming that the other party's weakness will somehow make his or her own strength greater. Parents may try to weaken the other parent by bullying, use of dominance or manipulation.

This is a common approach used in divorce litigation. Both parents, through their attorneys, do everything they can to create the perception that the other party is at fault, and that the settlement should reflect this fact by greatly penalizing the offending party and rewarding the offended party. The divorce is seen not only as a way of dissolving the marriage, but also a way of defeating and often punishing the other person. This approach requires a "loser." The loser often feels the need for revenge and the cycle begins again.

Another approach to conflict is avoidance. When parents are caught in high conflict, they usually appear as though they are not avoiding anything at all, but rather actively working to stay engaged in the conflict. However, there may be issues which are not on the surface or that have been articulated that are fueling the conflicts that are brought to the table. For example, there may have been unresolved issues between the parties which were avoided for a long time before the overt conflict emerged.

It is tempting to believe that conflicts will just go away if we pretend they do not exist. Avoiders simply pretend that there is no conflict or they may assume that time will heal all wounds. By ignoring the problem, they think or hope it will disappear. A variation of ignoring the problem is to sidestep confrontation. Unlike parents who pretend there is no conflict, these avoiders may acknowledge that there is a conflict, but they refuse to confront the other party. This may occur for several reasons. The parent may believe that it will do no good and therefore they aren't willing to waste their energy or time. Another reason is the fear that confrontation will lead to a battle and they may be so overwhelmed that they do not feel they can tolerate another battle. There is also the perception that if a battle ensues, someone will come out the loser—and it doesn't matter whether it is them or the other person—they don't want to risk being the loser.

Frequently, the avoider will focus on diversions to avoid confrontation. If enough peripheral or unrelated matters can be used to divert attention from the actual conflict, then they can get by without having to deal with their real issues and get lost in tangential or less emotionally charged conflicts. Unfortunately, avoidance merely postpones dealing with the conflict and often causes it to worsen. When a parenting coordinator notices either parent using this approach, it is important to identify what is occurring and point out that continuing to use this approach will prevent them from clarifying the disputes and creating the possibility of improvement.

Another approach to resolving conflict is to attempt to bargain with the other side. This approach focuses on the demands each parent is making. Demands are highlighted while needs, perceptions, values, goals, and feelings are ignored. Individuals who use this approach often believe that as long as both parties in a conflict trade somewhat equal portions of their demands, effective conflict resolution has taken place. There is also an element of power play in this approach since one party attempts to coerce the other to give up or concede a demand. This approach often generates more conflicts because each party attempts to position themselves to be at an advantage over the other party. An example of this approach is when one parent continues to make unrealistic demands that they know will not be accepted. Such demands create the *appearance* that the other parent is unwilling to compromise because they never agree to any of the demands.

Some parents are so uncomfortable with conflict or feel so unequipped to manage conflict effectively that they reach for whatever quick-fix solution they can find. This is often referred to as a "band-aid" because the net effect is similar to putting a band-aid on a wound that is infected and needs sutures. This approach covers up the fundamental problems of a conflict. "I can't see the infected wound, so there is no problem." Following the analogy, it is easy to see how this approach is not likely to be effective and is more likely to result in things getting worse. The core issues do not get clarified or resolved. This approach often results in no lasting improvement in either the conflict at hand or in their overall relationship. The band-aid approach does not work because it does not allow the parents to develop a *process* they can use effectively in future conflicts.

Identifying approaches to conflict resolution and helping parents see which approaches are likely to be more effective in resolving their conflict is a central strategy in the parenting coordination process. The parenting coordinator must be aware of different approaches and be able to readily identify the elements of an approach as it is occurring in order to invite parents to use a strategy that may be more effective. Allowing parents to continue to engage in conflict resolution approaches that do not work only serves to undermine each parent's confidence that resolution to their parenting disputes is possible. Fostering success in resolving disputes serves to reinforce trust in the parent coordination process.

ADDRESS PERCEPTIONS OF SELF, OTHER PARENT, AND CO-PARENT RELATIONSHIP

Just as unclear mirrors and windows can distort reality, it is also true that unclarified perceptions about oneself, the person with whom we are in conflict, and the relationship conflict can distort and obstruct the process of conflict resolution. Therefore, the parenting coordinator needs to help parents "clean the screen" through which they look at themselves, their partner in conflict, and the parenting issues in dispute. This is the process of clarifying perceptions.

Perceptions are formed early in life, and unless otherwise challenged, continue to develop into a screen through which one sees oneself, others, and the world around you. Perceptions are not "truth" and, while they are drawn from reality, over time they *create* reality or become a self-fulfilling prophecy. Perceptions, however, can change. New perspectives can be learned and it is incumbent upon the parenting coordinator to point out common interests and offer alternative perspectives. Opportunities to learn empathy may emerge as parents struggle with their children and their own adjustment post separation or divorce. The goal is to increase sensitivity and augment perspectives.

ABSENCE OF GOOD FAITH

Sometimes parents will enter into the parent coordination process with no intent to work out their parenting disputes by negotiating in good faith. Fisher et al. (1992) identify individuals who use this approach as those who use "tricks." Some parents will attempt to use unethical or coercive tricks in an attempt to gain an advantage in the parent coordination work. One of the tricks parents may use is *deliberate deception* about the facts or their intentions. It is not uncommon for parents entering parenting coordination to have lost all trust of the other parent because "tricks" of deception have been employed in the past. The strategy to mitigate the negative impact of deliberate deception is for the parent coordinator to seek verification of claims or assertions. It may help to ask each parent for further clarification of a claim, or to put the claim in writing.

The parent coordinator should adopt an attitude that conveys their impartiality in asking for verification. For example, "I do not know if your 'fact' is true or not. Do you have something that will support your claim?" This is similar to a court process where evidence must be presented to support the truth of a matter. In court, the judge is the trier of fact and does not accept unsubstantiated claims as facts. While the parent coordinator is not a judge, adopting a similar stance can be useful. The parent coordinator must ensure that this stance is uniformly applied to both parents at all times. In essence, the parent coordinator is communicating that it is not acceptable to make claims or assertions without something to support or back up the claim. It is very important that the parent coordinator not be seen as calling either party a liar which would serve to undermine the trust and respect that a parent coordinator seeks to model for parents. However, it is the parent coordinator's role to explicitly confront deceptions or falsehoods when present and to establish procedural ground rules for how deceptions will be handled within the parent coordination process.

Another common trick is *psychological warfare.* This often presents itself in parent coordination when one parent knows which "buttons" to push with the other parent and endeavors to press lots of buttons during the parent coordination session. When one parent is deliberately trying to provoke the other parent to get a reaction, the parent coordinator should intervene and ask the reacting parent what triggered their response if it is not obvious to the parenting coordinator. The parent coordinator may not recognize, initially, when subtle personal attacks are made so it is important to instruct participants in how to communicate their experience during the parent coordination process so the parent coordinator can intervene appropriately and establish a more constructive environment. For example, the parent coordinator may tell both parents to articulate when their "buttons" are getting pushed by saying so or using a symbolic gesture, like the universal time out sign. By stopping the process and interrupting the destructive interaction, the parent coordinator preserves the integrity of the process and provides reassurance to both parents that the parent coordinator is trustworthy and working to ensure that the working environment is emotionally safe and constructive.

Threats are also a way to apply psychological pressure. The parent coordinator should identify threats when they occur and intervene. Threats have no place in the parent coordination process and certainly serve to undermine any good faith initiatives to resolve conflicts.

Another technique some parents use that betrays their lack of good faith effort *coercion* or an attempt to pressure the other parent into a no-win situation. This may be done by making extreme demands or refusing to respond to interactions. When one parent refuses to negotiate or to use what Gottman (1999) refers to as stonewalling, the other parent is left with no opportunity to work toward consensus building. A parent may refuse to work toward any resolution of conflict, knowing that they can delay responding which may cause the other parent or the parent coordinator to have to ask for direction from the court which may take months. Or, a parent may make a take-it-or-leave-it offer. The parent coordinator should recognize this as a bargaining tactic and then explicitly identify this tactic to the parents. If a parent continues to utilize these tactics, and the parent coordinator does not have authority to make decisions to mitigate this sabotaging technique, then the parent coordinator may need to consider whether continuing the parent coordinator work is appropriate.

AVOIDING POWER STRUGGLES

The balance of power and struggles over power in a relationship is not unique to parents in parenting coordination. All relationships represent some form of power balance. It is often when relationships are in transition and new roles and responsibilities have not been clearly defined that issues of power between parents emerges. This is certainly true in divorce when issues related to children and money are at stake. In the initial phases of parenting coordination parents are often locked in power struggles which pervade their functioning. A common display of a power struggle can be seen when one parent believes they are "entitled" to more time with the children either by virtue of their gender or the amount of time they have spent in child-rearing activities prior to the separation.

In the book *Solomon's Sword*, Schutz, Dixon, Lindenberger and Ruther (1989) uses the biblical story of King Solomon as an analogy for dividing children between disputing parents. In this parable, the King is asked to decide who the real mother of the infant is. In the story, both mothers had infants, but one infant died in the night. The mother of the dead infant stole the infant of the other mother and claimed it was her own. This well-known parable highlights the intense investment each parent may bring to "proving" that they are right in a dispute. The wise King uses a *paradox* strategy to decide the issue between the two mothers: He suggests that they use the sword to divide the child in half with the expectation that the child's "true" mother would be willing to "give up" the child rather than have it killed. Parenting coordinators may also use paradox strategies to help parents identify their power struggles and learn how to disengage from this no-win situation, emotionally damaging circumstance for their children.

No single dispute resolution method can completely overcome differences in power. However, a parent coordination can introduce structure that helps balance the power equation. For example, the parent coordinator may rephrase statements in neutral language and introduce an alternative perspective or suggest a "time out" so that both parents have an opportunity to reflect on the issue before attempting to move forward in negotiating a resolution. The parent coordinator must model a nonhostile tone and response for parents even when faced with escalating emotions.

MEASURE PROGRESS IN RESOLVING DISPUTES

As mentioned in the beginning of this chapter, building consensus and resolving disputes can seem impossible at first. Parents need help analyzing the elements of the conflict, discovering alternate approaches to conflict resolution and learning how to take steps to disengage from the conflict crucible. This takes time and patience. The parent coordinator should take responsibility for helping parents identify specific actions or behaviors for which they will be responsible that will serve as steps toward the ultimate goal of conflict resolution. These steps need to have certain characteristics. Weeks (1992) identified such steps as "doables." He defined a "doable" as an action or behavior that

- stands a good chance of being accomplished
- does not favor one party at the expense of the other party
- meets one or more shared needs
- involves shared power
- helps build trust, momentum, and confidence in working together; and/or
- adds another stepping-stone along the pathway to improving the overall relationship

Breaking down steps that work toward resolution of conflicts accomplishes several goals. One goal is to help parents begin to see that resolution is possible. Often parents feel defeated in this goal before they begin. They do not trust their partner in conflict nor have they had success in resolving differences constructively. Therefore, they have little hope upon which to build. The parent coordinators job is to instill a dose of hope if possible. Successive approximation toward a goal has long been known in psychology terms to be a successful approach to addressing an issue or resolving a conflict. Successive approximation is also known as "shaping" which is a behavioral psychology term that refers to gradually molding or training someone to perform a specific response by reinforcing any responses that come close to the desired response. A parenting coordinator can help parents learn how to take small, measurable steps toward conflict resolution and notice the impact on themselves and their partner in conflict. Even when the conflict is not resolved, small steps toward the goal can be acknowledged and encouraged.

IS FORGIVENESS IN THE CARDS?

The stage model of forgiveness (Gordon & Baucom, 2003; Gordon, Baucom, & Snyder, 2000) proposes that forgiveness of major betrayals (e.g., infidelities, significant deceptions, and violations of trust) can closely parallel some aspects of recovery from more general traumatic events. The typical response to a traumatic event incorporates three phases: impact, a search for meaning, and recovery. Trauma research has suggested that posttraumatic stress reactions evolve from "violated assumptions" (e.g., Janoff-Bulman, 1989; McCann, Sakheim, & Abrahams, 1988; Resick & Calhous, 2001). The major betrayal that requires a forgiveness process can be seen as an interpersonal trauma that disrupts the person's previous assumptions and expectations of his or her partner and their relationship in general.

Parents engaged in high-conflict relationships may have no interest or need to engage in the forgiveness process. However, they likely are interested in regaining a sense of interpersonal control, predictability, and safety in the relationship with their co-parent, particularly if they can come to understand that forgiveness may be the key to moving on. In this approach, the motivation to forgive is not about the other person, but about a parent's own desire to move on with their life and not continue to expend energy, time, and financial resources to keep the conflict fueled.

If the forgiveness process is to occur, the parents must begin to realize the effect of the betrayal upon themselves and their relationships. This stage is a period of significant cognitive, emotional, and behavioral disruption (e.g., Enright et al., 1991; Gordon & Baucom, 2003; Hargrave & Sells, 1997; Rosenak & Harnden, 1992; Rowe et al., 1989; Smedes, 1984). Individuals in this phase are likely to report feeling as if the rug were pulled out from beneath them. Previously held assumptions about their relationship have been disrupted.

These violated assumptions often involve beliefs that one's partner (or previous partner) could be trusted, that the relationship is safe, that one can predict how one's partner will behave, and that one has reasonable control over one's own relationship. The betrayal can call these important assumptions into question; injured partners no longer can trust their assumptions to guide their daily interactions or to predict future events. Therefore they are likely to engage in a process of collecting details related to the negative event or betrayal in an attempt to explain to themselves what has happened.

These violated assumptions often leave the "victim" feeling out of control, powerless, and no longer able to predict future behaviors on the part of his or her partner. Consequently they are likely to lash out in a punitive manner toward their partners in order to "even the score." This type of interaction occurs with frequency in parenting coordination. Helping parents understand that some of these phenomena are natural reactions to a painfully traumatic event can be helpful in identifying underlying causes of unrelenting conflict (Horowitz, 1985; Horowitz, Stinson, & Field, 1991).

The second phase of forgiveness in the stage model involves the injured partners attempt to place the betrayal trauma in a wider context in order to understand why it occurred. The focus of this stage is to discover why the betrayal occurred in order to make the partner's behavior more understandable and predictable. Facilitating movement through the stages of forgiveness is not the principal role of the parenting coordinator. However, the parent coordinator may point out the possibility of forgiving so that each parent can understand that doing so may heighten the possibility of an increased sense of control over one's own life, a greater sense of safety and security for themselves and their children, and a decreased feeling of powerlessness.

The third stage of forgiveness involves the possibility of recovery and moving beyond the betrayal to stop allowing it to control his or her life. The understanding gained from stage two is consolidated during stage three of the forgiveness process. Under optimal circumstances, the injured partner develops a nondistorted view of his or her partner and their relationship. The injured individual may experience less intense negative feelings toward the partner, either from the increased understanding that has been obtained, or from the realization that clinging to high levels of anger has disruptive effects on the person experiencing those emotions. Similarly, the injured person recognizes that continuing to punish the partner will not "even the score" and makes it difficult to move forward with life. With high-conflict parents, both parties may feel like they are the injured or betrayed party. This means each parent must determine whether they are willing to work toward forgiveness.

If parents are able to forgive, then they are more likely to regain a balanced view of their co-parent; decrease their negative feelings towards them; and acknowledge their willingness to stop trying to punish their co-parent further.

MOVING ON

Acknowledging a history of previous hurts, aggressions, or actions is an important part of learning to move on and extract oneself from the crucible of conflict. Previous actions that led to complete erosion of trust are not easily forgotten. Denying these past realities does not remove them from history. On the contrary, denying or minimizing hurts or aggressions tends to exacerbate tensions and ensure future conflicts.

It is important to acknowledge the negative experiences and consequences of history between parents in order to reduce tensions. Tensions can thus be limited to contemporary issues over which control and change can be affected.

Summary Steps

1. Create an effective atmosphere
2. Clarify perceptions—self, other, relationship disputes
3. Focus on shared goals and needs
4. Build shared positive power
5. Look to the future
6. Generate options
7. Develop stepping stones to action
8. Develop mutually beneficial agreement

The parent coordinator can also point out that the best way to avoid future conflicts is to prevent them from arising. This is where a detailed parenting plan with enough structure and flexibility becomes an essential tool for helping parents transform themselves from adversaries to parenting partners.

8

Parenting Plans: Using Research on Child Development and Parenting Styles as a Guide

Mankind owes to the child the best it has to give.
—U.N. Declaration

One of the most difficult challenges facing parents at the time of separation is deciding how they will address issues concerning their children. The development of a parenting plan can be an invaluable tool for parents. Some parents will start parenting coordination with a very detailed *parenting plan* that was developed as part of their divorce proceedings, either with their attorney or with a mediator or by the court. Other parents may be referred to a parenting coordinator relatively early in their divorce proceedings and may not have a parenting plan in place. There are also parents who may have a general outline of a parenting plan, but who require assistance from the parenting coordinator to help finalize the detailed components they will need to best meet the needs of their children in this new co-parenting relationship. Therefore, it is critical for the parenting coordinator to know how to develop parenting plans and how to help parents decide which aspects of a parenting plan they will need.

A parenting plan document may have different titles and include different components depending on jurisdiction. Generally, there are legally required components to a parenting plan that must include elements such as name of the parents, names of the children, legal address, jurisdiction, child support arrangements, and so on.

In addition, a parenting plan will also include components which detail time-sharing arrangements, "custody" designation, and decision-making arrangements. Often, the custodial and time-sharing arrangements will be incorporated into a mediated Marital Settlement Agreement or a Final Judgment of Dissolution of Marriage order of the court. Regardless of the title of the document, a parenting plan is intended to be a formal statement of how the needs of the children are to be met following separation or divorce.

Typical components will include

- Residential and child care arrangements
- Time spent with each parent and the (wider) family
- Recreation and holiday arrangements
- Religion and education

Helpful components to include

- Conflict-resolution techniques
- Communication plan
- Decision-making plan
- When to modify

THE IMPORTANCE OF A "BEST INTEREST" APPROACH TO PARENTING PLANS

In Chapter 2, the current legal standard in the United States that provides direction to the court when making decisions regarding children in child custody matters was identified. That standard is referred to as the "best interest" standard. A similar standard is also well established in Canadian law and case law. This standard is intended to help the courts focus first on the children's needs and to use these needs as a guide in determining parenting arrangements including time-sharing and decision-making as it relates to the care and well-being of the children.

Objectives of a parenting plan are as follows:

- Provide for the child's physical care
- Maintain the child's emotional stability
- Provide for the child's changing needs
- Set forth the authority and responsibilities of each parent
- Minimize the child's exposure to harmful parental conflict
- Protect the best interests of the child

In addition, a well-designed parenting plan will

- Lessen disagreements
- Decrease conflict
- Help the entire family understand and accept change
- Provide a guide for parenting behavior and the co-parenting relationship

In developing a parenting plan, there are some important factors for parents to consider when developing the details of a parenting plan:

- MINIMIZE LOSS: Children experience divorce as a series of significant losses. To a child, parents' separating means losing home, family life, loving parents who care about each other, pets, financial security, familiar schools, friends, and a daily routine.
- MAXIMIZE RELATIONSHIPS: Parents should encourage all relationships which existed for the children before the separation (parents, grandparents, aunts, uncles, and friends.) A child's identity depends on their feeling that they belong to a family and children will keep the feeling of family when they have pleasant, free access to both parents and both extended families.
- PROTECT CHILDREN'S FEELINGS AND SENSE OF WELL-BEING: Parents should reassure the children that they are not responsible for the separation and try to avoid blaming the other parent for the separation as this forces a child to "take sides." Parents should not confide in children or share details of adult relationships.
- INCREASE SECURITY: Scientific research confirms that children will suffer now and later if they frequently see their parents in conflict. Raised voices, arguing, hateful remarks, and physical altercations are not suitable for a child's viewing. Do not discuss adult issues at the time of transfers or when the child is present and remember that children are harmed when they hear one parent say bad things about the other parent.
- AGE-RELATED NEEDS: Children of different ages need and benefit from different parenting arrangements. Parents should try to be flexible and tailor schedules as much as possible to reflect their child's developmental needs and individual requirements. As the child gets older, parents will need to be more flexible and will need to work harder at communicating effectively to adequately address an older child and adolescent's changing needs.

If parents do not have a parenting plan, or the plan they have is outdated or not working or not detailed enough to provide them with a guide for meeting the needs of their children within the context of their new co-parenting arrangement, then the PC may be asked to assist with the development of such a plan. This can be a critical intervention strategy to help parents disengage emotionally and provide the structured framework needed to minimize conflict between them. Parenting plans can be divided into four general outlines or structures which include basic, safety-focused, long-distance, and highly structured parenting plans. Figure 8.1 displays a self-assessment tool (12th Judicial Circuit, Florida, www.jud12.flcourts.org) which may be useful in determining which parenting plan best suits a particular family's needs.

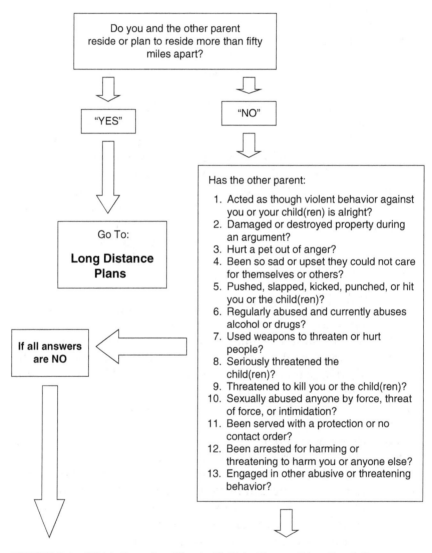

FIGURE 8.1   Which Parenting Plan Is Right for You and Your Family?

FIGURE 8.1   *(cont.)*

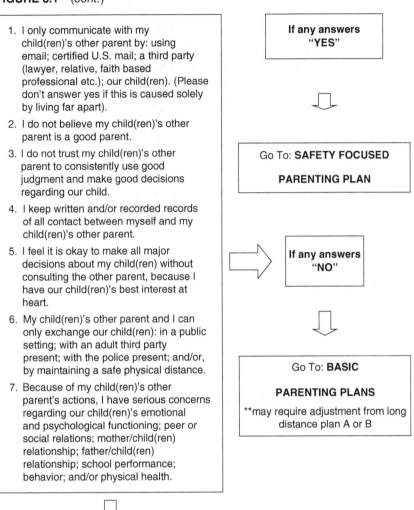

1. I only communicate with my child(ren)'s other parent by: using email; certified U.S. mail; a third party (lawyer, relative, faith based professional etc.); our child(ren). (Please don't answer yes if this is caused solely by living far apart).

2. I do not believe my child(ren)'s other parent is a good parent.

3. I do not trust my child(ren)'s other parent to consistently use good judgment and make good decisions regarding our child.

4. I keep written and/or recorded records of all contact between myself and my child(ren)'s other parent.

5. I feel it is okay to make all major decisions about my child(ren) without consulting the other parent, because I have our child(ren)'s best interest at heart.

6. My child(ren)'s other parent and I can only exchange our child(ren): in a public setting; with an adult third party present; with the police present; and/or, by maintaining a safe physical distance.

7. Because of my child(ren)'s other parent's actions, I have serious concerns regarding our child(ren)'s emotional and psychological functioning; peer or social relations; mother/child(ren) relationship; father/child(ren) relationship; school performance; behavior; and/or physical health.

If any answers "YES"

Go To: **SAFETY FOCUSED PARENTING PLAN**

If any answers "NO"

Go To: **BASIC PARENTING PLANS**
**may require adjustment from long distance plan A or B

If any answers "YES"

Go To: **HIGHLY STRUCTURED PARENTING PLANS**

The general outline for the Highly Structured Parenting Plan suggested above is included in the addendum. (The other three parenting plan outlines referenced above may be accessed through the Florida Twelfth Judicial Circuit website, www.jud12.flcourts.org/parenting plans.) All parenting plans need to include specific information about where the child will live on any given day. It should also include specific time frames for the child to be with each parent. The means of communication between each parent and child must be detailed along with where the child will be educated. Transportation and travel arrangements, holiday and school break time-sharing, as well as extracurricular activity arrangements. Generally, information regarding health care providers and any religious education or observance will also be included. Beyond the standard arrangements just listed, there are several aspects of parenting plan development that may be helpful to consider.

WHICH COMPONENTS ARE HELPFUL TO CONSIDER WHEN CRAFTING A PARENTING PLAN?

- Making decisions based on social science
- Child development research
- Postdivorce adjustment research
- Parenting style
- "Fit" between parenting and child
- Logistical considerations
- Special needs of children or adults

WHAT DOES THE RESEARCH TELL US?

- Children's developmental issues must be taken into consideration
- Parental conflict does damage
- Parenting style matters
- There are predictable phases of postdivorce adjustment that warrant consideration

CHILD DEVELOPMENT RESEARCH

Child development is not linear. Rather, it involves the child's inherent personality and temperament, which influences parent initiations and responses. It also involves the parent's personal, social, and cultural expectations, which influence the child's developmental changes. Child development is also influenced by the environment and relationships outside of the parents.

Infants: Birth to 10 Months

This is a very busy and important time. The infant is totally dependent on the adults around them while they touch, listen, and observe the world. Things are always changing. Infants learn very quickly. They are completely dependent on their caregivers to protect them and to provide constant attention to their needs. This includes their need for love, nurturing, and attention. They form attachments by consistent, loving responses such as holding, playing, feeding, soothing, and talking. When both parents have been actively involved, the child forms an attachment to both parents.

Changes and separations from the caregiving parent will cause discomfort and distress because an infant does not have a sense of time. They have a limited ability to remember the absent parent. Infants should have frequent contact with both parents. Infants trust their regular caregivers to recognize their signals for food, comfort, and sleep and trust their caregivers to meet these needs.

Infants need to feel secure with routine and familiarity. They require a predictable schedule. Their sleeping, waking, feeding schedules should be consistent. Parents need to adjust their schedules to meet the infant's needs as this is an important time for the child to develop a sense of security, trust, and comfort with others. If an infant's needs are not met, parents may notice that their child cries excessively, refuses food, fails to gain weight, has difficulty sleeping, fails to interact with the environment, or shows other signs of distress in one or both households. (Table 8.1)

TABLE 8.1   Designing a Parenting Plan for an Infant

When designing a parenting plan for an infant, remember:

- Frequent, repeated contact with each parent is recommended.
- Contact should provide time for feeding, playing, bathing, soothing, napping, and nighttime sleeping.
- Both parents must develop the required skills to be good caregivers.
- Infants should not be away from either parent for more than a few days.
- Parents will need to share their experiences in a way to provide consistency and stability. They must do this in a way that does not expose the child to anger and in a way that is comforting to the infant.

Baby/Older Infant: 10 to 24 Months

Older infants are beginning to explore their world. There is a great deal of rapid development. There are many motor accomplishments: sitting, crawling, standing, and walking. They are still very dependent on their caregivers and they continue to need holding, caressing, gentleness, and nurturing. While they can hold on to a memory of an adult they haven't seen for a day or two, they still may show fear or distress at the time of the next contact and cannot tolerate long separations.

The older infant is self-centered and believes the actions and moods of others are directly related to their actions and moods. They recognize anger and harsh words. They show and express a wide range of emotions through their own gestures, actions, and expressions. They will begin to communicate with sounds, smiles, and show simple emotions. They have special, familiar things that the parents ensure go with the child(ren) (toys, blankets, pacifiers).

The older infant still needs a great deal of holding, caressing, gentleness, and direct eye contact. They will now benefit greatly from repetitive play and having adults talk with them to share their language and their feelings. This is how they continue to feel safe while beginning to relate to the world around them.

A consistent routine increases their trust in others and their confidence that all of their needs will be met. They can become anxious if separated from familiar and comfortable surroundings. They will benefit from repetitive play and having adults talk to them. They will benefit from having similar routines in each household. Infants have emotional memories and can recognize anger and harsh words. If their needs are not met and they do not feel secure, excessive crying, irritability, withdrawal, feeding, or sleeping problems may develop.

A child will respond to multiple caregivers if each is sensitive to the child's cues and follows along with the required and routine activities (sleeping patterns, eating schedule, and wakeful activities). Long separations from either parent still feel like permanent losses, and they will show feelings of helplessness, abandonment, and sadness. (Table 8.2)

TABLE 8.2   Designing a Parenting Plan for a Baby

When designing a parenting plan for a baby, remember:

- Each parent should participate in the daily routines including feeding, bathing, putting the child down to sleep, and waking the child up from a nap. This will help the child develop a secure relationship and help both parents master the tasks of caretaking.
- Separations of more than 3 days may interfere with the child's sense of safety and stability. Work responsibilities must be balanced with the child's need for regular involvement with each parent during the weekdays and shared time of weekends.
- Each household should follow similar patterns and routines in child care to provide consistency.

Toddler: 25 to 36 Months

Toddlers experience rapid physical, emotional, and social growth. They are on the move! They are developing a sense of independence and more control over the world around them. Mastery of language and toilet training occurs during this period. The toddler has a desire to explore the world and learn how things work. As they try to understand the world, they also try to change the rules, limits, and boundaries set by the caregivers. They have discovered that new word, "no."

Toddlers require a balance between their need for greater independence and their equally strong need for fair and consistent limits to keep them safe. They need to develop self-control and learn that trustworthy adults are caring for them. They need supervision, encouragement, and a high level of caregiver involvement. Patient, consistent, loving, supportive care is essential.

During separations, the toddler needs reminders that the important people have not disappeared, will return, and continue to love them. Nightly phone calls can be reassuring. Only when the child feels safe and secure can they begin to explore their world.

If a toddler's needs are not met, parents may notice that their child becomes anxious or irritable. The child may become clingy or excessively aggressive. Their sleep may be interrupted by bad dreams. Sometimes they will become fearful when transitions take place and begin to display behaviors they had already outgrown. (Table 8.3)

TABLE 8.3   Designing a Parenting Plan for Toddlers

When designing a parenting plan for toddlers, remember:

- Transitions can be difficult unless both parents have soothing styles and can meet the child's needs for structure and reassurance.
- Parenting must be adjusted to meet the child's need for success. Similar ways of handling events will provide a sense of comfort.
- Telephone calls at a regular hour can be a good way to "touch base" for the child and the parent. This keeps the relationship in the present.
- A picture of each parent in the child's room along with the "special blanket or teddy" that travels back and forth can be reassuring.
- It is best that overnights be spaced throughout the week.

Preschool, Early Kindergarten: 36 Months to Age 5

Preschoolers are busy and creative in their thinking. They want to take charge of their ever-expanding world. They want to learn and try things out. They are beginning to enjoy time with other children and are learning how to cooperate and share. Because they have better co-operation and because they like to be "big" they can take more responsibility in caring for themselves such as getting dressed, using feeding utensils, and picking up toys. They can begin to understand the idea of a day and a week but do not really understand time.

They are beginning to understand "right" and "wrong". They are very observant. They begin to understand the difference between boys and girls and begin to watch the way their friends of the same gender make choices. They try to do the same things. They begin to understand that little boys grow into daddies and little girls grow into mommies. They begin to notice the ways that the parents relate to each other. They begin to imitate. This begins to set the stage for their own grown-up relationships as well as how they will relate to each parent.

They will get enjoyment out of most activities if they observe their parents cooperate in planning and sharing in activities. They can find routine and feel safe and comfortable in each residence. Naps are replaced by quiet time and a change of pace in activities. They need consistency and predictability from the outside so they can find a way to calm themselves.

If the child's needs are not met, parents may observe persistent sleeping and/or eating problems. The child may show long periods of being moody: sadness, withdrawal, crying, and anger. The child may refuse to engage in the activities provided. This is a time for them to learn how to become bigger than a toddler…they have work to do and need to be able to focus on their jobs. Transitions between households require positive support to help the child know that everybody is ok and gets along. (Table 8.4)

TABLE 8.4 Designing a Parenting Plan for the Preschool and Early Kindergarten Child

---

When designing a parenting plan for the preschool and early kindergarten child, remember:

- Take into consideration your child's temperament.
- Each parent should become competent and comfortable in helping the child be successful in the daily routine which includes getting ready for the school experiences. It is important to consider the amount of childcare each parent had provided prior to the separation.
- Participate in the daily routines like feeding, playing, bathing, reading.
- The child should be encouraged to take on some responsibility for self care actions (picking up toys, flushing the toilet, washing hands before meals) to develop independence and responsibility.
- If both parents have been involved in all aspects of care (before the separation) the child may be able to be away from either parent for 2 or 3 days. This may depend on the child's temperament.

Early Elementary School: 5 to 9 Years

This period begins a long, more settled period of childhood. The child begins to have a variety of experiences away from the home and the family. Children become involved in their school activities and find other sports and interests that they share with a number of friends and other adults. While they are interested in their teachers and peers, they still need to please their parents most of all. They can begin to adapt to different styles of parenting and see the differences in different places and situations. They need to check in and touch base. They want the security of stable patterns in caretaking, and regular contact with each parent, including individual time with each parent. They want help in grooming, dressing, eating, and remembering things, but the more they learn and succeed at such tasks themselves the better they feel. Doing well at school and well at home makes the child feel good.

Early school children can understand the concept of time and routine. They can look forward to things that will happen and can remember things that were done before. They are better able to express things that are important to them and can find ways to get others involved.

They are beginning to understand the difference between fantasy and reality. They know what is "fair." They begin to have definite opinions about what they like and what they don't like. They learn to solve simple problems. If the child's needs are not being met there may be physical problems (tummy aches, headaches), sleep problems, expressions of anger, and a return to more childish behaviors (bed wetting, baby talk). (Table 8.5)

TABLE 8.5   Designing a Plan for the Early School Child

When designing a plan for the early school child, remember:

- The child's schedule of school and after school activities must be considered so that the child can succeed in these areas.
- A consistent schedule and routine is necessary so that the child can focus on the job of school, friends, and team activities.
- Parents should select activities that match the child's interests and work together to balance these activities with the demands of school.
- Birthday parties and other peer activities will be important and may require some additional transportation and flexibility of parenting time.
- Provide support for the child's school program by setting a study routine and communicating with the teacher.
- Fewer midweek transitions make it easier for finishing school projects but both parents need to participate fully. Research shows that children with fathers involved in their schooling perform better in school.

Preteen: 10 to 12 Years

These children are preparing to make the leap into adolescence. They become far more independent and want to do things for themselves. They pay attention to the way they look and the acceptance of a peer group is very important. Their increased ability to think logically and their more developed sense of conscience may lead to stronger judgments, statements of opinion, and increased arguments. They can discuss issues in detail, want explanations for other's decisions, and want the freedom to solve problems on their own. They may side more with their peers and confide in them more readily. They will often choose to be with their friends over their family.

Children begin to develop and test values and belief systems. Children this age need to be able to express their feelings but must recognize that the parents make the final decisions.

They may choose to side with one parent over the other. This may change based on the specific issue or the parenting style. They need to be encouraged and given permission to love both parents and understand that the parents' separation matters are not their burden.

There is a difficult balance between providing structure and creating the chance for independence. Families need flexibility so the child may have the time required with friends and activities as well as with both parents. Parents need to encourage the move toward independence while providing reasonable and consistent limits and boundaries.

TABLE 8.6   Designing a Plan for a Preteen

When designing a plan for a preteen, remember:

- Parenting plans must provide frequent, meaningful contact with both parents.
- Preteen children do well with many different options of parenting plans as long as the contact is structured and consistent. When possible, plans should include overnights during the school week and on weekends so that both parents may be active participants.
- Schedules can provide longer times away from either parent (up to a week) but must take into consideration the child's activities and school responsibilities.
- Children should be given open telephone access to the other parent and be given privacy for the calls.
- Rules and routine between the households should have some consistency and continuity for increased success.
- Develop a format for discussing the child's academic and extra-curricular activities without including the child in discussions (journal, email communication, phone conference, "business-like" meeting).
- Children can be consulted about their views and suggestions, but the parents should still make the final decision.

There is cause for concern if a preteen child loses interest in friends and other relationships and begins to isolate (spending extended times in his room, skipping meals and activities, not going out, or not answering the phone). A child working too hard at being "too good" could suggest a high level of internal stress or desire to cover up. If the child begins to take sides or feels the need to take sides with one parent there is greater chance of depression and rebellion. A change in school performance and peer group may indicate some loss of well-being. (Table 8.6)

Early Adolescent: 13 to 15 Years

Children between thirteen and fifteen use the family as a base for support and guidance. Though they may not show it, young adolescents continue to need both the nurturing and the oversight of their parents. Decision-making ability varies widely in this age group as well as from one situation to another.

Girls tend to mature earlier than boys. The primary task for children of this age is one of increasing independence from the family and developing a separate identity. They are involved in the difficult task of preparing themselves to function as young adults.

As their bodies change and they begin to physically develop into adults, they may feel more self-conscious, they may feel more emotionally sensitive, and their need for privacy will increase. It is necessary to provide them privacy while staying aware of their activities. There is an increase in moodiness, tiredness, and sloppiness. They will want to have a "say" in things that matter to them. They want explanations, will voice their opinions more loudly, and may become argumentative.

Children have frequently formed close relationships with other teachers, adults, peers, and generally regard their relationships with their peers as the most important relationships in their lives. They want to spend much more time with their friends and less time with their parents. They have strong opinions and want to have more control over their lives. They should be expected to assume greater responsibility for their decisions and consequences of their actions. If they are given some flexibility in their schedules and the arrangements, most adolescents can adapt, compromise, and enjoy the limited time they chose to spend with the parent.

Parents need to provide safe options for this exploration while setting reasonable limits and appropriate rules (curfew, family tasks, responsibility for schoolwork). The challenge for parents of these early adolescents is to support their growing independence while maintaining basic structure and close contact with both parents. The guidelines must be reasonable, firm, and fair, as should the privileges and consequences. It will be important that the parents talk or communicate directly with each other to be certain that the child is safe and accountable. Children are exposed to a variety of situations that put them at risk, and parents must stay informed and able to discuss these hard topics (sexual behaviors, alcohol use, drug abuse).

If the teen's needs are not met, there may be excessive anger and negativity. Children this age may begin to hide out or stay away from others. School difficulties become evident as the demands of school become greater. There will be an increase in the acting out, sometimes with increased sneakiness, lying, and risky behaviors. Out and out defiance of rules is a real concern. (Table 8.7)

TABLE 8.7   Writing a Plan for an Early Adolescent

When writing a plan for an early adolescent, remember:

- The child's schedule, commitments, and obligations must be taken into consideration.
- Flexible creative plans that would not have worked for younger children may be considered.
- While each parent may have a longer period of time without the child in residence, the parent should increase contact and awareness through regular attendance at the child's athletic events, performances, academic events, and other activities.
- Frequent communication between parents is advised as children may distort the situation and seek to play one parent against the other. Consider communicating by using a journal, email, phone calls, or "business-like" meeting.

Older Adolescent: 15 to 18 Years

Children this age are preparing to become independent and self-sufficient young adults. It is necessary for them to have a gradual and healthy separation from both parents. These adolescents are making decisions about how they want to be and where they want their lives to go. They will establish their own sense of self with regard to rules and behaviors, taking into consideration the family, the peer group, and their community standards. Adolescents are developing their own personal standards. They have developed strong and lasting relationships with both boys and girls. Appearance and "fitting in" continue to be important. Closer groups begin to form that have something in common.

By late adolescence, they have begun to view their parents as individuals with qualities they both like and dislike. They begin to figure out how that may affect who they are and who they want to be. The peer group has great impact on choices that they make. Children are particularly vulnerable to changes in the family and pressure from outside the family. Maintaining stability and consistency can be challenging as an adolescent's feelings are often changeable and intense.

Increased schoolwork, extracurricular activities, and jobs become important. Many students begin to focus on future goals such as work, further education, or other post–high school plans. The freedom to set their own schedule (both between households and about driving, curfews, dating, and overnights) becomes a priority. Parents should be aware of a teenager's efforts to be in control while the teenager's judgment and experience is still limited. The driver's license adds freedom which increases the need for trust, communication, and accountability.

This is a "practice" for their being out on their own, so it becomes a period of teaching and learning. They need the opportunity to make plans while the parents maintain age-appropriate guidelines and structure. Privileges come with responsibilities. Compromise is encouraged when conflicts arise between the wishes of adolescents and their parents, including conflicts regarding the contact schedule. (Tables 8.8 and 8.9)

TABLE 8.8   Designing a Plan for an Older Adolescent

When designing a plan for an older adolescent, remember:

- Adolescents do well with a variety of parenting plans.
- Parents need to be aware of the adolescent's need to be consulted, informed, and involved when making the schedule and making family plans.
- Parenting times and schedules will need to take into consideration school demands, job hours, automobile access, and extra-curricular and social activities.
- Adolescents need to balance time between independent social time with peers and meaningful family time.

TABLE 8.9   Child-Focused Parenting Plan Essentials

In all plans it is important to remember:

- Children develop best when both parents have meaningful and stable involvement in their children's lives.
- Each parent has different and valuable contributions to make to their children's development.
- It is better for young children to spend more time with parents and less time with other caregivers. When both parents work, parents should make every attempt to choose mutually-acceptable and accessible caregivers.
- Communication and cooperation between parents is important. Consistent rules in both households and sharing of knowledge of events, creates a sense of security for children of all ages. Households must discuss and plan school activities and other events.
- If children are allowed to bring their personal items back and forth between the households, they develop a better sense of ownership and responsibility. Parents should purchase special things for the children but not merely for their own household.
- Children need to be protected from adult conflicts. They should not be exposed to arguments, hostility, and negative comments between the parents. They do not want to hear negative things about someone they love.
- They should not be messengers…they are the children. The parents should do the adult work so that children may complete the tasks of being children.

PARENTING STYLE MATTERS

Crafting appropriate time-sharing schedules is a difficult and, at times, daunting task as it requires consideration of more than just calendars and day-to-day activities. In many instances, parents and courts want schedules that are convenient and easy to follow, but these may not be child centered or in the child's best interest. To develop parent time schedules that serve a child's best interests, parents and mental health providers must factor in both developmental levels for children and parenting styles. Further, parent time schedules must be viewed as "dynamic" rather than "static" and must consider the changing needs of the child, the changing family structure, and combine those with the parenting style of each parent to arrive at the best possible fit for long-term positive development.

Parenting style is generally defined as the overall emotional climate of the parent–child relationship—an affective context of sorts that sets the tone for the parent's interactions with the child (Darling & Steinberg, 1993). Almost 50 years ago, parenting style was described globally along two dimensions: warmth–hostility and permissiveness–restrictiveness (Becker, 1962). Twenty years later (Maccoby & Martin, 1983), parenting styles were expanded to include a fourfold classification system which included

- Authoritarian-autocratic
- Indulgent-permissive
- Authoritative-reciprocal
- Indifferent-uninvolved

Parenting styles have been a major topic of study for the later part of the 20th century. Baumrind (1971) defined three specific parenting styles and their consequences for children: (a) authoritative, (b) authoritarian, and (c) permissive styles of parenting based on levels of warmth and control used by the parent in disciplining the child. According to Baumrind (1991), parenting styles are meant to capture normal variations in parents' attempts to socialize children.

Parenting styles can be both supportive and unsupportive in their tone, both of which affect developmental outcomes and consequences to personality development. Baumrind described how parenting styles affect measures of competence, achievement, and social development. There is also some evidence that parenting styles are related to social competencies of children (Baumrind,

1991; Dekovic & Janssens, 1992; Dishion, 1990; Lamborn, Mounts, Steinberg, & Dornbusch, 1991).

Parenting *styles* differ from parenting *practices* in that parenting styles set the tone for interactions, rather than being goal-directed attempts to guide and socialize a child. According to Baumrind, parenting styles change the nature of the interactions between parents and their children through the way interactions are presented. Darling and Steinberg (1993) theorized that while parenting practices have a direct effect on specific child behaviors, parenting styles influence development indirectly by moderating the relationship between parenting practices and child outcomes.

Authoritarian

The authoritarian parenting style consists of punitive and directive strategies (Querido, Warner, & Eyberg, 2002). This parent determines the rules and the child follows without question. Physical punishment is often used in this style of parenting. The authoritarian parent attempts to shape, control, and evaluate the behavior and attitude of the child in accordance with a set standard of conduct (Baumrind, 1971). Harsh and inconsistent punishment is normal in these high-control, low warmth homes. Authoritarian parents will likely use destructive criticism when they discipline their child. Barber (2000) suggested that although children of authoritarian parents behave and obey parents, they are living in fear of their caregivers and tend to avoid their company as much as possible.

As suggested by Hartup and Laurson (1993), authoritarian parents often put a child down, and give little or no explanation for punishment. These researchers also point out that authoritarian parenting is related to later development of dysfunctional relationships. Baumrind (1971) found children of authoritarian parents to be more often withdrawn, discontent, and distrustful. Children are provided with standards of behavior and are expected to adhere. They are given very little freedom, if any, in decision-making and are never asked for their opinion on any decision that is made for the family. In an authoritarian home, children are given no control over their environment and, therefore, have no opportunity to "practice" skills for independent functioning. According to Laible and Thompson (2002), forceful discipline such as that found in authoritarian homes has been shown to interfere with children's processing of parental messages.

Authoritative-Reciprocal

An authoritative parent encourages verbal expression, self-will, and autonomy (Baumrind, 1971). This parent uses some control while also using explanation and reinforcement techniques to modify their children's behaviors. Authoritative parenting consists of emotional support, bi-directional communication, firm limit setting, and responsiveness (Querido et al., 2002). Baumrind (1971) maintained that authoritative parents are more effective in teaching children acceptable social behavior, which they can internalize and draw upon in later interactions with their peers and others. (Table 8.10)

TABLE 8.10   Authoritarian/Autocratic Parenting Style

* Characterized by power assertion.
* Children are expected to obey rules and not permitted to make demands on parents.
* Little warmth or verbal give-and-take between parents and children.
* Physical punishment is a typical discipline method.
* Often restrict their children's access to peers, which can inhibit their opportunities to learn social skills and other important social adaptation skills.
* Adolescents with these parents score high on measures of obedience and low on measures of self-competence.

Authoritative parents have children who are characterized as being more self-reliant, curious, and content with themselves (Baumrind, 1971). When children receive consistent explanations regarding their behavior they have a better understanding of how to please others and feel freer to interact. Laible and Thomas (2002) found that mothers who were constructive during conflict had children who perceived relationships in a more prosocial manner. Authoritative parents put a lot of investment into their children while surrounding them with an atmosphere of love and acceptance.

Authoritative parents use directive strategies in combination with high amounts of nurturance, accepting attitudes, mutual responsiveness, patience and playfulness. Warmth, which includes affection and responsiveness, among other positive behaviors, has been shown to be associated with friendly, prosocial behavior with peers and lower levels of aggressive behavior (Attili, 1989; Mize & Petit, 1997; Domitrovich & Bierman, 2001). This information lends support to the idea that these children have greater success with acceptance within their peer group and tend to be more socially competent.

Authoritative parents allow their children opportunities to learn about the give-and-take of reciprocal relationships. A parent who is warm and accepting of their child is likely to respond positively when their child models some form of acceptable behavior, thus increasing the tendency of the child to behave this way more in the future. Authoritative parents provide children with opportunities to observe warm interactions. These parents understand that coaching their children on the appropriate ways to interact with other children and adults is important. This differs from authoritarian parenting, which focuses on a unilateral relationship. If children perceive others as accepting, it is likely that they will advance into interactions more positively, which suggests that authoritatively raised children will be more accepted by peers, which is an important developmental milestone and a foundation for healthy social interactions in peer and family relationships.

Permissive

There are two types of permissive parenting styles. A neglectful permissive parent uses low levels of control that reflect disengagement from child-rearing duties, while an indulgent permissive parent employs a low amount of control, which has a foundation in absolute trust, democracy, and indulgence (Lamborn et al., 1991). The permissive parent does not force any control over the child. There are few demands made and little to no limits on their behavior (Querido et al., 2002). These children are given no responsibility, and, in addition, the parent often consults with the child about the rules of the house. A caregiver in a permissive home does not force any responsibility on the child, nor do they have any expectations for their children's behavior (Baumrind, 1971). They may avoid controlling the child because they also want to avoid confrontations and temper tantrums. (Table 8.11)

TABLE 8.11 Authoritative-Reciprocal Parenting Style

- Parents are responsive to the demands of their children and expect their children to be responsive to their demands.
- Encourage verbal give-and-take.
- Enforce rules when necessary.
- Set clear expectations for mature behavior and encourage independence.
- Explain their assertions and provide rationales for rules and regulations.
- Adolescents with these parents are more competent, and have higher self-esteem, moral development, impulse control, and subjective feelings of independence.

These parents present themselves as resources for the child to use as he/she wishes (Baumrind, 1971). Children raised in permissive homes are given total control over their own environment with occasional input from the caregiver. According to Barber (2000), developmental outcomes of children in indulgent permissive homes are much like those of children raised in neglectful and abusive homes. Having a permissive parent who sets no boundaries may have serious effects on children's future development. These children are the least self-reliant, curious, and self-controlled of any group (Baumrind, 1971). Parents may not be aware of the disservice this parenting style provides children when they are outside of the home environment.

Of the research available concerning permissive parenting styles, a major portion is related to adolescents. Adolescents who describe parents as permissive report greater social competence and tend to have higher scores on measures of self-perception than those children raised in authoritarian homes (Lamborn et al., 1991). However, these children are seen as being more self-centered and have incredible difficulties controlling their impulses (Bornstein, 2002). This may be due to no authority figure setting any consistent limits on their behavior. Children in disengaged homes were also less conforming than children in both authoritarian and authoritative homes (Mounts & Schwartz, 1996). (Tables 8.12 and 8.13)

TABLE 8.12   Permissive-Indulgent Parenting Style

- Parents are reasonably responsive to their children.
- Avoid regulating their children's behavior and impose few rules.
- Make relatively few demands for mature behavior.
- Avoid the use of punishment.
- Tend to be tolerant of a wide range of behaviors in their children.
- Adolescents with permissive parents are self-confident but show higher levels of substance use and school problems.

TABLE 8.13   Permissive-Disengaged Parenting Style

- Parents often limit the amount of time they devote to parenting tasks.
- Set no expectations or rules.
- Important parenting functions are often absent, such as the long-term commitment to providing guidance and direction with consistency.
- Adolescents with these parents show the lowest scores on competence and the high scores on behavior problems.

Research on the impact of different parenting styles indicates that authoritative parenting yields the most favorable and successful outcomes for adolescents (Lamborn et al., 1991). In addition, children reared with authoritative parenting are more likely to be in a peer group that endorses both parent and peer values (Durbin, Darling, Steinberg, & Brown, 1993). According to Steinberg (1990), when one or more components of authoritative parenting are missing, adverse outcomes typically occur. He also concludes that "responsiveness" in parents appears to facilitate the development of self-esteem and social skills in children and "demandingness" appears to foster impulse-control and social responsibility in children. According to Dekovic and Janssens (1992), children raised under the authoritative parenting style demonstrate more involvement in groups, display less hostility, and work more proficiently with others than children raised under a more autocratic style of parenting.

It is important for the parenting coordinator to identify the type of parenting style for each parent and to be familiar with the outcomes likely to be associated with each style. Parenting coordinators may use empirically based education to help parents learn how to increase their competence as parents even if they have very different styles. Framing elements of a parenting plan into questions of how to match children's needs with parenting strengths creates a framework for working toward the "best fit" parenting plan. Rather than focus on parenting deficits, the parenting coordinator can help parents identify creative options for crafting and/or modifying their parenting plan so that every family member's needs and abilities are taken into account with the goal of fostering healthy adjustment and future growth.

9

Intervention Strategies for Families
With Extra Challenges

Hope is the thing with feathers
That perches in the soul—
And sings the tune without words
And never stops—at all
—Emily Dickinson

We know parental divorce has an impact on children and families. We also know that conflict between parents hurts children and that the quality of parenting after divorce has a significant impact on children. Understanding and responding to the challenges of families where one or both parents display a pattern of substance abuse and addiction, mental illness, child abuse, or alienating behaviors presents an extraordinary challenge for the court and for parenting coordinators. One of the goals of parenting coordination is to attempt to mitigate damage to children who are at greater risk for harm due to impairment or disability in one or both parents. This chapter will address those challenges and offer intervention strategies to help the parenting coordinator manage those families with special needs.

SUBSTANCE ABUSING AND ADDICTED PARENTS

The prevalence of addiction and substance abuse issues in family law cases poses an immense challenge for family courts. The U.S. Department of Health & Human Services (2000) indicates that adults with histories of child abuse and neglect are at high risk for developing substance abuse disorders, and that substance abuse contributes to almost three-fourths of the incidents of child abuse or neglect for children in foster care. Child welfare experts report a "frequently occurring correlation" between alcohol and other drug use and child abuse or neglect (Child Welfare League of America, 2008).

169

It is not surprising that substance abuse and addiction are frequently associated with the neglect and abuse of children. Parents battling substance abuse often put the needs created by their own alcohol or drug dependency ahead of the welfare of their families. At the same time, they and their children commonly have complicating physical and/or mental health problems. Often unable to maintain employment or provide a stable and nurturing home environment, addicted parents are often incapable of putting the needs of their children or family ahead of their addiction. Given the connection between substance abuse and issues such as child abuse and neglect, the courts must assess the risk factors for children of exposure to substance dependent or addicted parents without provisions for safety in place. The tension lies between protecting children's best interests and not discriminating against parents who have addictions.

Not all parents who use or abuse alcohol or other drugs neglect their children, and their children may not be in danger. It is critical for the parenting coordinator to differentiate between parents who have a substance abuse problem and do not neglect or abuse their children and those who place their children at risk for harm. As stated in earlier chapters, it is not appropriate for the parenting coordinator to conduct an evaluation to verify or discount whether a parent has a substance dependence disorder, but it is appropriate to identify these risks for the parents and facilitate appropriate intervention as well as any changes in parenting responsibilities to protect children until the substance dependent parent is considered safe again.

Indications of substance dependence may arise through allegations made by a parent or another individual in the child's life such as a teacher, family member, or babysitter. Collateral sources of information can be very helpful to the parenting coordination when they are attempting to develop a course of action to shield the children from risk or harm and facilitate, if possible, appropriate interventions for the impaired or dysfunctional parent. This will often require court intervention and support, particularly if the substance-dependent parent is in denial about their disease.

The parenting coordinator should notify child protection authorities immediately if they suspect that a parent is substance dependent and potentially placing their children at risk when they are in their care. If court appointed, the parenting coordinator should also notify the court which will have a number of options available to them. The court may change the time-sharing arrangements to limit the parenting time of the substance-dependent parent, order contact between the children and the substance-dependent parent to be supervised, order the parent into treatment, or suspend that parent's access entirely if circumstances warrant in order to protect the children. The parenting coordinator should not impose these types of substantive changes in the parenting arrangements, but they may provide information to the court so the court can determine an appropriate course of action.

In addition to allegations made by a co-parent or other person with reliable information, there may be a history of substance dependence which the parent readily admits or previous records which indicate a need for oversight and caution. In these circumstances, a parenting coordinator may ask the parent to agree to drug screening prior to contact with their children. This may serve to reassure the other parent and resolve the issue. However, if a parent is addicted to substances, a drug screening may not be sufficient to adequately protect children while in their care. Substance-addicted parents may go to extreme lengths to protect their addiction and maintain contact with their children, for example, using methods to ensure a false negative outcome of a drug screen.

It is important for the parenting coordinator to understand the science of addictions and appropriate treatments to avoid jumping to conclusions about the fitness of a parent and reinforcing negative stereotypes. For example, a positive drug test may create a *presumption* of an unfit parent, but more information is needed. Under these circumstances, for example, a judge may be tempted to remove children from their families, but many children may be able to remain safely with their parent if treatment and appropriate support services, such as family counseling and parenting skill development, are implemented and monitored.

Health care providers recognize that addiction and substance abuse are family problems that not only involve every family member but also affect generations. Even in cases where there is only one family member who abuses alcohol and/or other drugs, addiction professionals consider treatment of the family to be part of the treatment of addiction. While many treatment options are available for addiction, it is important to understand the impact that failure to treat or improper treatment has on an entire family, not just the addict (Stimmel, 2009).

Leis and Rosenbloom (2009) point out the complex variables which may emerge in working with addicted parents. They state, "more so than other populations of parents, addicted parents will pose important questions about social attitudes, negative stereotypes, and personal responsibility." In addition, there is very little research on the precise impact of substance abuse on parenting and on parent–child relationships. In the absence of data indicating otherwise and the societal pressure to rely on negative stereotypes, substance-abusing parents are likely to be dismissed as incompetent, irresponsible, uninvolved, and potentially dangerous. Family courts may greatly limit addicted parents' contact with their children or sanction them in other ways in an effort to promote the child's best interests. However, there are a number of risk factors for children with substance-abusing or substance-dependent parents that must be carefully weighed. For example, will the parent's presence or absence in their child's lives be better or worse for the child? Is the parent actively using or in recovery? Is the parent able to work and pay child support? Eliminating or greatly reducing contact between an addicted parent and a child should not be the only option considered particularly if the parent is willing to get proper treatment and structures can be put into place that protect the child and still allow them to maintain a healthy, loving relationship with their parent.

Therefore, a parenting coordinator must be aware of how to identify potential addictions in parents and the implications for monitoring parent–child access while protecting the best interests of children. If the court order of referral and parenting plan do not specify the safety parameters that should be in place for an addicted or substance abusing parent to have access to their child, then the parenting coordinator must be prepared to make such recommendations to parents and, possibly, the court. These parameters may include mandatory attendance at treatment sessions, urine toxicology screening, in-patient rehabilitation, and evidence of compliance by the addicted parent to the recommended treatment protocol.

MENTALLY ILL PARENT

Parents who are referred to parenting coordination, like the rest of the population, will have some incidence of mental illness. A parenting coordinator needs to be aware of the nature of a parent's mental health condition and any treatments indicated to ensure children's best interests are protected. Mental illness or a mental diagnosis does not necessarily mean that a parent will not be able to parent adequately. Researchers studying parenting competence following divorce found that parent sensitivity is a key ingredient for the development of a healthy relationship between parent and child. This sensitivity is based on parents' ability to reflect on their children's emotional states in a nondefensive and thoughtful manner (Fonagy, Steele, & Steele, 1991). Parents with untreated mental illness may lack this sensitivity. In addition, a parent's ability to be attuned may result from their preoccupation with their own needs and well-being (Ainsworth, Bell, & Stayton, 1974). Mentally ill parents may distort or incorrectly interpret their child's needs or signals or they may project their needs onto the child (Brisch, 2002).

Mood disorder symptoms, such as depression and anxiety, are not uncommon in the postadjustment period following divorce as parents may be adjusting to major changes in lifestyle, finances, parenting responsibilities, and emotional loss. Approximately one-half of all marriages now end in divorce, and about 30 to 40 percent of those undergoing divorce report a significant increase in symptoms of depression and anxiety (Brown & Harris, 1989). Vulnerability to depression and anxiety is greater among those with a personal history of mental disorders earlier in life and is lessened by strong social support.

Although some stressors, such as the breakup of an intimate romantic relationship and financial hardships, are so powerful that they may evoke significant emotional distress in otherwise mentally healthy people, the majority of stressful life events do not invariably trigger mental disorders. Rather, they are more likely to spawn mental disorders in people who are vulnerable biologically, socially, and/or psychologically (Brown & Harris, 1989; Kendler et al., 1995; Lazarus & Folkman, 1984). It is important for the parenting coordinator to determine whether a parent's mental health symptoms are a reaction to significant stress associated with separation and divorce and, therefore, may be relatively short-lived, or whether the symptoms reflect a longer-standing issue that will require ongoing treatment and intervention to allow that parent to function adequately when their children are in their care.

Treatment may involve therapy or medication or both in order to help the parent function adequately. If a parent has a thought disorder, such as schizophrenia, it does not necessarily mean that they are unable to parent, but great caution is indicated since this type of illness, and the symptoms associated with it, can cause impaired reality testing, poor judgment, and failure to tend to the basic needs of the individual much less their children. However, thought and mood disorders can readily be treated and many individuals are able to function very well in their parenting role with proper treatment and adequate supports.

One class of mental illness that manifests frequently in parenting coordination are parents with personality disorders. A personality disorder is an enduring pattern of inner experience and behavior that deviates markedly from the expectation of the individual's culture, is pervasive and inflexible, is stable over time, and leads to distress or impairment in interpersonal relationships. There are three main types, or clusters (American Psychiatric Association, 2000), of personality disorders. Individuals with a Cluster A personality disorder may be characterized as "odd and eccentric." Paranoid, schizoid, and schizotypal personality disorders fall in this cluster. The second cluster, Cluster B, includes individuals who are characterized by dramatic and erratic behavior and thinking. These include antisocial, histrionic, narcissistic, and borderline personality disorders. The last type is Cluster C which include individuals who are characterized as anxious and fearful. These include avoidant, dependent, and obsessive compulsive personality disorders. Eddy (2006) asserts that "persons with Cluster B personality disorders appear to have characteristics that draw them into intense, ongoing conflicts on a regular basis—much more than other clusters." The parenting coordinator should not evaluate a parent to determine whether a personality disorder is present, but may need to refer a parent for evaluation if they recognize signs and symptoms which suggest the presence of a personality disorder that may impact safe and effective parenting.

We do not have incidence or prevalence rates for the number of parents with personality disorders who are ordered to parenting coordination. However, practitioners who work with high-conflict parents are likely to report a higher incidence of parents displaying symptoms similar to individuals who have one of the Cluster B type of personality disorders.

The first type in this cluster is entitled Borderline which is commonly misunderstood by individuals who are not mental health practitioners as a disorder which is on the edge of or borders some other mental or behavioral condition. Borderline personality disorder is a distinct type of personality disorder that refers to a specific set of personality traits which include:

- Fears of being alone
- Volatile and unstable relationships
- Identity disturbance or unstable self-image or sense of self
- Impulsivity in potentially self-damaging ways (spending, sex substance abuse, reckless driving, binge eating)
- Suicidal behaviors/gestures/threats or self-mutilating behavior
- Wild or erratic moods—affective or emotional instability
- Chronic feelings of emptiness
- Inappropriate, intense anger, or difficulty controlling anger
- Transient, stress-related paranoid ideation

The second type of disorder in Cluster B is called Narcissistic and includes personality traits such as:

- Extreme preoccupation with self
- Need to be seen and treated as superior
- May exaggerate achievements and talents
- Has a sense of entitlement, that is, expects special privileges or favors
- Lacks empathy and tends to dismiss the feelings or needs of others
- Acts arrogant
- Tends to be very envious of others

The third type of personality disorder in this cluster is titled Histrionic and includes the following traits or symptoms:

- Needs to be the focus of attention in all situations
- Interacts with others in a sexually seductive or provocative manner
- Extreme focus on physical appearance
- Dramatic in speech and presentation, for example, "drama queen/king"
- Easily influenced by others or circumstances
- Shallow expression of emotions
- May fabricate events

The fourth and final type of personality disorder in Cluster B is Antisocial. A person with these traits will likely display the following behaviors/attitudes:

- Extreme disregard for the rules and norms of society
- Impulsive
- Irritable and aggressive
- Willing to hurt others for personal gain
- Lying and deceitful
- Feels no remorse and rationalizes their behavior

A parenting coordinator may not have knowledge of a parent's mental diagnosis prior to beginning work, but may quickly recognize some of the characteristics or traits described above. More important than the diagnostic label, however, is knowing how to work with individuals who display these traits in the parenting coordination process. Pointing out the self-destructive nature of some parent's behaviors is not likely to be effective any more than trying to "reason" away behaviors or traits. Even if parents are behaving in such a bizarre, erratic, impulsive, self-damaging manner, they may not be able to change without effective intervention.

Unfortunately, there are no "cures" for a personality disorder, but some symptoms may be managed effectively through the use of psychotropic medication and/or therapy. The challenge for the parenting coordinator is to recognize a parent's strengths and attempt to structure interventions that mitigate damage to the children, while managing character traits in parents that may undermine progress toward resolution of conflicts.

It is important for the parenting coordinator to build a working alliance with parents if they are to establish a foundation of trust and maintain the integrity of the parenting coordination process. Working with parents who have a personality disorder is challenging and the parenting coordinator should carefully evaluate their approach and interaction style to increase the likelihood of a successful working environment. Following are some general guidelines or tips to assist the parenting coordinator in their work when they recognize personality traits that are similar to personality disorder characteristics.

BORDERLINE

Do establish and maintain consistent boundaries in all interactions
Do not criticize
Do not try to "match" their mood
Do model emotional and behavioral stability
Do provide repeated guidance, but limited reassurance

NARCISSISTIC

Do not keep them waiting
Do not blame
Do not overtly disagree or challenge
Do show great respect to form a working alliance
Do blame "absent" participants: system, statutes, and so on

HISTRIONIC

Do not ignore or fail to notice
Do not respond to seductiveness
Do acknowledge feelings but without agreement
Do model stable emotion regardless of dramatic presentation
Stay focused on goals

ANTISOCIAL

Do not compare or compete
Be respectful
Do not be swayed by charm
Do not try to appeal to their empathy
Do stay at reward-consequence level
Do collaborate on goals without engagement

The above-noted tips are for individuals who may fall into the Cluster B personality disorder types that were discussed earlier in the chapter. Parenting coordinators may encounter parents who display traits or characteristics that fall outside of this cluster and may also encounter circumstances where both parents have a personality disorder. These are some of the most challenging cases and require careful consideration for intervention. It is also helpful to be aware of the types of personality disorder traits that do not match well with others. For example, a very difficult dyad to work with occurs when one parent has a Borderline personality disorder and the other a Narcissistic personality disorder. In these circumstances, the parenting coordinator must work to maintain clear behavioral and emotional boundaries at all times during the parenting coordination process in spite of the challenges that will be presented regularly by both parents. The parenting coordinator must be alert to one parent wanting affirmation of their superiority and expect to be accused of bias toward one parent or the other. The parenting coordinator must also address unrealistic expectations of a parent without coming across as critical or demeaning.

Other challenging dyads occur when one parent has a Dependent personality disorder and the other an Antisocial personality disorder. Parents with dependent type traits may easily be lured into agreements that are not realistic or fall for the charismatic approach of the parent with antisocial traits. The parenting coordinator may be the subject of adoration or idealization by the parent who is looking for someone upon whom they can depend to help them with their life. It is important for the parenting coordinator to encourage the dependent parent to rely upon individuals within the support team for such reassurance. The antisocial parent may be used to taking advantage of the parent with dependency needs and the parenting coordinator must recognize the power and control imbalance explicit in these type of dyads and intervene accordingly.

Another example of a challenging dyad occurs with parents when one is Histrionic and the other has Obsessive compulsive traits. The histrionic parent is by nature dramatic and imprecise and constantly needing to be the center of attention. The obsessive compulsive parent needs precision, control, and organization. A classic example of escalation occurs when the histrionic parent is chronically late for the appointments and begins immediately to describe with great flourish the drama of the week. The obsessive compulsive parent becomes enraged and hyperfocused on the lateness which is met by dismissal from the other parent. Then, name calling begins, "you're so anal...that's why the kids can't stand being around you," and the interaction quickly becomes destructive. The parenting coordinator must intervene by redirecting the focus back to parenting issues and the children.

When one or both parents have personality disorders, it is often very helpful to have a mental health professional as a part of the professional team to assist the parenting coordinator in providing the structure and support needed to these parents who may otherwise deteriorate in functioning given the stressors of their divorce and postadjustment phase.

ALIENATION, ESTRANGEMENT, ALIGNMENT, AND AFFINITY

Children in high-conflict divorce and custody cases may align with one parent and show signs of visitation refusal or beliefs about the other parent that may be distorted and lead to rejection of that parent. It is important for the parenting coordinator to determine whether the child is a victim of alienation or has become estranged from a parent for other reasons. With a comprehensive custody evaluation, the parenting coordinator may have the history of the parent–child relationship and know how to intervene if visitation refusal issues arise. Without a custody evaluation to rely on for a history, the parenting coordinator will need to gather information from the parents, children, and others involved to determine an appropriate intervention strategy. The court order of referral and the parenting plan should detail the time-sharing arrangements that the parenting coordinator is to monitor and help parents implement.

There are many circumstances when issues of alienation or estrangement do not arise during the process of divorce or separation, but manifest during the course of parenting coordination. There are specific assessment procedures (Lee & Olesen, 2001) to determine the "child's stance, the degree of entrenchment, and the child's vulnerability to alienating pressures" and a continuum of criteria to differentiate between children exposed to high conflict who are estranged, aligned, or alienated (Lampel, 2002). The parenting coordinator may want to refer the family for a comprehensive evaluation when a child resists or refuses contact with a parent in order to direct intervention for the alienated or estranged child and the parent.

The issue of resistance to visitation has undergone a number of formulations over the past 30 years, from the "pathological alignment" between an angry parent and child (Wallerstein & Kelly, 1976, 1980) to Richard Gardner's (1987, 1992, 1998, 2001, 2002, 2003) "parental alienation syndrome," and the most recent reformulation as "child alienation" (Kelly & Johnston, 2001). Kelly and Johnston's model uses a more holistic, family systems approach acknowledging the role of context, multiple contributing factors, and a broader range of potential interventions. Stolz and Ney (2002) suggest that Kelly and Johnston's model should be reformulated to also include contextual variables, namely the adversarial legal context and the mislabeling of *unreasonable* attitudes and behaviors as symptomatic of child alienation. Kelly and Johnson's model uses the following definition:

> An *alienated* child is defined as one who expresses, freely and persistently, unreasonable negative feelings and beliefs (such as anger, hatred, rejection and/or fear) toward a parent that are significantly disproportionate to the child's actual experience with that parent.

Stolz and Ney describe the problem of visitation resistance and refusal as one which is significantly impacted by an adversarial legal system. "The influence of the adversarial paradigm is such that all parties involved—the divorcing couple, lawyers, helping professionals, and even the children themselves—are drawn into the dynamic of escalation and retaliation" (Stolz & Ney, 2002). From a child's perspective, divorce produces massive shifts in the family system and in their social environment. If divorce is accompanied by parental conflict, the child must learn new rules of engagements. The child may be pulled in two different directions: one that says "stay connected with both parents" and one that says "you must choose sides." This places the child in an untenable vise and, out of sheer psychological survival, the child may choose one parent or "side" over the other to reduce the intolerable pressures and to simplify their life.

When parents and others around them are engaged in an adversarial system, the child is likely to buy into this system also. However, the price for the child in trying to extricate themselves from this vise is having to choose between parents. This is precisely what alienated children do. Therefore, it is important for the parenting coordinator to understand the family dynamics and what created the vise for the child in order to formulate intervention strategies and goals. Presumably the goal is to change the nature of the child's relationship with the rejected or targeted parent, if possible, and to facilitate compliance with access agreements in a way that is not damaging for the child.

Stolz and Ney (2002) formulate the problem of visitation resistance and refusal in such a way that takes into account the goal of compliance and the continuing influence of the adversarial system and minimizes the potential harm of that influence on the parties involved (especially children). They offer the following definition:

> *Resistance to visitation* is defined as any set of behaviors on the part of the child, parents, and other involved in the conflict that leads to the cessation of or significantly impedes visitation with the noncustodial parent.

They also offer specific suggestions for dialogue and interventions within their "resistance dynamic framework" as a more effective model based upon risk-benefit analysis and the goals of all interventions to reduce resistance and increase trust.

Garber (2007) added a developmentally informed approach to understanding visitation resistance and refuse, including a definition grounded in attachment theory (Ainsworth & Witting, 1969; Bowlby, 1969, 1973) which defines alienation as "the dynamic in force when any party (actor) presents information (message) which causes a child to accommodate his/her mental schema of the caregiver (target) such that the child becomes less secure with that caregiver." In other words, a child's secure attachment to one caregiver (alienating parent) can be used as a weapon against the other parent (target parent) in an attempt to threaten the child's security of attachment to either caregiver. This is a very powerful weapon because children need a secure attachment to a caregiver in order to emotionally, and often literally, survive.

There are no reliable statistics on the prevalence of alienation in parenting coordination and the role of the parenting coordinator in working with families impacted by alienation or estrangement is not clear. However, many parenting coordinators will be faced with the very difficult task of assisting families where parental alienation or estrangement phenomena are present. Although there has been much debate amongst professionals regarding the defining characteristics of parental alienation "symptoms" or "syndrome," all those who have worked with high-conflict families know that there are parents who attempt to influence children to develop and/or maintain a negative view of the other parent. There are also circumstances where a child refuses or resists contact with a parent for a variety of reasons that are not related to either parent's efforts to influence the child. In addition, there are circumstances where a child is more "aligned" with one parent or another because of temperament, gender, age, familiarity, greater time spent with that parent, or shared interests.

Regardless of whether the refusal or resistance to contact is due to alienation, estrangement, alignment, or affinity, the "rejected" parent often wants to re-establish and maintain contact with their child and may insist that the court enforce their rights to access to their child. These are some of the most difficult and tragic families to work with because there are no reliable or empirically proven interventions that will guarantee a repair in the ruptured relationship between a parent and child. The parenting coordinator must be prepared to both identify and understand the phenomena if they are to be effective in assisting the children caught in this vise.

One intervention to consider is a *family-systems approach* for mild and some moderate cases (Fidler & Bala, 2010). This approach involves the participation of the entire family in various combinations, will always involve both parents and may include relatives such as stepparents, step-siblings, and grandparents as well as third-party professionals such as treating physicians and therapists (Friedlander & Walters, 2010). A similar approach, called family restructuring therapy, is practiced by a team of psychologists in Edmonton, Canada (Carter, Haave, & Vandersteen, 2008). Eddy (2009) has also developed a short-term and highly structured, early intervention program based on cognitive-behavioral principles, called new ways for families, for high-conflict family court cases, including those involving allegations of alienation.

Much of the research in the area of alienation and estrangement points to the need for early identification, triage, and appropriate intervention. There is also an important role for the court which is primary education in all but the most intractable cases where custody reversal may be ordered. If a parenting coordinator is ordered to work with a family where visitation refusal or resistance is present, it is critical that the parenting coordinator have an intervention strategy, very specific parenting plan ordered by the court, and the support of the court in establishing a team of professionals to assist.

SEXUAL ABUSE ALLEGATIONS IN CUSTODY AND ACCESS DISPUTES

One of the most challenging tasks for a parenting coordinator is how to manage child sexual abuse allegations in the context of high-conflict parenting interactions. If the parenting coordinator is presented with information that indicates that a child is at risk for abuse or neglect, either by a parent or another person involved with the family, they must report this to child protection services. Being appointed as a parenting coordinator does not relieve a professional from a mandatory obligation to report abuse or neglect. However, high-conflict parents may make wild and alarming allegations of abuse about the other parent with no evidence or reliable data to support their claim. Some parents make a series of abuse allegations, which may be later determined to be unfounded, in an effort to thwart contact between a child and the other parent or to get back at the other parent with whom they remain enraged and bitter.

It is helpful to consider these serious and alarming allegations of child sexual abuse in the broader context of high-conflict parents in general. Although the vast majority of couples divorcing with children or returning to court with conflict over custody and access may not allege abuse, the cases that are referred to custody evaluators and sexual abuse specialists are likely to be cases in which the two are linked. Faller (1991) reviewed several types of sexual abuse allegations that arise in connection with divorce and custody disputes:

- Discovery of sexual abuse results in one parent filing for separation and subsequent divorce to protect the child
- The parents separate and the child feels safe, and able to reveal long-standing victimization, once the perpetrator is out of the home
- A marital breakup occurs and sexual abuse begins in the context of one parent's (usually father) emotional regression and neediness

One of the first considerations when allegations of sexual abuse arise in the context of a disputed custody battle is whether the allegations are true or false. Attempts to distinguish between children who have and have not been sexually abused produce significant risks. If abuse is reported, but determined to be unfounded, the child may not have the opportunity to get the treatment needed. An even greater concern is that the abuse may continue. On the other hand, if abuse is alleged but did not occur, the child, his or her family, and the alleged perpetrator may be exposed to devastating emotional, financial, and relational distress.

To begin to understand this high stakes circumstance more fully, the parenting coordinator should consider the environment in which false allegations may arise. For example, there are important situational factors such as extreme marital discord and family dysfunction that may have been occurring in the family for some time. In addition, one parent may have vilified the other parent to an extreme degree that they have come to believe, and to convince others, that the other parent is capable of harming the child. There are also circumstances where making of a claim of sexual abuse gives the accuser a clear strategic benefit in accomplishing a legal, financial, or emotional goal. The parenting coordination should consider all of these factors when determining an intervention strategy.

It is also important to be aware of what research tells us about child sexual abuse in the general population. Traditionally, men have been shown to be the most common perpetrators of child sexual abuse, with incidence rates ranging from 80% to 95% (Finkelhor, 1986; Finkelhor, Hotaling, Lewis, & Smith, 1990), and the victims are more often female (Cawson et al., 2000). Sexual abuse is inflicted most commonly by a person known to the child, such as a family friend, rather than by a family member or a stranger (Tomison, 1995) and one quarter to one third of the perpetrators are juveniles (Cawson et al., 2000). While males are the most common perpetrators, fathers or father equivalents are not. However, girls are more likely to be abused by a family member than are boys. One study (Cawson, 2002) found that emotional abuse versus sexual abuse was inflicted equally by mothers and fathers and that victims of emotional abuse were divided equally between male and female children.

Two studies of custody and contact disputes in the Family Court of Australia where allegations of child abuse had been made explored the fathers' roles in the abuse (Brown et al., 1998, 2001). They found that more allegations came from mothers than from fathers or from any other source. However, most fathers were found not to be the perpetrator as had been alleged. When the sexual abuse was said to have begun after separation, the incidence of fathers as substantiated abusers was reduced by half, and other males became more prominent as alleged abusers (e.g., the mothers' and fathers' male relatives and/or mothers' boyfriends).

In the early 1990s, research in the area of child sexual abuse sought to identify reliable indicators of abuse such as overt sexual behaviors, increased trauma symptoms, moodiness, nightmares, and regressive behaviors (Kendall-Tackett et al., 1993). However, Kuehnle and Connell (2009) point out that even with some of the advances made by research into some aspects of child sexual abuse evaluations, "there is no clear set of behaviors or symptoms to affirm the occurrence of abuse."

Faust, Bridges, and Ahern (2009) recently reviewed the literature on child sexual abuse and highlighted the need for more research to identify a methodology for reliably identifying sexually abused children. They assert that, in order to be useful, indicator variables, or variables that are associated with child sexual abuse occurrence, must be valid and differentiating. If an indicator is valid, it means that there is an association between the indicator and the occurrence of child sexual abuse. A child sexual abuse evaluator will typically focus on the association between abuse and some behavioral, emotional, or cognitive symptoms in the child. A differentiating indicator variable is one which helps to separate children who have been sexually abused from children who have not been abused or other children in general. The parenting coordinator will not be conducting the child sexual abuse evaluations, but they should be aware that there are specific protocols and methodologies which must be followed in such evaluations in order to produce results and recommendations that can be relied on for future interventions. The parenting coordinator may need to refer a parent or child for a sexual abuse evaluation and should be knowledgeable about the expertise and training required of the evaluator in order to make an appropriate referral.

Ultimately, it will be up to the court to determine whether a child has been sexually abused and what interventions are necessary to protect the child in the future and address their needs. The parenting coordinator may be faced with the challenge of a parent making allegations that the other parent or someone they have allowed the child to be around has sexually abused their child. These allegations should always be taken seriously and reported to the proper authorities. Pending the outcome of an investigation or evaluation, parenting coordination may continue. Whether there should be contact between the alleged perpetrator and the child is an issue that should be decided by the court or other authority. If allegations that a parent has abused their child are substantiated, there are likely to be significant changes to the parenting plan and access schedule and parenting coordination may be discontinued. However, if allegations are proven to be unfounded or are unsubstantiated, parenting coordination will likely continue. The parenting coordinator should continue to be alert to the possibility of false allegations, but should not assume that all future allegations are false. At all times, the parenting coordinator must monitor the potential risks of child maltreatment and work to ensure the safety of all members of the family.

10

Managing the Parenting Coordination Process

Healing is a matter of time, but it is sometimes also a matter of opportunity.
—Hippocrates, *Precepts*

PROTECTION FOR ALL: PHYSICAL SAFETY

Of utmost importance throughout the parenting coordination process is the need to make sure everyone involved in the process is physically safe. This includes parents, children, other family members, the parenting coordinator, staff of the parenting coordinator, and other professionals working with a family. It is important to remember that in high-conflict cases, emotions are likely to run high and when individuals are consumed with anger, rage, and frustration, they may act in ways that are uncharacteristic for them in general. There is the old joke about criminal lawyers working with bad people at their best. Parenting coordinators often work with good people at their worst.

Some individuals embroiled in conflict may be more impulsive and prone to threaten harm to others. The parenting coordinator should be alert to this possibility and, to the degree possible, take preventive measures to ensure safety for all. Most parenting coordinators will see parents in a private office which is not likely to have metal detectors or monitors for detecting firearms. In most jurisdictions, parenting coordination does not take place in a setting where there are guards or bailiffs to provide protection.

Therefore, a parenting coordinator should establish a safety policy to ensure physical safety for all. An example of this might be a policy where parents are not allowed to bring large bags or briefcases into the appointment with them which might conceal weapons or listening devices. The parenting coordinator may ask each parent whether they have a weapon and whether they carry that weapon on their person or in their vehicle. If so, parents should be directed not to carry into the appointment any weapons, concealed or otherwise.

The parenting coordinator also has an obligation to provide a safe environment for parents in and around the office setting as well. If one or both parents tend to escalate quickly or upon the sight of the other, the parenting coordinator may direct one parent to arrive in advance of the other and to wait in a different area of the office so that the parents have no time when they are alone and unattended. The parenting coordinator may also direct one parent to leave the office and parking lot prior to the other leaving as an additional safety measure.

The parenting coordinator should also be cautious about scheduling parents embroiled in high conflict at a time when no other individuals are around, that is, after hours when staff may have left for the day or during the evening when other individuals in nearby offices may not be present. In general, the more volatile the circumstance, the more protections should be in place to mitigate risks.

If a parent makes a direct threat to the other parent or the parenting coordinator or others involved with the family, the parenting coordinator should report the threat directly to local law enforcement and notify the court immediately. The parenting coordinator should not take on the responsibility of determining whether the parent threatening "really meant it." All threats should be taken seriously and acted upon immediately to ensure safety for all.

CALLING IT QUITS

When the parenting coordination process works well and families are no longer caught in a crucible of conflict and are able to co-parent effectively, terminating the parenting coordination process is often a decision easily reached by parents and the parenting coordinator. There may be some concern about losing the parenting coordinator as a resource even when things are going very well, but with encouragement and support, the parenting coordinator can assure parents that they have the tools they need to move forward without the need for parenting coordination. The parents may still have third party professional supports in place such as therapists or support groups.

There are other circumstances when parenting coordination seems to no longer be effective or appropriate. While much parenting coordination work from the onset may be challenging and frustrating for the parenting coordinator, it is important to distinguish between circumstances when the work requires more structure and patience versus circumstances when parenting coordination is not likely to be effective no matter how much time and money is invested in the process. These circumstances can arise at any time throughout the process and are helpful to use as a guide in determining an appropriate course of action for the parenting coordination. Examples of these circumstances might include

- when one or both parents lose trust in the parenting coordinator
- when the parenting coordinator has violated boundaries or acted in an unprofessional manner
- when financial circumstances change dramatically and do not allow for one or both parents to continue to pay for parenting coordination services
- when a significant change in functioning of one or both parents (i.e., illness) occurs
- when there is a substantial change in family dynamics or make up that requires a complete overhaul of the parenting plan
- when jurisdiction changes; and/or
- when the youngest child reaches the age of majority

The parenting coordinator has an obligation to advise parents and the court if the parenting coordination process is not appropriate at any time during work with a family. In earlier chapters, screening tools and procedures to determine safety risks were reviewed. These procedures are designed to determine whether parenting coordination is appropriate in the earliest phase of the work. It is important to remember that screening for safety is an ongoing process. If, at any time, the parenting coordination process places the parents, children, or anyone involved at risk, the parenting coordinator must notify the court and cease work.

There are circumstances when parenting coordination may have been very helpful to parents in the beginning of the process, but due to a change in family circumstance or dynamics, is no longer effective or appropriate. The parenting coordinator must determine whether additional direction and/or support from the court will allow the integrity of the parenting coordination process to be preserved and assist parents. If so, then it is appropriate for the parenting coordinator to request such direction or support directly from the court. Depending on jurisdictional procedures, this may take the form of a status or case management conference.

REQUESTING A CASE MANAGEMENT
OR CASE STATUS CONFERENCE

The procedure for initiating a request for a case management conference will differ depending upon jurisdiction. Some jurisdictions will allow the parenting coordinator to make the request, while other areas will require that parties themselves or their attorneys make such a request. A case management conference is generally a more informal proceeding than a formal hearing, but procedures for noticing all parties and attorneys should be followed. Each jurisdiction will have their own procedures for providing notice of the date, time, and location of the conference. The notice will specify who is expected to be present at the case management conference, but will generally include the parties, their attorneys if represented, the parenting coordinator and the jurist who is presiding over the conference.

When one or both parties are obstructing or sabotaging the parenting coordination process, the parenting coordinator may be tempted to ask the court for an Order to Compel Mature Adult Behavior and Cooperation by the parents. However tempting this may be, this is not an appropriate reason to request a case management conference since the court cannot control an individual's behavior by entering an Order. A case management conference is different from an evidentiary hearing where the court will hear "evidence" presented by parties or their counsel to "prove up" a matter of law. Ideally, the case management or status conference is a review of how the parenting coordination work is proceeding and an opportunity to determine whether additional services or parameters need to be included to assist the parenting coordinator in the work.

If the parenting coordinator requests a case management or status conference, they should be prepared to present factual information about the parenting coordination process to the court with a clear and specific request from the court as to the reason for making the request. Depending on jurisdiction and whether the parenting coordination process is confidential, the parenting coordinator may be limited as to the information presented. In addition, some jurisdictions do not allow a nonlawyer parenting coordinator to petition or "motion" the court directly for any reason, including a case management conference. Filing a motion may be considered practicing law without a license which is strictly prohibited. This may not be an issue for parenting coordinators who are also attorneys, since they will presumably have a license to practice law in the jurisdiction where the case management conference is requested. However, many jurisdictions do allow parenting coordinators to notice the court that direction or a "conference" is needed by sending a letter to the court and providing a copy to each party and counsel. In these circumstances, the court, on its own motion, may set the date/time for the conference and notice all parties who are expected to attend.

If the parenting coordination process is not confidential, the parenting coordinator must still be wary of presenting information that may compromise, or appear to compromise, the neutrality or "unbiased" position that they must preserve in order to be effective. The parenting coordinator may provide factual information to the court such as the date when the parenting coordination work began, the number of appointments to date. The parenting coordinator must be careful when presenting information that may border on "expert" opinions such as a parenting coordinator's perception of whether each party is participating in a good faith effort or whether each parent is complying with the court-ordered parenting plan. As discussed in earlier chapters, parenting coordinators should avoid engaging in behaviors that place them in a dual role.

Parenting coordinators should review the court's order and know their mandates and limitations, as well as what they are asking of the court, before making a request of the court. An example of this occurred with Sarah and Carl who had reached an impasse in parenting coordination about a difference of opinion regarding their 7-year-old son, Carl Jr. Sarah had recently refused to allow Carl Jr. to visit his father because Carl had allowed him to walk alone to the corner grocery and she believed this put Carl Jr. in serious danger. Carl thought it was perfectly safe and ignored Sarah's requests to either accompany him or not allow him to walk alone. The parenting coordinator offered several ideas to resolve this dispute, but the conflict was escalating between them to the point where Carl had recently appeared at Sarah's house unannounced and started yelling and banging on her door demanding that she send Carl Jr. outside. The parenting coordinator felt it was necessary to ask the court for direction and requested a case management conference. In this example, the court set an evidentiary hearing where both sides were able to present their concerns and then made a ruling that directed each parent's behavior regarding access to the child. The court also reaffirmed their confidence in the parenting coordinator and directed Sarah and Carl to go back to work with the parenting coordinator to learn how to resolve their differences in a more constructive manner.

Jurists who are knowledgeable about the parenting coordination process can be very helpful to the parenting coordinator. It is not appropriate for the parenting coordinator to request direction from the court every time there appears to be an impasse between the parents or if the parents are unwilling to work cooperatively. This is generally the reason they were ordered to go to parenting coordination in the first place. However, it is appropriate to request direction and support from the court if the parenting coordinator needs the court to modify an order or a parenting plan if these are necessary to continue the work. They court may also give the parenting coordinator more authority or provide encouragement to the parties to continue working with the parenting coordinator to resolve their disputes.

WHEN TO WITHDRAW

Parenting coordinators also need to know when they need to withdraw from a case for personal or professional reasons. This may be because the parenting coordinator identifies an issue that they are unqualified to address, for example, if one of the parents develops a serious mental illness or has a "relapse" in mental health symptoms and the parenting coordinator is a legal professional with no experience or training in the mental health arena. The parenting coordinators should also withdraw if they determine that they are no longer able to be objective or unbiased in their work.

One such occasion occurred very early in a parenting coordination case. During a prior appointment, the parenting coordinator had arbitrated a minor decision regarding time frame for pick up for mid-week contact between the children and their father. The father wanted to pick up the children at 5 P.M. rather than 6:30 P.M. during his mid-week contact because he had to go to work early the next day. The mother insisted that he stick to the regular pick up time because two of the children had tutoring after school which did not end until 6 P.M. The parenting coordinator had the authority to arbitrate the dispute and suggested that the father pick up the children from the tutoring center at 6 P.M. At the beginning of the next appointment, the father started telling the parenting coordinator that he had read about her young son in the local newspaper and commented that the son had gotten a "hat trick" (three goals) in a soccer game he played. The father then proceeded to comment in detail about the parenting coordinator's son's soccer skills that he had observed while watching the son at several practices. At the time, the parenting coordinator's son was playing on two different travel teams which held practices at different locations and times that were unpublished. It was immediately clear to the parenting coordinator that the father was sending a threatening message. In essence, he admitted to stalking the parenting coordinator's son and was sending the message that he knew who her son was and that he could get to him at any time. While the father made no direct threat and presented the information as a "compliment", the parenting coordinator clearly understood the message and felt enraged and protective of her child. It was clear to her that she would not be able to remain objective in working with this family. Therefore, she suspended the parenting coordination appointment and notified the court immediately of her intent to withdraw from the case.

Parenting coordinators may also need to withdraw if their schedule changes and they no longer have time to meet the demands of the family. The parenting coordinator may also have a personal circumstance arise that warrants shielding themselves from the stress of working with high-conflict families. There are numerous circumstances that may arise during the course of parenting coordination work that might cause a parenting coordinator to withdraw from a case. It is important for parenting coordinators to pay attention to their own physical and emotional well-being and any stressors in their life that may impede their ability to be effective with a family. The parenting coordinator should consider whether it may be better for the family to work with another parenting coordinator or whether the parenting coordination process is likely to be effective regardless of the provider.

WHAT IF A PARENT FILES A GRIEVANCE OR REGULATORY BOARD COMPLAINT AGAINST THE PARENTING COORDINATOR?

Working with highly litigious parents who may have an investment in maintaining conflict, even if it is not in their conscious awareness, may redirect their anger and wrath toward the parenting coordinator in addition to their ex-partner. This may come in the form of a "grievance" against the parenting coordinator. Depending on jurisdiction, grievances may be directed back to the court which referred the parties to parenting coordination or may involve complaints filed with the professional's regulatory or certification board and/or filing civil lawsuits. Parenting coordinators must consider whether they can continue to be objective in the light of these complaints and lawsuits. Given that the parenting coordinators may need to "defend" their work before a regulatory or certification board or in a civil court, it is unlikely that a parenting coordinator could remain objective during this type of process. Therefore, the parenting coordinators should probably withdraw from the case as soon as they are alerted that a pending regulatory complaint or lawsuit has been filed against them. The parenting coordinator may recommend to the court that another parenting coordinator be appointed in order to avoid a party's manipulation of the system. Some parties may use filing of a grievance without good cause as a means of getting themselves out of the parenting coordination process or as a deliberate attempt to thwart resolution of conflict. A well-crafted court's order requiring parties to present their grievance to the court order of referral to determine whether there has been any wrongdoing on the part of the parenting coordinator, before filing a complaint to the parenting coordinator's license board, may help avoid this type of manipulative maneuver by an angry parent.

PROFESSIONAL LIABILITY

Any professional can be sued for negligence or harm by violating the standard of care for that particular profession. The professional can also be the subject of a complaint to any regulatory board governing their profession or removed from a voluntary professional organization. There is no effective method to prevent a disgruntled party from attempting one of these actions.

Court-appointed professionals may be accorded a quasi-judicial immunity for actions appropriately taken under the court's order depending on law and jurisdictional rules. For a parenting coordinator, the professional liability risk increases due to the fact that the process of parenting coordination is not uniformly defined by law and is not governed by any nationally recognized standards or regulatory body. The Association of Family and Conciliation Courts has published Guidelines for Parenting Coordinators (2005), but these are primarily aspirational in nature and are not nationally endorsed by any organization that requires parenting coordinators to adhere to them. The American Psychological Association has also developed guidelines for the practice of parenting coordination (http://www.apapracticecentral .org/ce/guidelines/index.aspx) which are designed to describe best practices for the ethical and competent functioning in this unique role, but they are written primarily for psychologists.

Because parenting coordination is a new and emerging type of alternative dispute resolution and merges different professional functions, the court-expert type of quasi-judicial immunity may be in jeopardy. In other words, there may be no actual "expert designation" for these particular duties. For this reason, it may be prudent to include all duties and authorities for the parenting coordinator appointment that are possible in the court order of referral (COR). The parenting coordinator should be familiar with the Statutes/Rules in their jurisdiction which may allow for quasi-judicial immunity for court-appointed experts or third party neutrals, such as a parenting coordinator, and maximize opportunities for professional protection. A parenting coordinator may also want to consider consultation with their own attorney to determine the best course of action to protect their professional practice while working with high-conflict, litigious parties.

Unless the parenting coordinators are practicing in an area of the country that specifically provides for immunity while acting as a parenting coordinator, they should make the assumption that no immunity exists and, therefore, all precautions to protect their professional practice should be exercised. This should include, at the very least, professional liability insurance with a specific provision that includes practice in the forensic or family law area. Some carriers will provide this coverage as part of the typical liability policy for professional practice. Others will require the provider to notify them, in writing, if they are providing services which may be outside the scope of their typical services. It is important for the parenting coordinator to obtain, in writing, assurance that their liability carrier is aware of and providing coverage for parenting coordination services. It is also important for the parenting coordinator to obtain as much liability coverage as possible in terms of a legal defense fund which some liability carriers offer at an additional expense. This type of fund often provides reimbursement for legal fees incurred when the parenting coordinator must defend themselves against either regulatory board complaints or civil litigation.

ADDITIONAL CONSIDERATIONS TO MINIMIZE RISK

Some states have used "conciliation" courts with the idea that parents will be encouraged to agree and cooperate if they have the benefit of a parenting coordinator. After all, the goal of parenting coordination is to achieve "conciliation" between the parents for the benefit of the child. In this role, the parenting coordinator should consider:

- Having the parties sign an agreement indicating that the parenting coordinator has appropriate professional qualifications and skills for the appointment. This agreement should be reflected in the order of appointment and the professional services agreement.

▪ Not serving unless the parties stipulate to the order with broad powers. Such a stipulation may insulate the coordinator from liability more than a court appointment without the parties' consent.

▪ Requesting that the order of referral acknowledge that there is judicial or quasi-judicial immunity and that there will be no liability unless there is actual malice when there is no public policy or law prohibiting such a limitation of liability.

Suggested language to include in the order appointing a parenting coordinator follows:

> It is the intent of this order to include the broadest possible authority for the parenting coordinator to facilitate the smooth and cooperative implementation of the parenting schedule and plan for the full family's benefit under _____ (insert State Statute). Thus, the parenting coordinator may use the powers of a mediator and arbitrator under ___ (Insert State Statute) _____, or guardian ad litem for the child under ___ (Insert State Statute or Rule) _____, where those functions will assist in carrying out this Court's adjudication of a parenting plan. It is also the intent of the Court that the parenting coordinator shall have full benefit of quasi-judicial immunity as a Court-appointed expert and the immunity provisions provided for in _____(Insert Statutes/Rules that apply)_____. The parties have stipulated to this appointment and the powers granted herein to the parenting coordinator, and that the person appointed has the requisite professional qualifications and professional skills to do the work required.

All efforts to provide the maximum liability protection for professionals should be with the advice and consultation of an attorney because of the sophistication of the legal concepts involved.

HANDLING THREATS OF A LAWSUIT

For most providers, the thought of facing civil litigation for the professional services they provide is terrifying. However, many high-conflict clients are familiar with litigation and may have been embroiled in court processes for years. A party or their attorney may also believe that threatening to file a lawsuit may be enough to intimidate a professional into agreeing to what that party is requesting or withdrawing from the case which may be what the threatening parent wants to achieve. Every professional has their own tolerance for risk taking and working with parenting coordination clients may cause the practitioner to examine their risk tolerance more carefully than they have in times past. Regardless of whether the party is threatening or actually pursuing legal action against a parenting coordinator, the parenting coordinator must take the threat seriously and should consult with their attorney for advice.

In some circumstances, the threatening party may be "testing" the parenting coordinator to see whether they will react to threats or to see whether the parenting coordinator can be intimidated. In some circumstances, the parenting coordinator may be able to work more effectively with clients once they have "proven" themselves to be resilient and uncompromising in terms of maintaining the integrity of the parenting coordination process and adherence to professionalism under all circumstances.

Generally, civil litigation will not be the first step of a grievance against the parenting coordinator because the party must prove "harm" done which is difficult except in the most egregious cases where there has been a clear violation of ethics and professional standards by the practitioner. What is more likely to come first is a complaint against a practitioner's license or certification to practice filed with the oversight regulatory body.

HANDLING THREATS OF A PROFESSIONAL REGULATORY BOARD COMPLAINT

Most practitioners go through their career hoping to never have to face a complaint against their license or certification which allows them to provide professional services. However, working with highly litigious, angry parties increases the risk that a complaint may be threatened or filed. The parenting coordinator should be prepared for regulatory board complaints and be prepared to defend them. Most governing bodies which grant licensure or certification to provide professional services within a state or jurisdiction have a process whereby "probable cause" must be determined before a grievance or administrative complaint against a practitioner will be acted upon.

In most cases, a complainant must provide their allegations of misconduct or wrongdoing in writing to the governing agency. Any "evidence" the complainant has to support their allegations is reviewed along with the written complaint against the practitioner. The regulatory agency may then appoint a "probable cause" panel of experts to investigate the veracity of the claims. This panel may request specific information from the parenting coordinator as well as their "response" to the complaint.

The panel may ask an independent practitioner familiar with the services provided that are the subject of the complaint to review the parenting coordinator's file and any additional information the parenting coordinator provides. The panel of appointed experts will then determine whether "probable cause" exists to move forward with the complaint against the practitioner or whether to dismiss the claim.

If the complaint is dismissed, the parenting coordinators may continue their work with no action needed. If the complaint is found to meet probable cause criteria, then the parenting coordinators are likely to receive notice of an Administrative Complaint filed against them by the regulatory agency. The parenting coordinators would be wise to have legal representation throughout this process, but certainly if probable cause has been determined. The parenting coordinators must then respond and defend their actions in an effort to mitigate any consequences for alleged or actual misconduct.

Consequences vary from jurisdiction to jurisdiction depending on the severity of the complaint. Consequences for the parenting coordinator may range from a fine to suspension or revocation of license or certification. The practitioner may also be required to obtain additional continuing education to practice or to limit their practice to specific practice areas. They may also be required to work under supervision of another licensed practitioner in their profession for a set period of time.

If a complainant is successful in "proving" that a practitioner has violated a professional standard or acted unethically or in an unprofessional manner, the parenting coordinator may need to notify the court of the sanctions placed upon him/her by their licensing or certification board. The court then has the responsibility to determine whether the parenting coordinator should continue to provide services for other individuals appointed by the court under the sanctions imposed. In addition, the complainant may have a much stronger case to pursue civil litigation. If a regulatory board affirms the complainant's grievance that the professional has acted in an unethical or unprofessional manner, the complainant may be able to assert that harm was done to him/her and, therefore, he/she should be entitled to monetary compensation.

In addition to the fear factor involved when complaints are filed, practitioners also run the risk of their professional reputation being tarnished which may have long-standing consequences in terms of their livelihood. There may also be significant financial penalties involved over and above legal fees for defending themselves. The impact of a regulatory board complaint is significant for practitioners both in terms of their professional practice, but also in terms of the emotional toll it takes to be under scrutiny and have to defend one's actions in public. In addition, some areas impose a "gag" order on the practitioners prohibiting them from discussing the case with other practitioners while the case is pending which makes it very difficult to get professional support at a time when it is sorely needed.

The best course of action, of course, is to avoid complaints when possible. One option is to include a provision in the professional services agreement that requires a party to notify the parenting coordinator in writing as to the nature of the grievance and agree to meet with the parenting coordinator to attempt to resolve the issue before taking any other action. It is also reasonable to include in the professional services agreement, an affirmation by parties that any grievance will first be taken back to the court which referred the parties to the parenting coordinator to determine whether "good cause" exists to pursue additional actions including regulatory complaints or civil litigation. The parenting coordinator might also consider an additional provision in the professional services agreement that informs parties of their "proactive duty" to report to the parenting coordinator any perceived violation of the court's order, the client's rights, or any law/regulation.

Establishing a procedure whereby parties can make their grievances known and have an avenue where their complaints can be resolved informally may be sufficient to thwart additional action by a grieving party. It also provides the grieving party with information regarding the parameters of the work and what issues will not be considered as misconduct or inappropriate action.

MANDATORY REPORT OF SUSPECTED ABUSE OR NEGLECT

Regardless of their background or training, most parenting coordinators are obligated to report any suspicion of or actual abuse or neglect to a child or disabled person. Parents or other involved individuals may present information to the parenting coordinator that requires the parenting coordinator to file a report of suspected abuse/neglect. Does this mean that the parenting coordinator must immediately withdraw from the case? Not necessarily. Sometimes a parenting coordinator may feel that a report of suspected abuse or neglect is warranted, but, for example, has some strong suspicions that the claims are spurious, exaggerated, or false. The parenting coordinator may suspect that the parent making such claims is merely trying to hinder the other parent's access to the child and/or use the abuse claims as a form of harassment.

The parenting coordinator, like other mandatory reporters, must use their judgment in determining the motivation which may underlie the allegation of abuse or neglect. However, the parenting coordination should err on the side of caution and trust that the professionals involved in child protection cases will investigate and determine an appropriate course of action. If a suspected case of abuse/neglect has been reported, investigated, and ultimately determined to be unfounded, the parenting coordination process may proceed without modification. If, however, the suspected abuse or neglect of a child is determined to be founded, then the parenting coordinator must notify the court and seek direction. Often, the court will need to modify parental access to a child to protect the child from further risk of abuse or neglect. Further discussion of this issue was presented in chapter 9.

The issue for the parenting coordinators, if they must file a report of suspected abuse or neglect of a child by a parent, is whether they can preserve their neutrality and unbiased position with the parents. One such case occurred when the mother of a 4-year-old boy reported to the parenting coordinator that her son had started "humping" her after the shower and licking the drain stopper in the bathtub in a very "suggestive" manner. The mother said these behaviors only occurred after the son had spent time with his father and she suspected that the father was abusing their son. The parenting coordinator felt he had to call child protection services. The father was understandably outraged when the mother presented this information in a parenting coordination appointment. The parenting coordinator notified both parents of his intent to file a report of suspected abuse and proceeded to do so during the appointment with both parents listening to what was said. The parenting coordinator wanted to assure both parents that proper action had been taken, but was not offering an opinion about the veracity of the claims. In this case, the parenting coordinator did not think his neutrality was compromised and continued to work with the family until the child protection team had concluded their investigation. Ultimately, child protection services made a determination that the allegations were unfounded and the case was closed.

If the parenting coordinator withdraws every time they are required to file a report of suspected abuse/neglect, then the family may be left without the structure and support of an independent third party at a crucial time. However, the decision must be carefully considered. As with many other complex and vexing circumstances, a parenting coordinator is wise to consult with trusted colleagues to help think through a decision that has serious implications for the family and for the parenting coordinator.

KNOW THE APPLICABLE PROFESSIONAL STANDARDS AND GUIDELINES FOR YOUR PROFESSION

An essential component of professional liability protection is to know and follow the applicable professional standards and guidelines for your individual profession. For example, practitioners in the United States have standards of practice that apply regardless of regulatory or specialty area, that is, Ethical Guidelines, Record Keeping Guidelines, and so on. In addition, there are often "specialty" guidelines that a practitioner must know and adhere to that are applicable for their particular discipline. While many of the guidelines for certain professions may not apply directly to the provision of parenting coordination service, a parenting coordinator must know these guidelines and identify areas where their professional standards and parenting coordination practice may conflict. Parenting coordinators must attempt to resolve any perceived conflict of standards or guidelines and determine which set of standards supersedes the other.

For example, in psychology there are Specialty Guidelines for Forensic Psychologists (American Psychological Association [APA], 1991) which govern the practice of psychologists who provide services to clients in conjunction with court proceedings. Each discipline will have guidelines and standards of practice that apply to their practice. Providing service as a parenting coordinator does not relieve a practitioner from adherence to their industry standards. Because parenting coordination services is a hybrid role and newly emerging field, definitive standards of practice have not been established across the industry. Each practitioner must be aware of and adhere to all laws and rules that apply to their profession.

MONITORING PROFESSIONAL BOUNDARIES AND WELL-BEING

Boundary challenges will occur in parenting coordination work. Some are expected and predictable, like scheduling difficulties, resistance or refusal to pay for services, "forgetting" what was agreed upon, or lavish compliments and gifts to the parenting coordinator. Boundary challenges may also take the form of power struggles wherein a parent attempts to engage the parenting coordination in a power struggle much as adolescents do with parents. The parenting coordination must be prepared for these boundary challenges and have procedures in place to manage them. Management techniques should include procedures whereby the integrity of the parenting coordination process is reinforced, parameters set forth in the order of referral and professional services agreement are enforced, and a steadfast refusal to engage in the challenges a parent presents.

In spite of advanced planning, a parenting coordinator may still have reactions and feelings that are triggered by a parent and, therefore, are vulnerable to their own countertransference issues. Counter transference is a psychological term which refers to the emotional feelings and reactions that are triggered by an individual or circumstance that are based on the parenting coordinator's own needs and conflicts. Counter transference reactions may be outside the awareness of the parenting coordinator, as distinguished from conscious responses to the parent's behavior. It is imperative that the parenting coordinators recognize the possibility of this occurring and guard against it or they are likely to act outside their professional role in an inappropriate manner. For example, a parenting coordinator's competence may be challenged by a parent if the parenting coordinator doesn't agree with their perspective. If a parenting coordinator allows themselves to get too fatigued or has too many challenging cases, they may react to the challenge with anger or defensively. This will only serve to fuel the challenge and places the parenting coordinator in a compromising position.

There is a push/pull phenomenon in these boundary challenges that is common in work with parenting coordination clients. A parent may "idealize" the parenting coordinators by proclaiming how brilliant, wise, and skilled they are in their work and how no one else has been able to help them until they found this "fabulous" parenting coordinator. While the compliments may be flattering and may reinforce how the parenting coordinator feels about themselves, the flowery compliments should be a clear warning that there is likely to be an "agenda" behind the compliments even if the parent is not openly proclaiming what the agenda entails or if it isn't obvious at the time.

Another potential "pull" for the parenting coordinator may be the clients themselves particularly if they are well-known and respected individuals or individuals with celebrity status. The same holds true when clients enjoy a lifestyle that the parenting coordinator may find enviable. Remember, parenting coordinators are human beings who have their own day-to-day struggles in life which may include financial stressors, relationship difficulties, and needs for attention, respect, and recognition. Parenting coordinators may admire the accomplishments and success of their clients or be impressed with the material things some clients have. Certainly, the goal is not to pretend that the "pulls" are not there, but rather to recognize them and guard against the temptation to be drawn out of the neutral, unbiased, professional role.

The other side of the dilemma is when clients "push" the parenting coordinator by making threats or demands, challenging the parenting coordinator's competence or integrity, and basically displaying bad behavior. Most individuals will have emotional reactions to having their competence and honesty challenged. Parenting coordinators are no different simply because they have advanced training and are serving in a professional role. Some clients are particularly good at reading others and knowing where the tender spots or hot buttons are in their personality. These clients, many of whom have personality disorders, may quickly identify these tender spots within the parenting coordinator and attempt to press every button until they get a reaction. If the parenting coordinator reacts out of anger, hurt, or frustration, then the parenting coordinator's neutrality is likely to be compromised. Depending on the circumstances, the parenting coordinator may need to withdraw from the case. However, it may be possible for the parenting coordinators to acknowledge their action or reaction as inappropriate and move forward in reinforcing boundaries.

Another "push" is when clients are constantly or regularly noncompliant with the parenting plan or agreements reached during the parenting coordination work. A parenting coordinator may want to consider building sanctions into the parenting plan and getting parents to suggest what these ought to be. The parenting coordinator should also anticipate potential areas of conflict (e.g., lack of detailed parenting plan and time-sharing schedule) and avoid them if possible. The parenting coordinator may suggest eliminating or modifying specific areas of the parenting agreement if they are causing constant conflicts, such as the right of first refusal clause. Ultimately, the parenting coordinator has no power to enforce compliance. It is the court's prerogative to deal with noncompliance issues via contempt motions and possible sanctions.

Parent noncompliance is a common issue in parenting coordination work. The parenting coordinator should be prepared for noncompliance and have a plan for how to manage it. The parenting coordinator should guard against making judgments against a noncompliant parent and being pulled into a desire to "punish" the client or decide to "sanction" the parent themselves. These would represent clear boundary violations on the part of the parenting coordinators and very likely compromise their neutral stance and the integrity of the parenting coordination process. If a parent is constantly not complying with the parenting arrangements or court orders, the parenting coordinator may need to report this to the court and be prepared to arbitrate the issue for later enforcement by the court.

BURNOUT AND SETTING LIMITS

There is an acronym often used in 12-step programs, HALT, which stands for the saying that one should never allow oneself to be too hungry, angry, lonely, or tired. This is a good rule of thumb for parenting coordination work as well. If the parenting coordinator does not take care of themselves physically, emotionally, spiritually, or otherwise, they are vulnerable to the stressors and pressures that are inherent in work with high-conflict individuals. If parenting coordinators are not healthy themselves, they are much more vulnerable to compromising their professional role.

Setting limits on the number of parenting coordination cases one takes at any given time or the number of parenting coordination clients seen during a work day is important to monitor. Everyone has their own tolerance levels and should be aware of what they need to be healthy, physically and emotionally. Another important limit to set is maintaining the rules of engagement that were outlined at the beginning of the parenting coordination process and may need to be repeated often. For example, the parenting coordination should enforce:

- No yelling or berating the other parent or parenting coordinator
- No interrupting or speaking over the other person: Everyone gets a turn
- No distractions: Stay focused on issue at hand
- Stay focused on children's best interests

NEED FOR SUPPORT AND CONSULTATION GROUP

It goes without saying that work with high-conflict clients is not for the faint of heart and can be very demanding work. However, it can also be extremely rewarding. But, having a professional support network is a critical piece of helping parenting coordinators maintain their own health and well-being as well as help them keep clear boundaries at all times. Additional options for support include professional supervision and parenting coordination mentoring groups. It is important to debrief with colleagues (without revealing confidential information), balance your practice, listen to your own instincts, be mindful of the type of cases that you accept, and get out of cases that you feel unequipped to handle for any reason. Setting clear limits for the practice of parenting coordination and maintaining consistent self-care will help avoid burnout and potential harm to all.

ETHICAL CONSIDERATIONS

In the absence of Ethical Guidelines for parenting coordinators that encompass the practice of parenting coordination across the United States and beyond, it is important for the practitioner to establish and adhere to some general ethical parameters. One of those parameters is whether the parenting coordinator acquires and maintains competence to perform this hybrid role. Competence involves hybrid knowledge and skills. It also involves core competences in the areas of psychological knowledge, applicable legal knowledge, and conflict resolution skills. The parenting coordinator should also make sure they have the skill and expertise in any special issues specific to a case.

Another ethical parameter to consider is whether clients have consented to the parenting coordination process. Generally the court ordering parties to the process will have explained the role of the parenting coordinator and the reasons why the court believes this process will be helpful. It is important that parties understand, and ideally agree to, the parenting coordinator's role at the outset. The parenting coordinator should provide information about responsibilities and areas of decision-making and clarify the process of decision-making. The parenting coordinator should also provide information about the limits of confidentiality and/or privilege, the duties of the parenting coordinator, and limitations of the parenting coordinator's role. Informed consent is an ongoing process. If any changes occur, updated consent to the process should be obtained.

Ethical practice of parenting coordination also includes making sure the parenting coordination role is firmly established and inviolate. The parenting coordinator should not "shift" roles, that is, assume one professional role and then shift to another. An example would be a professional who had served as the parents' mediator and then becomes their parenting coordinator or if the professional had been the custody evaluator and then becomes their parenting coordinator. The parenting coordinator should avoid personal and business relationships with parties or relatives; avoid multiple professional relationships, for example, therapeutic and forensic; and avoid services to parties directly related to parenting coordination process.

Maintaining impartiality and an unbiased approach is an essential parameter for ethical parenting coordination practice. The parenting coordinator should gather information fairly and evenly, ensure decisions represent interests of each party, clearly articulate rationale for decision made, and address perceptions of bias promptly. Records should provide a sufficient foundation for any decisions made and be detailed, legible and comprehensive. All agreements made by the parents should be dated and written as much as possible in a bilateral manner.

TROUBLE—BEWARE

No matter how many precautions are taken, the parenting coordinator should be aware that rules and parameters are faulty and cannot possibly anticipate every circumstance. However, if the parenting coordinators fail to detail rules of engagement or maintain boundaries, they are asking for trouble. The parenting coordinator should also be aware of personal biases and prejudices and guard against them influencing the parenting coordination work.

If the court order of referral and professional services agreement lack definition of scope of authority and does not provide clear role definition, the parenting coordination process and likelihood of success is compromised from the beginning. If the order of referral is not detailed enough, the parenting coordinator should ask for clarity from the court before beginning the process. Parenting coordinators should make sure they are not attempting to address issues that are outside of their expertise. Even when asked to do so by the court or attorneys who are regular referral sources, or because there seems to be little other options available for the clients you want to help, STOP. Do not proceed. Explain to all that you do not have the qualifications to address the specific issues of a case and suggest other options for the court to consider.

OFFICE ADMINISTRATIVE STAFF COMPORTMENT AND RESPONSIBILITY

Training administrative staff to set and maintain boundaries is also a critical component of parenting coordination work. They are often the front line for a professional and they need to model clear boundaries in their dealings with clients. Clients may be rude, demanding, and at times threatening both on the telephone and in person. Staff should be trained on how to address these behaviors and to report details of their interchanges to the parenting coordinator immediately. Staff should also be trained to interact with clients with professionalism and respect and maintain confidentiality at all times.

Along with the hybrid skills and experience needed to provide quality parenting coordination services, the parenting coordinator must also have the skills to oversee and manage the process. The best strategy to manage risk and maintain integrity in the parenting coordination process is to have a clearly defined court order, a detailed professional services agreement, and practice policies and procedures set forth that establish and reinforce the structure needed for this unique and challenging work. Parenting coordinators should make sure they are qualified and competent and that they continue to hone and refine their skills through proper training, continuing education in relevant areas, and consultation with experienced peers and other professionals.

Parenting coordination presents unique challenges and opportunities for parents and children and the professionals who strive to help them make their lives better. Most families entering parenting coordination need help and a lot of it. Or, in the words of one famous doctor, "when you're in a Slump you're not in for much fun. Un-slumping yourself is not easily done" (Seuss, 1990). But patience, perseverance, wisdom, and compassion can go a long way in helping families heal their wounds and lead healthy, happy, and productive lives.

Appendix A

Examples of Court Orders of Referral for Parenting Coordination

I   Twelfth Judicial Circuit in and for Manatee
and Sarasota County, Florida

II   Stipulation and Order Appointing Special Master—California

**IN THE CIRCUIT COURT OF THE TWELFTH
JUDICIAL CIRCUIT**

IN AND FOR _____COUNTY, FLORIDA

Petitioner,

and   **Case No.**

Respondent.
_____/

ORDER OF REFERRAL TO PARENTING COORDINATOR

The Court considered the ❑ motion of the court, ❑ joint motion of the parties, ❑ motion of a party, reviewed the court file, considered the testimony presented. Based on this information, the court finds that:

A. **Appropriateness of Process.** This matter is appropriate for parenting coordination and it is in the best interest of the child(ren). This is not a Chapter 741 proceeding.

B. **Parenting Coordination Process.** Parenting coordination is a child-focused alternative dispute resolution process whereby a parenting coordinator assists the parties in creating or implementing their parenting plan by facilitating the resolution of disputes, providing education and making recommendations to the parties; and, with the prior consent of the parties and approval of the court, making limited decisions within the scope of this order of referral.

209

C. **Parenting Coordinator.** A parenting coordinator is an impartial third person whose role is to assist the parties in successfully creating or implementing a parenting plan.

D. **Selection of Parenting Coordinator.** The parenting coordinator was selected by:

- the parties' agreement.
- the court.

E. **History of Domestic Violence.** Based upon testimony and evidence presented and a review of related court records, the court has determined:

- There is no history of domestic violence.
- There has been a history of domestic violence, and there is an injunction for protection in place, and:
  - Each party has had an opportunity to consult with an attorney or domestic violence advocate before this court has accepted the parties' consent.
  - Each party has consented to this referral and the consent has been given freely and voluntarily.
- There has been a history of domestic violence, and there is no current injunction for protection, and:
  - Each party has had an opportunity to consult with an attorney or domestic violence advocate before this court has accepted the parties' consent.
  - Each party has consented to this referral and the consent has been given freely and voluntarily.

Domestic Violence safeguards should be considered.

It is therefore, **ORDERED:**

1. **Parenting Coordinator.** The parties are referred to the following parenting coordinator for an initial period of ___months:

Name: _____

Address: _____

Telephone No. _____

Fax Number: _____

a. The parenting coordinator shall file a response to this Order within 30 days accepting or declining the appointment. The response to the appointment must be in substantial compliance with the form Response by Parenting Coordinator adopted by the 12th Judicial Circuit.

b. The parties or their attorneys must provide to the parenting coordinator copies of all pleadings and orders related to domestic violence and any other pleadings and orders requested by the parenting coordinator related to parenting coordination.

2. **Meetings.** Unless prohibited herein as a domestic violence safeguard or by another court order, the parenting coordinator may meet with the parties and/or child(dren) together or separately, in person or by any electronic means.

3. **Domestic Violence Safeguards.** The parties shall adhere to all provisions of any injunction for protection or conditions of bail, probation, or a sentence arising from criminal proceedings.

▩ There has been a history of domestic violence, and there is no current injunction for protection. Therefore, the following domestic violence safeguards should be implemented:

   ▩ None are necessary
   ▩ No joint meetings
   ▩ No direct negotiations
   ▩ No direct communications
   ▩ Other: _____

4. **Role, Responsibility, and Authority of Parenting Coordinator.** The parenting coordinator shall have the following role, responsibility, and authority:

a. Assist the parties in creating and implementing a parenting plan;

b. Facilitate the resolution of disputes regarding the creation or implementation of the Parenting Plan;

c. Recommend to parties strategies for creating or implementing the Parenting Plan. Such recommendations may include that one or both parents avail themselves of accessible and appropriate community resources, including, but not limited to, random drug screens, parenting classes, and individual psychotherapy or family counseling, if there is a history or evidence that such referrals are appropriate;

d. Recommend to the parents changes to the Parenting Plan;

e. Educate the parties to effectively:

  i. Parent in a manner that minimizes conflicts;
  ii. Communicate and negotiate with each other and their child(ren);
  iii. Develop and apply appropriate parenting skills;
  iv. Understand principles of child development and issues facing child(ren) when their parents no longer live together;
  v. Disengage from the other parent when engagement leads to conflicts and noncooperation;
  vi. Identify the sources of their conflict with each other and work jointly to minimize conflict and lessen its deleterious effects on the child(ren); and,
  vii. Allow the child(ren) to grow up free from the threat of being caught in the middle of their parents' disputes.

f. Report or communicate with the court concerning nonconfidential matters as provided in paragraph 7 of this order;

g. Communicate with the parties and their child(ren), separately or together, in person or by telephone, unless otherwise prohibited by court order or applicable law;

5. **Scope of Authority.** The parenting coordinator shall make limited decisions within the scope of this order of referral. A parenting coordinator shall not have decision-making authority to resolve substantive disputes between the parties. A dispute is substantive if it would:

a. Significantly change the quantity or decrease the quality of time a child spends with either parent;

b. Modify parental responsibility;

The parenting coordinator may have additional authority with express written consent. If there has been a history of domestic violence the court must find that consent has been freely and voluntarily given.

a. With the expressed written consent of both parties, the parenting coordinator may:

  i. Have temporary decision-making authority to resolve specific nonsubstantive disputes between the parties until such time as a court order is entered modifying the decision.
  ii. Make recommendations to the court concerning modifications to the parenting plan or time-sharing.

b. With the express written consent of a party, a parenting coordinator may:

  i. Have access to confidential and privileged records and information of that party;

ii. Provide confidential and privileged information for that party to health care providers and to any other third parties.

c. Unless otherwise prohibited by the court, the parenting coordinator may:

 i. Have access to a child's confidential and privileged records and information.

 ii. Provide confidential and privileged information for that child to health care providers and to any other third parties.

6. **Fees and Costs for Parenting Coordination.**

a. ▣ The parties have consented to this referral to parenting coordination and have agreed that they have the present ability to pay parenting coordination fees.

 ▣ The parties have consented to this referral to parenting coordination and the Court finds that:___petitioner___respondent ___both parties has/have the present financial ability to pay parenting coordination fees.

 ▣ This order is without the consent of the parties and the court has determined that:___petitioner___respondent___ both parties has/have the financial ability to pay the parenting coordination fees and costs.

b. The court allocates payment of fees and costs for parenting coordination as follows:

 _____% shall be paid by the Father.

 _____% shall be paid by the Mother.

c. If a party has caused the parenting coordinator to expend an unreasonable and unnecessary amount of time, the Court may later determine that party will be solely responsible for payment of the parenting coordinator's fees and costs for such time expended or that the party shall reimburse the other party for the parenting coordinator's fees and costs paid by the other party for such time expended. Failure to pay the parenting coordinator's fees and costs in a timely manner may subject the party to sanctions for contempt of court.

d. The parenting coordinator shall not proceed until he/she is satisfied with the terms and conditions of payment for his/her services. Further, the parenting coordinator shall not perform nor continue to perform the parenting coordination services in this case unless all of his/her fees and costs are paid by the parties as ordered, and, in the event of nonpayment, the parenting coordinator shall file a Request for Status Conference, and the court will address the issue of nonpayment of fees and costs.

7. **Confidentiality.** All communications made by, between, or among the parties and the parenting coordinator during parenting coordination sessions are confidential. The parenting coordinator and each party may not testify or offer evidence about communications made by a party or the parenting coordinator during the parenting coordination sessions, except if:

a. Necessary to identify, authenticate, confirm, or deny a written agreement entered into by the parties during parenting coordination;

b. The testimony or evidence is necessary to identify an issue for resolution by the court without otherwise disclosing communications made by any party or the parenting coordinator;

c. The testimony or evidence is limited to the subject of a party's compliance with the order of referral to parenting coordination, orders for psychological evaluation, counseling ordered by the court or recommended by a health care provider, or for substance abuse testing or treatment;

d. The parenting coordinator reports that the case is no longer appropriate for parenting coordination;

e. The parenting coordinator is reporting that he or she is unable or unwilling to continue to serve and that a successor parenting coordinator should be appointed;

f. The testimony or evidence is necessary pursuant to s. 61.125 (5) (b) or s. 61.125(8);

g. The parenting coordinator is not qualified to address or resolve certain issues in the case and a more qualified coordinator should be appointed;

h. The parties agree that the testimony or evidence be permitted; or

i. The testimony or evidence is necessary to protect any person from future acts that would constitute domestic violence under Chapter 741; child abuse, neglect, or abandonment under Chapter 39; or abuse, neglect, or exploitation of an elderly or disabled adult under Chapter 825.

8. **Agreement on Nonconfidentiality.** The parties can agree to waive confidentiality of a specific communication or all communications. The waiver must be in writing, signed by the parties and their respective counsel. The waiver shall be filed with the court and a copy served on the parenting coordinator. Either party may revoke their waiver of confidentiality by providing written notice signed

by the party. The revocation shall be filed with the court and a copy served on the other party and the parenting coordinator.

9. **Scheduling.** Each party shall contact the parenting coordinator within 10 days of the date of this order to schedule the first appointment. The parenting coordinator shall determine the schedule for subsequent appointments.

10. **Withdrawal Procedure.** With Court approval, the parenting coordinator may withdraw from the role of parenting coordinator. The parenting coordinator shall apply directly to the Court with a request to be discharged, and shall provide notice to the parties and their counsel of their request to withdrawal. Either party may seek to terminate the parenting coordinator's services by filing a motion with the Court. The parenting coordinator's services may not be terminated by either of the parties (or at the request of both parties) without order of this court.

11. **Reservation of Jurisdiction.** This Court specifically reserves jurisdiction to enforce and/or modify the terms and conditions of this Order.

DONE AND ORDERED in _____ County, Florida, on this _____ day of _____, 20___.

_____
Circuit Judge

Copies to:
    Parenting Coordinator
    Address of Parenting Coordinator

Name of Party:
    Counsel for Party
    Address of Counsel

Name of Party: Guardian ad Litem:
    Counsel for Party   Address of GAL
    Address of Counsel

SUPERIOR COURT OF CALIFORNIA
COUNTY OF _____

In re the Marriage of

)

)

_____

Petitioner:)

)

)

and)

)

Respondent:)

)

)

)

**STIPULATION AND ORDER
APPOINTING
SPECIAL MASTER**

Case No.:

_____

PURSUANT TO THE STIPULATION OF THE PARTIES hereinafter set forth, and good cause appearing therefore,
IT IS ORDERED, ADJUDGED AND DECREED THAT:

APPOINTMENT:

1. _____ is appointed Special Master under Code of Civil Procedure Section 638, until resignation of _____ or written agreement of the parties, further court order, or 2 years from the date of appointment, whichever first occurs.
2. This appointment is based upon the expertise of the Special Master as a licensed mental health professional and/or family law attorney.
3. The Special Master may make orders resolving conflicts between the parents which do not affect the court's exclusive jurisdiction to determine fundamental issues of custody and visitation. Each party specifically agrees that the Special Master may make decisions (this may involve making and changing orders) regarding possible conflicts they may have on the following issues[1], and that such decisions

[1] *By agreement, signed by both, the parties may exclude specified items from the following list. Each party is to initial each item to which they agree.*

are effective as orders when made and will continue in effect unless modified or set aside by a court of competent jurisdiction:

___/___ a. Dates and times of pick up and delivery:

___/___ b. Sharing of vacations and holidays:

___/___ c. Method of pickup and delivery:

___/___ d. Transportation to and from visitation:

___/___ e. Participation in child care/daycare and baby sitting:

___/___ f. Bedtime:

___/___ g. Diet:

___/___ h. Clothing:

___/___ i. Recreation:

___/___ j. After school and enrichment activities:

___/___ k. Discipline:

___/___ l. Health care management:

___/___ m. Alterations in schedule which do not substantially alter the basic time share agreement:

___/___ n. Participation in visitation (by significant others, relatives, etc.):

___/___ o. In the case of infants and toddlers, increasing time share when developmentally appropriate:

___/___ p. Making orders more specific or clarifying existing orders so as to help the parties to avoid violation of the Court's orders:

___/___ q. Alteration of the child(ren)'s appearance, such as haircuts, pierced ears, body piercing, and tattoos:

___/___ r. Telephone contact by noncustodial parent which the child(ren) are in the custody on the custodial parent:

___/___ s. Changing the times for religious observances and training by the child(ren):

___/___ t. Decisions regarding large purchases made by either parent for children, e.g., cell telephone, blackberry, cars, horses, animals to be transported with the child(ren):

___/___ u. Other: _____

4. The Special Master will have authority to make recommendations on the following issues[2], which recommendations shall be submitted to the court, which may approve them and enter them as court orders.

---

[2] *By agreement, signed by both, the parties may exclude specified items from the following list. Each party is to initial each item to which they agree.*

These recommendations will be effective when adopted by the court, and can be reviewed only upon a hearing de novo at which time the moving party has the burden of proof.

___/___ a. Private school education:

___/___ b. Religion and religious training:

___/___ c. Church attendance:

___/___ d. Large changes in vacation and holiday time shares:

___/___ e. Supervision of visitation:

___/___ f. Time share changes which do not alter the child(ren)'s primary residence:

___/___ g. Appointment of counsel for child(ren):

___/___ h. Other: _____

Once a court order is made relating to any item in this paragraph, the Special Master may make decisions, implementing the court order.

5. The Special Master shall not make any orders which substantially alter[3] the parties' time-sharing arrangements, alter an award of physical custody, alter an award of legal custody, or substantially interfere with a party's contact with his/her children. These decisions and others relating to the best interests of the child(ren) are reserved to the San Francisco Superior Court for adjudication, and may be presented to the court by either party upon the recommendation of the Special Master in the form of an order to show cause or notice of motion. In an emergency, the Special Master may ask the court to initiate an Order to Show Cause on its own motion.

6. The Special Master may recommend to the court and/or the parties that the child(ren), and/or either or both parents participate in adjunct services including physical and psychological examinations and assessments, and psychotherapy (including selection of a therapist for the children when the parties cannot agree); alcohol and drug monitoring/testing; domestic violence counseling, attendance at Batterer's intervention programs, or parenting classes for the parents. The cost for psychotherapy for the children shall automatically be shared by the parties equally in the absence of any provision to the contrary in a current court order.

7. On notice to both parties and the court, the Special Master may recommend in writing or in open court that a custody evaluation or assessment be conducted. Such recommendation shall set forth the issues to be evaluated or assessed. Unless the parties agree to the evaluation or assessment within 15 days, the matter will be set

---

[3] *Ordinarily defined as more than 2 nights per week.*

by the court for an order to show cause with written notice to all parties. The parties may choose to respond.

8. The Special Master may request instructions from the court, either in open court or in a writing directed to the court, on 15 days written notice to all parties, unless shortened by the court. The parties may choose to respond.

QUASI-JUDICIAL IMMUNITY:

9. The Special Master is an officer of the court/referee, acting as a private judge for the parties to this action, to the extent of this stipulation. The Special Master has quasi-judicial immunity. The Special Master cannot be sued based on her actions in this matter. The Special Master cannot be compelled to testify and is subject to the restrictions of Evidence Code Section 703.5. Any testimony given pursuant to this stipulation or in furtherance of her appointment as Special Master shall not constitute a waiver of the Special Master's quasi-judicial immunity.

10. The Special Master may not testify without the express agreement of the Special Master and the parties. Any testimony given pursuant to this paragraph shall not constitute a waiver of the Special Master's quasi-judicial immunity.

11. Notwithstanding the above, the Special Master may elect to testify in any hearing to remove the Special Master, in any request of the Special Master to the Court to terminate the appointment, in any request for instructions, or to enforce fee collection. Any testimony given pursuant to this paragraph shall not constitute a waiver of the Special Master's quasi-judicial immunity.

PROCEDURE:

12. **Statement of Policies and Procedures:** Both parties shall participate in the dispute resolution process as defined by the Special Master and shall be present when so requested by the Special Master. The Special Master shall provide the parties with a written agreement for services containing her policies, including specifically the policy concerning confidentiality of information obtained by the Special Master. The Special Master shall have the authority to determine the protocol of all interviews and sessions including, in the case of meetings with the parties, the power to determine who attends such meetings, including individual and joint sessions with the parties and/or the child(ren). In the event a party does not attend a meeting set by the Special Master, the Special

Master may make orders despite the party's absence. **Both parties understand that they do not have the right to confidentiality with any information they provide to the Special Master as this is not a confidential process.**

13. **Hearings/Sessions:** The Special Master may conduct hearings/ sessions which are informal in nature, by telephone or in person, and need not comply with the rules of evidence. No record need be made, except the Special Master's written recommendations. If either party wants an issue decided by the Special Master, he or she may submit a written or telephonic request to the Special Master, as directed by the Special Master, clearly setting forth the issues in dispute. The hearings may be informal and need not comply with the rules of hearsay or civil procedure. The testimony need not be sworn. **There is no confidentiality as to any evidence presented at such hearings.**

14. **Use of Assistants/Consultants:** On reasonable notice to the parties, the Special Master may utilize consultants and/or assistants as necessary to assist the Special Master in the performance of the duties contained herein. Fees for such consultants or assistants will be advanced by the parties as directed by the Special Master. In making such directions, the Special Master will consider the financial circumstances of the parties. In the event of a dispute regarding the allocation of such fees, the court retains jurisdiction to resolve the dispute.

15. **Interviews:** The Special Master may talk with and base orders or recommendations upon conversations with parties, attorneys, witnesses, or examinations of writings which may take place without anyone present. No record need be made. The Special Master may talk with each party and without the presence of either counsel. The Special Master shall have the authority to determine the protocol of all interviews, including the power to determine who attends such meetings.

DECISIONS:

16. Decisions of the Special Master relating to the items listed in paragraph 3, by their very nature are often made in circumstances involving severe time constraints, and, possibly, emergencies; therefore, these decisions may be made orally. Oral orders are binding and effective when made in a fashion communicated to both parties, and such orders shall be further confirmed in writing to both parties and counsel as soon as practicable. Orders made by the Special Master in writing, shall be binding and effective when

signed by the Special Master. All Orders will be submitted to the Judge at a later time, but their date of effectiveness is as stated in this paragraph. The parties will not obstruct the Special Master's ability to communicate with them to impart oral decisions. If either party does, it will be as if the oral decision of the Special Master has been communicated and said order will be binding.

WARNING: In signing this agreement, both mother and father should assume that the Special Master's decision on the issues listed in paragraph 3 will be final. Because of time constraints and because of the language of this stipulation, the possibility of obtaining a court order changing a Special Master's decision on these issues is unlikely. Any party challenging the Special Master's decision on any of these issues will have a burden of proving, with clear and convincing evidence, that the Special Master's decision was legally incorrect and/or not in the best interest of the child(ren).

17. If the Special Master makes recommendations on issues addressed in paragraph 4, above, these recommendations should be in writing, and filed with the court. If either party disagrees with any recommendation thus made, he/she may make a timely motion, requesting a judicial review of the order. In that event, the party challenging the Special Master's recommendation has the burden of proof according to law as set forth in paragraph 4. Once the court adopts the recommendation and it becomes a court order, the Special Master may make decisions implementing the court order.

18. **Copies of all motions, objections, or other documents submitted to the Court or issued by the Court shall be served in accordance with Code of Civil Procedure Section 1005 on all parties, counsel and the Special Master by the person or entity generating such documents.**

COMMUNICATION WITH SPECIAL MASTER:

19. The parties and their attorneys shall have the right to initiate or receive ex parte communication with the Special Master. The parties agree, however, that ex parte communications should be minimized whenever possible and the Special Master shall have the right to disclose all ex parte communications. If the Special Master is requested to make orders based upon an ex parte communication, she shall make reasonable efforts to contact the other party before making such orders. Any party may initiate contact in writing with the Special Master, provided that copies are provided to opposing counsel and/or all parties simultaneously.

20. The Special Master may communicate with the parties' child or children outside the presence of the parties. The Special Master may communicate with the therapists who are treating the parties' child or children, as well. If the Special Master is of the opinion that the information or notes generated by the Special Master's communications with the children and/or with the children's therapists contain information which may be harmful to the child or which may be damaging to the child's relation with his or her therapist or with either parent, the Special Master may withhold such information. If either parent wishes to review such information, such review can only be allowed upon noticed motion, after in camera review of the information by the Court, in consultation with the Special Master. If, after such review, the Commissioner or Judge agrees with the Special Master that the divulging of such information could be harmful to the child or damaging to the child's relationship with his/her therapist or either parent, the court may order that such information need not be divulged.

21. The Special Master may communicate ex parte with the Judge, at the discretion of the Special Master and the Judge. Such communications shall be made only after giving notice to both parties; provided, however, that notice may be excused if notice would frustrate the very purpose of the communication. If the Special Master communicates with the Judge without having given notice she shall notify the Judge of that fact and her reasons for not giving notice.

22. The parties shall provide in a timely fashion all reasonable records, documentation, and information requested by the Special Master.

23. Counsel for Petitioner/Plaintiff Respondent/Defendant shall provide, within 15 business days from the date this order is mailed, copies of all:
    ❏ Pleadings
    ❏ Orders and correspondence between counsel or the court and counsel related to the action.

24. No therapist–patient relationship and/or privilege is created between the Special Master and the parties by this stipulation. No attorney–client relationship and/or privilege is created by this stipulation between the Special Master and the parties.

DATA COLLECTION:

25. The parties have been informed that they are not required to give up privileges or rights to privacy, and they do not have to agree to disclose information. However, they agree that records and

information regarding either party and/or the child(ren) may be released to the Special Master by the following:

a. Child(ren)'s current/previous pediatrician;
b. Child(ren)'s current/previous psychologist/psychiatrist or mental health professional;
c. Child(ren)'s current/previous teacher(s) and schools;
d. Hospital and medical records of child(ren)'s current/previous physician;
e. Law enforcement agencies, police department/sheriff's office;
f. Prior Special Master;
g. Custody Evaluator;
h. Daycare providers;
i. Other: _____

The parties will sign the consent to the release of the above-listed information form(s) provided to them by the Special Master and any required by the persons, schools, and/or agencies noted in A through I above to release the information to the Special Master. In addition, the parties shall provide nonprivileged documents to the Special Master on request.

CHILD ABUSE REPORTING:

26. **The Duty to Report:** The penal code mandates that all child care custodians and health care practitioners (doctors, marriage counselors, family and child counselors, psychologists, social workers and others) report to child protective services any information regarding possible child abuse that comes to the attention of the health care practitioner. The reporting requirement is an exception to the confidentiality privilege. **This means that all incidents of child abuse or suspected child abuse that meet the mandatory reporting standards for mental health professionals will be reported by the Special Master to appropriate authorities.** Communications to this Marriage Family Therapist are not privileged or confidential because the therapist, in her role as a Special master, is not representing a client.

27. **Attorney Special Master:** The child abuse reporting statute does not apply to attorneys because attorneys are not named in the statute as a class of persons who are mandated to report a child abuse allegation. However, because this Special Master is a licensed Marriage Family Therapist in addition to being an attorney, she is a mandated reporter and must report as set forth in paragraph 26 above. Communications to an attorney Special Master are not privileged or confidential communications because the attorney, in her role as a Special Master, is not representing a client.

28. **False Allegations of Child Abuse:** The Family Code provides for a monetary sanction and attorney fees for any knowingly false allegation of child abuse made during a child custody proceeding. This section does not apply to Special Masters who report an allegation made to them, but does apply to the person making the allegation to the Special Master if the court finds that the initial allegation was made knowing that it was untrue.

29. **Immunity for Child Abuse Reporting:** Health care practitioners who are required to report allegations of child abuse are immune from civil suits or liability for making their required reports. They cannot be sued either for the report or for the violation of the confidentiality privilege. Specific statutes provide for the immunity from civil suits and also provide an exception to the confidentiality privilege.

FEES:

30. **Charges and Costs:** The Special Master's fees are $350.00 per hour. Time spent in interviewing, report preparation, preparing letters, faxes, statements of decision, recommendations, orders, review of records and correspondence, telephone conversation, travel, court preparation and any other time invested in connection with serving as Special Master will also be billed at the $350.00 hourly rate. The Special Master's fee for court appearances and settlement conference is $350.00 per hour (4 hour minimum) while in court and at the settlement conference (4 hour minimum) and $350.00 per hour travel time to and from her office.

31. It is understood that despite the fact that the Special Master may make decisions or orders in favor of one party, both parties will continue to be responsible for the payment of fees associated with such services at the allocated percentage set forth in paragraph 37 below. Ultimately, The court shall determine the proper allocation between the parties of the fees of the Special Master for such services and may require reimbursement by one party to the other for any payment to the Special Master.

32. The Special Master shall be reimbursed for any expenses she incurs in association with her role as Special Master. These costs may include, but are not limited to, the following: photocopies, messenger service, long distance telephone charges, express and/or certified mail costs and excess postage to foreign countries, parking, tolls, mileage, travel expenses and word processing.

33. **Payment:** Prior to the initial interview, the parties will provide the Special Master with an advance retainer totaling $_____, $_____ from each party. The aforementioned hourly fees and costs as set forth above shall be drawn against this retainer. Any funds remaining at the termination of the Special Master's services shall be refunded to the parties. In the event the retainer is expended within 4 hours of her fees prior to the termination of the Special Master's services, the parties agree to provide a like amount as and for an additional advance retainer within 15 days of the request. The Special Master shall not become a creditor of the parties.

34. **Objections to Fees or Costs:** Any objection to the Special Master's bills must be brought to her attention in written form within ten business days of the billing date; otherwise the billing shall be deemed agreed to and accepted.

35. **Enforcement:** In the event that arbitration proceedings or a legal action become necessary to enforce any provision of this order, the non-prevailing party shall pay attorney's fees and costs as may be incurred. The Special Master may proceed by noticed motion to the court in the event his/her fees are not timely paid. A willful failure to advance an initial or later retainer within 15 days of a demand therefore may be the subject of monetary or issue sanctions or contempt action.

36. The court reserves jurisdiction in the family law action to enforce the provisions of this stipulation.

ALLOCATIONS:

37. Except as otherwise provided herein, the fees and advance deposit of the Special Master retainer shall be shared by the parties in the following manner: Father shall pay____% of the Special Master's fees, expenses, advance and ongoing retainer; and Mother shall pay_____% of the Special Master's fees, expenses, advance and ongoing retainer. The Special Master shall have the right to *recommend* the reallocation of payment of her fees at a percentage different from the above if she believes the need for her services is attributable to the conduct of one party or if changed financial circumstances of one party or both parties warrant it.

38. Telephone calls to the Special Master by either party are part of the process and appropriately paid for the parties according to their percentage share as ordered, unless otherwise determined by the Special Master.

39. In the event that either party fails to provide 24 hours telephone notice of cancellation of any appointment with the Special Master, such party shall pay all of the Special Master's charges of such missed appointment at the full hourly rate, at the discretion of the Special Master.

RENEWAL, WITHDRAWAL, REMOVAL, GRIEVANCES:

40. **Renewal of Term of Appointment:** The parties and the Special Master agree to renew or extend the term of the Special Master by written stipulation and order.

41. **Resignation of Special Master:** The Special Master may, on notice to all parties and counsel, ask that the court remove her as Special Master. Such request shall set forth the reason for such request and 30 days written notice will be given to the parties.

42. **Removal of the Special Master:** The Special Master can be removed or replaced at any time by written stipulation and order signed by all parties. If there is not agreement by the parties and Special Master, paragraph 44 will apply.

43. **Disqualification:** The Special Master may be disqualified on any of the grounds applicable to the removal of a judge, referee or arbitrator. In the event the parties do not agree to remove the Special Master, either party may request the removal of the Special Master by noticed motion. Such motion shall proceed on the written documents submitted by both parties and the Special Master, unless the court orders an evidentiary hearing. Each party and the Special Master may respond to the initial submissions in writing.

44. **Contested Removal/Grievances:** Neither party may initiate court proceedings for the removal or disqualification of the Special Master, nor initiate any complaints or grievances, nor bring to the court's attention any grievances regarding the performance or actions of the Special Master, nor complain about the Special Master to the Special Master's licensing boards (either or both licensing boards) without first following this procedure:

    a. A person having a complaint or grievance regarding the Special Master must discuss the matter with the Special Master in person before pursuing it in any other manner.

    b. If, after discussion, the party decides to pursue a complaint, he/ she must submit a written letter detailing the complaint or grievance to the Special Master, to the other party, to both parties' attorneys (if any), and to the attorney for the child(ren), if one exists. The Special Master will within 30 days provide a written response to the grievance to both parties, both attorneys and the attorney for the child(ren).

c. If appropriate, given the circumstances, the Special Master will then meet with the parties and their attorneys (if any), to discuss the matter.

d. If it is a licensing matter and no resolution was reached after pursuing (a), (b), and (c) above, the parties and Special Master shall attend a judicially supervised settlement conference on the court's regularly scheduled settlement conference calendar prior to any licensing action being undertaken.

e. If the grievance or complaint is not resolved after following items (a) through (d) above, the complaining party may proceed by noticed motion to the court for removal of Special Master.

f. The court shall reserve jurisdiction to determine if either or both parties and/or the Special Master shall ultimately be responsible for any portion or all of said Special Master's time and costs spent in responding to the grievance and the Special Master's attorney's fees, if any.

WAIVER OF RULE OF COURT 3.904

45. Both parties agree that the Special Master shall be advised of the grounds for objection to appointment under Code of Civil Procedure Section 641, and the Special Master shall disclose to both parties, or their counsel if represented, within 30 days the existence of any such grounds. The failure of either party to file with the Court within 15 days any objection under Code of Civil Procedure Section 641 shall be deemed a waiver of grounds for objection to the Special Master under Code of Civil Procedure Section 641. Both parties agree that the requirement to post a notice indicating the case number and the telephone number of the person to contact to arrange for attendance in any Special Master proceeding under California Rule of Court Section 3.904 is waived. To that extent, the records in this case are deemed confidential.

IT IS SO STIPULATED

_____   _____
Mother   Father

APPROVED AS TO FORM

_____   _____
Attorney for Mother   Attorney for Father

Special Master

ORDER

Upon reading the foregoing stipulation, and good cause appearing therefore, IT IS SO ORDERED.

_____
DATE

_____
JUDGE OF THE SUPERIOR COURT

Appendix B

Sample Parenting Plans

TWELFTH JUDICIAL CIRCUIT IN AND FOR MANATEE
AND SARASOTA COUNTIES, FLORIDA

A. Introduction and Self-Assessment

B. Highly Structured Parenting Plan

INSTRUCTIONS AND ASSESSMENTS FOR YOUR PARENTING PLAN

(This section should be completed prior to the purchase
or downloading of any plan.)

12TH JUDICIAL CIRCUIT

MANATEE, SARASOTA, AND DESOTO COUNTIES, FLORIDA

*Legal matters can be very complex. If you have questions or concerns about the use of these forms, instructions, or your legal rights, it is strongly recommended that you talk to an attorney. All instructions and forms distributed by the Twelfth Judicial Circuit are provided merely to serve as a guide. The Twelfth Judicial Circuit does not guarantee that either the instructions or the forms will achieve the result desired by the parties or ensure that an individual judge will follow the procedures exactly or accept each and every form drafted. Any person using these forms and/or instructions does so at their own risk, and the Twelfth Judicial Circuit shall not be responsible for any losses incurred by any person in reliance on the instructions and/or forms.

A PLANNING GUIDE FOR PARENTS LIVING APART

One size does not fit all!

INTRODUCTION

One of the most difficult challenges facing parents at the time of separation is deciding how they will address issues concerning their children. Each family is different. However, putting the best interest of our children first must come first. Parents often fear that the end of their adult relationship means an end of their child–parent relationship. **THIS IS NOT TRUE.** Parents often do not know that conflict hurts children. **THIS IS ABSOLUTELY TRUE.** Therefore, parents who are concerned about how their separation will affect their children's healthy development are already ahead of the curve.

> HONESTLY RECOGNIZING YOUR FAMILY'S SITUATION AND YOUR ABSOLUTE RESPONSIBILITY TO ALWAYS SERVE YOUR CHILDREN'S "BEST INTEREST" IS KEY FOR DEVELOPING A PARENTING PLAN WHICH WILL WORK FOR YOU.

It is not the purpose of this guide to establish a single standard or even an "ideal" parenting arrangement. Likewise, it is beyond the ability of this guide to offer "customized" recommendations for every family. This information is intended to make you think, reflect, discuss, plan, and help you develop a parenting plan for your children's healthy future. **This assessment is just a tool and is <u>not</u> intended to be used as evidence in court.**

Although this booklet is intended primarily as a guide to parents at the original time of separation or filing of court action, it should continue to serve as a reference as your children grow and your situations change. Parents are encouraged to review their parenting plans as their children reach new developmental stages; as well as, when significant events such as remarriage and relocation are planned.

DESIGNING THE PLAN ...

YOU NEED TO **HONESTLY** ANSWER THE QUESTIONS BELOW TO
SERVE THE "BEST INTEREST" OF YOUR CHILDREN.

*REMEMBER YOU **MAY** NEED TO PROVE YOUR ANSWERS IN COURT.*

STEP ONE: FAMILY ASSESSMENT

Has the other parent:

1. Acted as though violent behavior against you or your child(ren) is all right?
2. Damaged or destroyed property during an argument?
3. Hurt a pet out of anger?
4. Been so sad or upset they could not care for themselves or others?
5. Pushed, slapped, kicked, punched or hit you or the child(ren)?
6. Regularly abused and currently abuses alcohol and/or drugs?
7. Used weapons to threaten or hurt people?
8. Threatened to never return the child(ren)?
9. Threatened to kill you or the child(ren)?
10. Sexually abused anyone by force, threat of force or intimidation?
11. Been served with a protection or no contact order?
12. Been arrested for harming or threatening to harm you or anyone else?
13. Engaged in any other abusive or threatening behavior?

NOTE: The taping or recording of others without their consent is usually illegal.

If you answered "YES" to one or more of the above questions, you may need a Safety Focused Plan. Please purchase this plan from the Clerk of Court or download the plan at www.jud12.flcourts.org

If you answered "NO" to all the above questions, please continue.

STEP TWO: HIGHLY STRUCTURED ASSESSMENT

1. I only communicate with my child's other parent by: using email; certified U.S. mail; a third party (lawyer, relative, faith based professional etc.); our child(ren). (Please don't answer yes if this is caused solely by living far apart).
2. I do not believe my child(ren)'s other parent is a good parent.
3. I do not trust my child(ren)'s other parent to consistently use good judgment and make good decisions regarding our child.
4. I keep written and/or recorded records of all contact between myself and my child(ren)'s other parent.
5. I feel it is okay to make all major decisions about my child(ren) without consulting the other parent, because I have our child(ren)'s best interest at heart.
6. My child(ren)'s other parent and I can only exchange our child(ren): in a public setting; with an adult third party present; with the police present; and/or by maintaining a safe physical distance.
7. Because of my child(ren)'s other parent's actions, I have serious concerns regarding our child(ren)'s emotional and psychological functioning; peer or social relations; mother/child(ren) relationship; father/child(ren) relationship; school performance; behavior; and/or physical health.

NOTE: The taping or recording of others without their consent is usually illegal.

If you answered "YES" to one or more of the above questions, you may need a Highly Structure Parenting Plan. Please purchase this plan from the Clerk of Court or download the plan at: www.jud12.flcourts.org	If you answered "NO" to all the above questions, please continue.

STEP THREE: DISTANCE ASSESSMENT

Do you and the other parent:

1. Live or plan to live more than 50 miles apart?

(contact during the week unlikely)

If you answered "YES", you may need a Long Distance Parenting Plan. Please purchase this plan from the Clerk of Court or download the plan at: www.jud12.flcourts.org

If you answered "NO" please continue.

THESE QUESTIONS WILL HELP YOU RECOGNIZE YOUR
ABILITIES AND NEEDS.

STEP FOUR: SELF-ASSESSMENT

DAILY SCHEDULE

If you are employed outside the home: What time do you leave? _____
    Return? _____
If employed in the home, do you need to be home certain hours?
    ❑ *Yes* ❑ *No*
Can your schedule be changed? ❑ *Yes* ❑ *No*
Are there any demands on your time after normal work hours?
    ❑ *Yes* ❑ *No*
Is out-of-town travel required? ❑ *Yes* ❑ *No   If yes, how often?*_____
How long are you gone? _____

OUTSIDE HELP

*Do you have any additional help from other family or friends to care for your
child(ren)?* ❑ *Yes* ❑ *No   If so, describe:*
_____
_____

Are you a caregiver for anyone other than your child(ren)? ❑ *Yes* ❑ *No*
_____

TRANSPORTATION

Do you have reliable transportation? ❑ *Yes* ❑ *No*
A valid driver's license? ❑ *Yes* ❑ *No*
Do you have any health issues which might affect your driving ability?
    ❑ *Yes* ❑ *No*

PARENTING

In what events or situations does the child(ren):
    *Ask you for help?*_____
    *Respond to your direction?*_____
    Not respond to your direction? _____

*What do you do well as a parent?*_____

What do you have trouble with as a parent? _____

COMMUNICATION

Do you have problems communicating with the other parent? ❑ *Yes* ❑ *No*
Do you have e-mail access? ❑*Yes* ❑ *No*
Internet access? ❑ *Yes* ❑ *No*
Cell phone? ❑*Yes* ❑ *No*
Text messaging? ❑ *Yes* ❑ *No*

FAMILY EVENTS

*What events or holidays are the most important to you?*_____

_____

DISCIPLINE

What kind do you use? _____

What kind works for your child(ren)? _____

THESE QUESTIONS WILL HELP YOU RECOGNIZE THE OTHER
PARENT'S ABILITIES AND NEEDS.

STEP FIVE: CO-PARENT ASSESSMENT

DAILY SCHEDULE

If the other parent is employed outside the home: What time do they leave?
_____ *Return?* _____ *If the other parent is employed in the home, do
they need to be home certain hours?* ❑ *Yes* ❑ *No*

Can their schedule be changed? ❑ *Yes* ❑ *No*

Are there any demands on the other parent's time after normal work hours?
    ❑ *Yes* ❑ *No*

Is out-of-town travel required? ❑ *Yes* ❑ *No   If yes, how often?* _____
How long are they gone? _____

OUTSIDE HELP

Does the other parent have any additional help from other family or friends?
    ❑ *Yes* ❑ *No   If so, describe:*
_____

Are they a caregiver for anyone other than your child(ren)?
    ❑ *Yes* ❑ *No*

TRANSPORTATION

Does the other parent have reliable transportation? ❑ *Yes* ❑ *No*
A valid driver's license? ❑ *Yes* ❑ *No*

Do they have any health issues that affect their ability to drive?
    ❑ *Yes* ❑ *No*

PARENTING

In what events or situations does the child:
    Ask for the other parent's help? _____
    Respond to the other parent's direction? _____
    Not respond to their direction? _____
What does the other parent do well as a parent? _____
What does the other parent have trouble with as a parent? _____

COMMUNICATION

Does the other parent have problems communicating with you? ❏ *Yes* ❏ *No*
Does the other parent:

Have e-mail? ❏*Yes* ❏ *No*
Internet? ❏ *Yes* ❏ *No*
Cell phone? ❏*Yes* ❏ *No*
Text messaging? ❏*Yes* ❏ *No*

FAMILY EVENTS

What events or holidays are important to the other parent? _____
_____

DISCIPLINE

What kind does the other parent use? _____
What kind are works for your child(ren)? _____

STEP SIX: CHILD ASSESSMENT

THESE QUESTIONS ARE WRITTEN TO HELP YOU MAKE
CHOICES THAT FIT THE NEEDS OF YOUR CHILD(REN), AND
BOTH PARENTS.
Complete one for each child

FULL NAME
OF CHILD: _____   DATE OF BIRTH: _____

1. What is the child's age? _____ School?_____
   Grade?_____

2. Is the child closer to one parent than the other? ❑ Yes ❑ No
   If Yes, which parent? _____

3. Has the child experienced any separations or deaths? ❑ Yes ❑ No
   If Yes, when? _____ Describe: _____

4. Has the child ever been diagnosed by a licensed professional with
   any academic needs, physical problems or emotional disorders?
   ❑ Yes ❑ No
   Evaluated by: _____
   Diagnosis: _____ When Diagnosed? _____
   If Yes, Treatment plan: _____

5. Has this child:
   a. Changed schools other than for normal progression? ❑ Yes ❑ No
   b. Been held a grade in school? ❑ Yes ❑ No
   c. Skipped a grade in school? ❑ Yes ❑ No
   d. Had difficulty in school? ❑ Yes ❑ No
   e. Been provided an Individualized Educational Plan (IEP)?
      ❑ Yes ❑ No
   f. Been found to be academically gifted? ❑ Yes ❑ No

6. How long is the travel time from your home? from your work?

   a. Child's school?   _____   _____
   b. Tutors?   _____   _____
   c. Sporting activities?   _____   _____
   d. Pediatrician?   _____   _____
   e. Extracurricular activities? _____   _____
   f. Place of worship?   _____   _____
   g. _____   _____   _____

7. How long is the travel time from other parent's home? from other parent's work?

a. Child's school?   _____   _____

b. Tutors?   _____   _____

c. Sporting activities?   _____   _____

d. Pediatrician?   _____   _____

e. Extracurricular activities?   _____   _____

f. Place of worship?   _____   _____

g. _____   _____   _____

8. List the activities in which this child *currently* participates and check the days of the week on which these events occur.

_____ ❑ Mon ❑ Tues ❑ Wed ❑ Thurs ❑ Fri
❑ Sat ❑ Sun ❑ Monthly

_____ ❑ Mon ❑ Tues ❑ Wed ❑ Thurs ❑ Fri
❑ Sat ❑ Sun ❑ Monthly

_____ ❑ Mon ❑ Tues ❑ Wed ❑ Thurs ❑ Fri
❑ Sat ❑ Sun ❑ Monthly

_____ ❑ Mon ❑ Tues ❑ Wed ❑ Thurs ❑ Fri
❑ Sat ❑ Sun ❑ Monthly

_____ ❑ Mon ❑ Tues ❑ Wed ❑ Thurs ❑ Fri
❑ Sat ❑ Sun ❑ Monthly

_____ ❑ Mon ❑ Tues ❑ Wed ❑ Thurs ❑ Fri
❑ Sat ❑ Sun ❑ Monthly

_____ ❑ Mon ❑ Tues ❑ Wed ❑ Thurs ❑ Fri
❑ Sat ❑ Sun ❑ Monthly

_____ ❑ Mon ❑ Tues ❑ Wed ❑ Thurs ❑ Fri
❑ Sat ❑ Sun ❑ Monthly

9. List any future planned activities:

_____

_____

_____

10. How do you and this child spend time together? When?

_____

_____

_____

_____

BE HONEST ABOUT WHAT IS WORKING NOW. CHILDREN NEED A REGULAR SCHEDULE. **HOWEVER,** THERE ARE OFTEN TIMES WHEN SOMEONE WHO WAS NOT AN ACTIVE PARENT BEFORE THE SEPARATION MAY WISH TO BECOME MORE INVOLVED AFTER SEPARATION. THE INITIAL PLAN SHOULD PROVIDE THAT PARENT ENOUGH TIME TO DEVELOP A CLOSER RELATIONSHIP.

The Do's and Don'ts of Parenting
Both Parents

DO:

- Maintain healthy communication with your children.
- Make it a priority to communicate regularly with the other parent.
- Religiously follow the parenting plan to make the process routine, easy and positive for your children.
- Strive to keep your word to the children.
- Contact the other parent immediately if there is an emergency involving the children while they are with you.

DON'T:

- Be uncooperative. The children will suffer consequences if their parents do not cooperate.

Parent A
(The parent with whom the child has more time-sharing)

DO:

- Share information about school, teachers, activities, friends and relatives with the other Parent.
- Be flexible and supportive of the children's relationship with the other Parent.
- Encourage excitement for the anticipated communication and/or travel with the other Parent.

DON'T:

- Edit, coach, monitor, or otherwise interfere with the children's communication with the other Parent.
- Take it personally if the children do not wish to call you regularly when they are with the other parent.

<u>Parent B</u>
(The parent with whom the child has less scheduled time-sharing)

DO:

- Make an extra effort to initiate contact with the children and educate yourself of their daily activities.
- Provide an itinerary to the other parent to prepare the children for the trip and to advise the other parent of the activities you are planning.
- Strive to keep your word to the children.

DON'T:

- Take it personally if the children do not wish to stay on the phone too long or do not call right back.
- Don't unreasonably limit the children's contact with the local parent during their stay.

REMEMBER

> As you develop your parenting plan
> *our child(ren)'s needs and......interests.*

BE HONEST! Think about your child(ren)'s ages, personalities, their likes and dislikes, interests, activities, ability to talk to the other parent, etc. Each family is different. There is no single parenting plan that is right for every family. Each parent will be asked to define a schedule that works best for your child(ren).

This is your chance to create a schedule that works for your child(ren). Remember your parenting schedule may change as your child(ren) grow.

REVIEW YOUR PARENTING PLAN WHEN:
* a child starts school   * a child's schedule changes * a parent remarries   * anyone experiences any major change

IN THE CIRCUIT COURT OF THE TWELFTH JUDICIAL CIRCUIT

IN AND FOR _____ COUNTY, FLORIDA

_____

Petitioner

Case No._____   Family Division:_____

AND

_____

Respondent

HIGHLY STRUCTURED PARENTING PLAN

1. PARENTING PLAN OF: *Check all that apply*
- ❏ Both Parents
- ❏ Mother
- ❏ Father
- ❏ Court-Ordered Plan
- ❏ Temporary
- ❏ Final Judgment
- ❏ Modification

	Name	**Address**	**Phone**	**E-Mail**
Father:				
Mother:				

THIS PARENTING PLAN INVOLVES THE FOLLOWING CHILD(REN):

	Name	**Date of Birth**	**Current Address**	**Future Address**
Child 1:				
Child 2:				
Child 3:				
Child 4:				
Child 5:				

LIST ANY MINOR CHILDREN YOU HAVE NOT
ADDRESSED BY THIS PLAN.

	Name	Date of Birth	Current Address
Child 1:			
Child 2:			
Child 3:			

*IF THE PARENTING ARRANGEMENTS ARE DIFFERENT FOR
SOME OF YOUR CHILDREN, YOU SHOULD WRITE UP A
SEPARATE PARENTING PLAN FOR EACH CHILD.*

2. JURISDICTION

▨ The United States is the country of habitual residence of the child(ren).

▨ The State of Florida maintains the most significant contacts with the child(ren) and is the most appropriate forum for addressing parenting contact.

▨ This Parenting Plan is a child custody determination for the purposes of the Uniform Child Custody Jurisdiction and Enforcement Act, the International Child Abduction Remedies Act, 42 U.S.C. ss 11601 et seq., the Parental Kidnapping Prevention Act, and the Convention on the Civil Aspects of International Child Abduction enacted at the Hague on October 25, 1980.

▨ The State of Florida is the child(ren)'s home state for purposes of the Uniform Child Custody Jurisdiction and Enforcement Act.

Venue is proper in the county of: ✓ *Select your County*
❑ Manatee   ❑ Sarasota   ❑ DeSoto County

3. PARENTING PRINCIPLES

A. General

▨ Each Parent shall make decisions regarding the day-to-day care and control of the child(ren) while they are with that parent.

▨ Each parent will make emergency decisions affecting the health or safety of the child(ren), notifying the other parent at the earliest opportunity.

▪ Each parent shall have access to all academic, medical, and other health related information pertaining to the child(ren), and they shall sign any necessary documentation ensuring that both parents have access to said records.

▪ Each parent shall be responsible for getting their own copies of records and reports directly from the school and medical facilities.

▪ Each parent has independent authority to confer with the child(ren)'s school, day care, medical and health related providers and other programs with regard to the child(ren)'s educational, emotional and social progress.

▪ Both parents shall be listed as emergency contacts for the child(ren).

▪ Each parent shall make sure the other parent has current contact information for the other parent.

▪ Each child has a right to be absent, insulated and protected from the parents' differences with each other and arguments or discussions.

▪ Each child has a right to be free of negative comments and behavior by one parent about the other.

B. In the event the parties do not agree on a parental decision: ✓ *Check only one*

❑ The parents shall submit the issue to the following Parenting Coordinator _____(name). If the parents are unable to agree on a parenting, one will be found or appointed from the 12th Judicial Circuit approved list.

Unless otherwise agreed the professional shall be
Paid by: ❑ Mother _____ % ❑ Father _____%

❑ If eligible, the parents will use the mediator appointed by the Court's mediation program.

❑ The parents shall first submit the issue to mediation.

If the parents are unable to mutually agree on a mediator, the parents shall use: _____

Unless otherwise agreed during mediation, the mediator shall be paid by: ❑ Mother _____ % ❑ Father _____%

The parents shall submit the issue to the court at the earliest available date.

❑ Other: _____

C. The ultimate decision-making authority shall be made by:
✓ *Check only Mother or Father for the following*

■ Academic/educational needs of   ❏ Mother   ❏ Father
the child(ren)

■ Medical/health related needs of   ❏ Mother   ❏ Father
the child(ren)

■ Extracurricular needs of the   ❏ Mother   ❏ Father
child(ren)

■ Religion   ❏ Mother   ❏ Father

■ Discipline   ❏ Mother   ❏ Father

■ _____ needs of the
child(ren)   ❏ Mother   ❏ Father

■ **Remember if you cannot resolve these parenting issues, the court will step in to assign one parent to resolve these parenting issues.**

4. CHILDREN'S RIGHTS

Each child has a right:

■ **To have two parents to love without fear of anger or guilt from the other; and**

■ **To develop an independent and meaningful relationship with the other parent and to respect the differences of each parent and their home; and**

■ **To be absent, insulated and protected from disparaging, belittling or alienating statements about the other parent; and**

■ **To not be used as a messenger, delivery means or means of communication with the other parent; and**

■ **To not be questioned about the other parent.**

5. EDUCATION

The children shall be enrolled/registered in school by: ✓ *Check only one*
❏ Mother
❏ Father

NOTE: This assignment does not determine <u>where</u> the child(ren) shall attend school. That determination shall be made by the school district rules.

The child(ren) shall attend (if known): ✓ *Check all that apply*
❑ Child Care:_____
    Paid by: ❑ Mother ____ %   ❑ Father ____%
❑ Preschool: _____
    Paid by: ❑ Mother ____ %   ❑ Father ____%
❑ Public School
❑ Private School: _____
    Paid by: ❑ Mother ____ %   ❑ Father ____%
❑ Before School Program:_____
    Paid by: ❑ Mother ____ %   ❑ Father ____%
❑ After School Program:_____
    Paid by: ❑ Mother ____ %   ❑ Father ____%
❑ Special Education:_____
    Paid by: ❑ Mother ____ %   ❑ Father ____%
❑ Tutoring:_____
    Paid by: ❑ Mother ____ %   ❑ Father ____%

6. EXTRACURRICULAR ACTIVITIES ✓ *Check all that apply*
❑ Either parent may register the child(ren) and allow them to participate in the activity of the child(ren)'s choice during that parent's parenting time.
❑ The parent with the minor child(ren) shall transport the minor child(ren) to and/or from extracurricular activities, providing all necessary uniforms and equipment are within the parent's possession, during that parent's parenting time.
❑ The costs of the extracurricular activities shall be
    Paid by: ❑ Mother ____ %   ❑ Father ____%
❑ The uniforms and equipment required for extracurricular activities shall be
    Paid by: ❑ Mother ____ %   ❑ Father ____%
❑ Other: _____
❑ No changes shall occur without court order.

❑ If the child(ren) attend summer camps, the costs and efforts shall be:

Paid by: ❑ Parent scheduled to have the child(ren) during that time period;

or

❑ Mother _____ %   ❑ Father _____%

7. MEDICAL

▪ Parents shall obtain on their own all medical, psychological, counseling, therapeutic, optical, orthodontic, dental or other health related care and needs of the child(ren) as allowed by court order.

▪ In the event of serious illness, accident or hospitalization affecting the health of the child(ren), the parent with the knowledge of such event shall immediately notify the other parent.

▪ A parent scheduling a routine appointment for the child(ren) shall notify the other parent in writing within 7 days, in writing, that the appoint occurred. The notice shall include the health care provider's name and contact information.

✓ *Check all that apply*

❑ Uncovered medical expenses of the child(ren) shall be

Paid by: ❑ Mother _____ %   ❑ Father _____%

❑ Uncovered dental and/or orthodontic expenses of the child(ren) shall be

Paid by: ❑ Mother _____ %   ❑ Father _____%

❑ Uncovered psychological, counseling, therapeutic or other health related needs of the child(ren) expenses shall be

Paid by: ❑ Mother _____ %   ❑ Father _____%

8. RELIGION ✓ *Check all that apply*

❑ Each parent may provide religious instruction in the faith they so desire.

❑ The parents have agreed that the child(ren)'s religious training shall be in the faith of:

_____

A. The costs of such training shall be

Paid by: ❑ Mother _____ %   ❑ Father _____%

B. The efforts and transportation needed for training shall be

Paid by: ❑ Mother _____ %   ❑ Father _____%

9. SCHEDULING

A. School Calendar

■ **On or before 01 August each year, both parents shall obtain a copy of the school calendar for the next school year.**

A. The parents shall follow the school calendar of:
✓ *Check all that apply*

❏ the oldest child

❏ the youngest child

❏ the school calendar for:
❏ Manatee   ❏ Sarasota   ❏ DeSoto County

❏ the school calendar for _____ School

B. Definitions

■ **Unless otherwise specified in this Agreement, the academic break periods or holidays,**

Begin: **At the end of the last scheduled day of classes before the holiday or break, and**

End: **On the evening before the first day of regularly scheduled classes after the holiday or break.**

C. Schedule Conflicts

■ **In the event holiday or vacation time conflicts with the ongoing parenting contact, the scheduled holiday or vacation time shall be observed.**

10. COMMUNICATION WITH THE CHILD(REN)

■ **Each parent shall notify the other parent within 7 days of any change to his/her contact information.**

■ **Each parent shall maintain a working phone.**

■ **Scheduled telephone contact shall not be monitored by or interrupted by the other parent.**

■ **Scheduled telephone contact shall be between the calling parent and child(ren).**

The child(ren) shall have access to the following:
✓ *Check all that apply*

❏ Cell Phone   ❏ Computer   ❏ Web Cam

Scheduled telephone contact shall be as follows: ✓ *Check all that apply*

❑ Monday ❑ Tuesday ❑ Wednesday ❑ Thursday
❑ Friday ❑ Saturday ❑ Sunday

During the hours of _____ to _____
The: ❑ Other parent initiates contact
❑ Child(ren) initiates contact

❑ Telephone contact shall not exceed: _____ minutes per call
_____ times per day

The cost of the cell phone and service shall be paid by:
❑ Mother _____ % ❑ Father _____%

The child(ren) may maintain internet/online access with either parent:
✓ *Check all that apply*

❑ Anytime

❑ Monday ❑ Tuesday ❑ Wednesday ❑ Thursday
❑ Friday ❑ Saturday ❑ Sunday

❑ During the hours of _____ to _____ The:
❑ Other parent initiates contact ❑ Child(ren) initiates contact

❑ The child(ren) may send/receive email.

❑ The child(ren) may make calls using the computer.

❑ The child(ren) may communicate on the following blogs, internet scrapbooks and/or photo services _____
_____.

The child(ren) may e-mail each parent at the following e-mail addresses:

Mother: _____

Father: _____

The cost associated with maintaining internet online access shall be paid by:
❑ Mother _____ % ❑ Father _____%

▪ **The parents shall monitor the child(ren)'s use of the computer to insure their safety:** ✓ *Check all that apply*

❑ The parents agree to install parental controls on all computers used by the child(ren).

❑ The parents agree that the child(ren)'s computer access will be supervised as follows:

_____

DEFAULT COMMUICATION PLAN BETWEEN PARENTS AND CHILD(REN) IF THE PARTIES CANNOT AGREE THE FOLLOWING SHALL APPLY:

1. The parent not with the child(ren) shall talk to the child(ren) every Sunday, Tuesday and Thursday at 7 P.M. in the time zone where the child(ren) are located for a maximum of 30 minutes. The parent not with the child(ren) shall place the call.
2. The child(ren) shall be permitted to call the other parent at any reasonable time they request. The parent with the child(ren) shall assist the child(ren) in making the call if needed.

11. COMMUNICATION BETWEEN PARENTS

Parents shall communicate by: ✓ *Check all that apply*
❑ E-mail   ❑ Text message   ❑ Third party
❑ Letter   ❑ Other: _____

DEFAULT COMMUNICATION PLAN BETWEEN THE PARENTS IF THE PARTIES CANNOT AGREE THE FOLLOWING SHALL APPLY:

The parents shall communicate about issues concerning the child(ren) by fax, email, or certified U.S. mail.

12. CHILD CARE PROVIDERS   ✓ *Check all that apply*
▪ **Child Care Provider means any party other than the parent who is caring for the child(ren).**
  ❑ Parents may individually select appropriate child care providers.
  ❑ Parents agree the following individuals can be used as child care providers:

  _____

  ❑ Each parent must offer via email or fax the other parent the opportunity to care for the child(ren) before using a child care provider for any period exceeding 48 hours.

13. MODIFICATIONS TO THIS AGREEMENT
  ▪ **If both parents agree to make a change to this agreement, such modification must be in writing, signed by both parties and filed with the court.**

14. RULES THAT APPLY TO EXCHANGE AND TRAVEL

- All necessary information will accompany the child(ren) including:
  - Medicine and dosage in its original packaging
  - Homework assignments, school projects and directions
  - Social and extracurricular activities with uniforms/equipment
  - Appointments
  - Sleep / meal schedules
- During all transportation exchanges neither parent shall display anger, sarcasm or profanity in the presence of the child(ren).
- Required child(ren)'s belongings will accompany them or be provided to the other parent by a third party.
- Each parent shall ensure each child has adequate clothing and personal effects for the duration of parenting time.
- Each parent shall return each child clean, fed, with the clothes, personal effects, and toys they took with them.

✓ *Check all that apply*

❑ In addition to the parents, the following person(s) may pick up or deliver a child:

_____

❑ Either parent shall be permitted to take the child(ren) on vacation away from their usual residence as allowed by the Highly Structured Parenting Plan time-sharing schedule.

❑ A written itinerary shall be provided to the other parent 30 days prior to the trip or, if a vacation is planned on short notice, as soon as the trip is planned.

❑ Neither parent shall be permitted to take the child(ren) out of the U.S.A. without the written permission of the other parent or a court order.

A. Exchanges:

If Driving, Exchanges Shall Occur: ✓ *Check only one*

❑ The parents shall meet at the following central location, and each shall remain in their vehicle (*e.g., Exit 213 off I-75, police substation*):

Drop-off location:_____

Pick-up location:_____

❑ Other: _____

<u>If the parties don't agree on an exchange location, the following shall apply:</u>   ✓ *Check only one*

❑ Child's

School (specify):_____

❑ Third party's residence
(specify):_____

❑ At law enforcement office
(specify):_____

<u>If Using Public Transportation:</u>   ✓ *Check all that apply*

❑ Cost of transportation of a child to share time with a parent is to be paid by:
  ❑ Mother _____ %   ❑ Father _____%

❑ Cost of transportation of an adult to travel with the child to share time the other parent is to be paid by:
  ❑ Mother _____ %   ❑ Father _____%

❑ The parents agree to meet in the following location:_____

▪ Neither parent shall be more than 30 minutes late without prior notice.

If the parties don't agree on an alternate exchange arrangement, the following plan shall be followed: ✓ *Check all that apply*

❑ The inconvenienced parent will return home with the child(ren) to be picked up by the tardy parent.
❑ The inconvenienced parent shall be entitled to an additional _____ with the child(ren) to be used with prior notice.
❑ The tardy parent will deposit $50 in the child(ren)'s savings account within seven days.

B. <u>Restrictions on Out of Country Travel:</u>   ✓ *Check all that apply*

❑ Is permitted when notice is provided to the other parent _____ days in advance. Such notice shall provide the child(ren)'s itinerary, travel mode, address and contact information for each destination of travel.

❏ Is not permitted without the prior written consent of the other parent. Such consent shall provide the child(ren)'s itinerary, travel mode, address and contact numbers.

❏ Travel is permitted only to countries that are signatory members of the Hague Convention on Civil Aspects of Child Abduction.

15. TIME-SHARING PLAN

Parent "A"_____

Parent "B"_____

Complete blanks above with name of parties.

Fill in which days each Parent (A or B) will spend over night time with the child(ren):

	Monday	Tuesday	Wednesday	Thursday	Friday	Saturday	Sunday
Week One	Parent __	Parent __	Parent __	Parent __	Parent __	Parent __	Parent __
Week Two	Parent __	Parent __	Parent __	Parent __	Parent __	Parent __	Parent __
Week Three	Parent __	Parent __	Parent __	Parent __	Parent __	Parent __	Parent __
Week Four	Parent __	Parent __	Parent __	Parent __	Parent __	Parent __	Parent __

Begins: ✓ *Check beginning time*
   ❏ End of school day

   ❏ _____ P.M.

   ❏ _____ A.M. on the day after the end of school day

Ends: ✓ *Check ending time*

   ❏ Beginning of school day

   ❏ _____ P.M. on the day before beginning of school

DEFAULT TIME-SHARING PLAN

IF THE PARTIES CANNOT AGREE THE FOLLOWING TIME-SHARING PLAN SHALL APPLY:

The child(ren) will spend every other weekend with the Parent A from 6 P.M. on Friday until 6 P.M. on Sunday, and every Wednesday from after school and/or day care until 8 P.M.

This schedule shall be extended to include school holidays and any teacher planning or in-service days where school is not in session that takes place on Friday or Monday. In event of such occurrence, the schedule shall be extended from Thursday 6 P.M. to Monday 6 P.M.

	Monday	Tuesday	Wednesday	Thursday	Friday	Saturday	Sunday
Week One	Parent B	Parent B	Parent A (P.M. only)	Parent B	Parent A	Parent A	Parent B
Week Two	Parent B	Parent B	Parent A (P.M. only)	Parent B	Parent B	Parent B	Parent B
Week Three	Parent B	Parent B	Parent A (P.M. only)	Parent B	Parent A	Parent A	Parent B
Week Four	Parent B	Parent B	Parent A (P.M. only)	Parent B	Parent B	Parent B	Parent B

16. HOLIDAYS, ACADEMIC BREAKS, SIGNIFICANT DAYS

▪ This schedule follows:
Even if your child(ren) are home schooled, or not in school at this time you must: ✓ *Check one.*

❑ Public school calendar (Specify County)

_____

❑ Private school calendar (Specify School)

_____

The calendar is available at: _____

Holiday time-sharing takes priority over regular weekday or week-end visits. ✓ *Check all that apply*

❑ **Martin Luther King Jr. Day**   *School Holiday: Third Monday in January*

  ❑ The ❑ Mother ❑ Father shall have parenting contact for this holiday every year.
  ❑ During even numbered years, the ❑ Mother ❑ Father has parenting contact. The other parent has contact in odd years

  Begins: *Check beginning time*
    ❑ End of school on last day of classes before the holiday
    ❑ _____ A.M. Saturday morning before the holiday
    ❑ _____ A.M. on the holiday
  Ends: *Check ending time*
    ❑ Beginning of school on first day of classes after the holiday
    ❑ _____ P.M. on the holiday

❑ **Presidents' Day**   *Holiday: Third Monday in February*

  ❑ The ❑ Mother ❑ Father shall have parenting contact for this holiday every year.
  ❑ During even numbered years, the ❑ Mother ❑ Father has parenting contact. The other parent has parenting contact in odd years.

  Begins: *Check beginning time*
    ❑ End of school on last day of classes before the holiday
    ❑ _____ A.M. Saturday morning before the holiday
      _____ A.M. on the holiday
  Ends: *Check ending time*
    ❑ Beginning of school on first day of classes after the holiday
    ❑ _____ P.M. on the holiday

❑ **Good Friday/Easter**   *Holiday: March/April*
  ❑ The ❑ Mother ❑ Father shall have parenting contact for this holiday every year.

❑ During even numbered years, the ❑ Mother ❑ Father has parenting contact. The other parent has parenting contact in odd years.

Begins: *Check beginning time*
    ❑ End of school on last day of classes before the holiday
    ❑ _____ A.M. Saturday morning before the holiday.
    ❑ _____ A.M. on the holiday
Ends: *Check ending time*
    ❑ Beginning of school on first day of classes after the holiday
    ❑ _____ P.M. on the holiday

❑ **Passover First Night**   *Holiday: March/April*

❑ The ❑ Mother ❑ Father shall have parenting contact for this holiday every year.

❑ During even numbered years, the ❑ Mother ❑ Father has parenting contact. The other parent has parenting contact in odd years.

Begins: *Check beginning time*
    ❑ End of school on last day of classes before the holiday
    ❑ _____ A.M. morning before the holiday
    ❑ _____ P.M. evening before the holiday
    ❑ _____ A.M. on the holiday

Ends: *Check ending time*
    ❑ Beginning of school on first day of classes after the holiday
    ❑ _____ P.M. on the holiday
    ❑ _____ A.M. morning after the holiday
    ❑ _____ P.M. evening after the holiday

❑ **Passover Second Night**   *Holiday: March/April*

❑ The ❑ Mother ❑ Father shall have parenting contact for this holiday every year.

❑ During even numbered years, the ❑ Mother ❑ Father has parenting contact. The other parent has parenting contact in odd years.

Begins: *Check beginning time*
- ❑ End of school on last day of classes before the holiday
- ❑ _____ A.M. morning before the holiday
- ❑ _____ P.M. evening before the holiday
- ❑ _____ A.M. on the holiday

Ends: *Check ending time*
- ❑ Beginning of school on first day of classes after the holiday
- ❑ _____ P.M. on the holiday
- ❑ _____ A.M. morning after the holiday
- ❑ _____ P.M. evening after the holiday

❑ **Passover Last Night**   *Holiday: March/April*

- ❑ The ❑ Mother ❑ Father shall have parenting contact for this holiday every year.
- ❑ During even numbered years, the ❑ Mother ❑ Father has parenting contact. The other parent has parenting contact in odd years.

Begins: *Check beginning time*
- ❑ End of school on last day of classes before the holiday
- ❑ _____ A.M. morning before the holiday
- ❑ _____ P.M. evening before the holiday
- ❑ _____ A.M. on the holiday

Ends: *Check ending time*
- ❑ Beginning of school on first day of classes after the holiday
- ❑ _____ P.M. on the holiday
- ❑ _____ A.M. morning after the holiday
- ❑ _____ P.M. evening after the holiday

❑ **Spring Break**   *Holiday: Defined by School Calendar*

- ❑ The ❑ Mother ❑ Father shall have parenting contact for this holiday every year.
- ❑ During even numbered years, the ❑ Mother ❑ Father has parenting contact. The other parent has parenting contact in odd years.

Begins: *Check beginning time*
- ❑ End of school on last day of classes before the holiday
- ❑ _____ A.M. Saturday morning before the holiday
- ❑ _____ A.M. on the holiday

Ends: *Check ending time*
- ❑ Beginning of school on first day of classes after the holiday
- ❑ _____ P.M. on the holiday

❑ **Memorial Day**   *Holiday:Last Monday in May*

- ❑ The ❑ Mother ❑ Father shall have parenting contact for this holiday every year.
- ❑ During even numbered years, the ❑ Mother ❑ Father has parenting contact. The other parent has parenting contact in odd years.

Begins: *Check beginning time*
- ❑ End of school on last day of classes before the holiday
- ❑ _____ A.M. Saturday morning before the holiday
- ❑ _____ A.M. on the holiday

Ends: *Check ending time*
- ❑ Beginning of school on first day of classes after the holiday
- ❑ _____ P.M. on the holiday

❑ **Mother's Day**   *Holiday: Second Sunday in May*

Begins: *Check beginning time*
- ❑ End of school on last day of classes before Mother's Day
- ❑ _____ A.M. Saturday morning before Mother's Day
- ❑ _____ A.M. on Mother's Day

Ends: *Check ending time*
- ❑ Beginning of school on first day of classes after Mother's Day
- ❑ _____ P.M. on Mother's Day

❏ **Father's Day**   *Holiday: Third Sunday in June*

> **Begins**: *Check beginning time*
> ❏ End of school on last day of classes before Father's Day
> ❏ _____ A.M. Saturday morning before Father's Day
> ❏ _____ A.M. on Father's day
> **Ends**: *Check ending time*
> ❏ Beginning of school on first day of classes after Father's Day
> ❏ _____ P.M. on Father's Day

❏ **Independence Day**   *Holiday: 4th of July*

> ❏ The ❏ Mother ❏ Father shall have parenting contact for this holiday every year.
> ❏ During even numbered years, the ❏ Mother ❏ Father has parenting contact. The other parent has parenting contact in odd years.

> **Begins**: *Check beginning time*
> ❏ _____ P.M. on the 3rd of July
> ❏ _____ A.M. on the 4th of July
> **Ends**: *Check ending time*
> ❏ _____ P.M. on the 4th of July
> ❏ _____ P.M. on the 5th of July

❏ **Labor Day**   *Holiday: First Monday in September*

> ❏ The ❏ Mother ❏ Father shall have parenting contact for this holiday every year.
> ❏ During even numbered years, the ❏ Mother ❏ Father has parenting contact. The other parent has parenting contact in odd years.

> **Begins**: *Check beginning time*
> ❏ End of school on last day of classes before the holiday
> ❏ _____ A.M. Saturday morning before the holiday
> ❏ _____ A.M. on the holiday

Ends: *Check ending time*
   ❑ Beginning of school on first day of classes after the holiday
   ❑ _____ P.M. on the holiday

❑ **Rosh Hashanah**   *Holiday: September*
   ❑ The ❑ Mother ❑ Father shall have parenting contact for this holiday every year.
   ❑ During even numbered years, the ❑ Mother ❑ Father has parenting contact. The other parent has parenting contact in odd years.

   Begins: *Check beginning time*
      ❑ End of school on last day of classes on the day of Rosh Hashanah.
      ❑ _____ A.M. on the day of Rosh Hashanah Eve
      ❑ _____ P.M. Rosh Hashanah Eve
   Ends: *Check ending time*
      ❑ Beginning of school on first day of classes after Rosh Hashanah
      ❑ _____ P.M. Rosh Hashanah day.
      ❑ _____ A.M. after one overnight, if celebrating on first day only.
      ❑ _____ P.M. after Rosh Hashanah if celebrating after two overnights

---

❑ **Yom Kippur**   *Holiday: September / October*

   ❑ The ❑ Mother ❑ Father shall have parenting contact for this holiday every year.
   ❑ During even numbered years, the ❑ Mother ❑ Father has parenting contact. The other parent has parenting contact in odd years.
   Begins: *Check beginning time*
      ❑ End of school on last day of classes before Yom Kippur
      ❑ _____ A.M. Yom Kippur Eve
      ❑ _____ P.M. Yom Kippur Eve

Ends: *Check ending time*
- ❏ Beginning of school on first day of classes after Yom Kippur
- ❏ _____ P.M. Yom Kippur
- ❏ _____ A.M. morning after Yom Kippur
- ❏ _____ P.M. morning after Yom Kippur

❏ **Columbus Day**   *Holiday: Second Monday in October*

❏ The ❏ Mother ❏ Father shall have parenting contact for this holiday every year.

❏ During even numbered years, the ❏ Mother ❏ Father has parenting contact. The other parent has parenting contact in odd years.

Begins: *Check beginning time*
- ❏ End of school on last day of classes before the holiday
- ❏ _____ A.M. Saturday morning before the holiday
- ❏ _____ A.M. on the holiday

Ends: *Check ending time*
- ❏ Beginning of school on first day of classes after the holiday
- ❏ _____ P.M. on the holiday

❏ **Eid al-Fitr**   *Holiday: Date varies*

❏ The ❏ Mother ❏ Father shall have parenting contact for this entire holiday every year.

❏ During even numbered years, the ❏ Mother ❏ Father has parenting contact. The other parent has parenting contact in odd years.

Time-sharing schedule as follows:
Day 1: Mother ___ A.M. to ___ P.M. Father ___ A.M. to ____ P.M.
Day 2: Mother ___ A.M. to ___ P.M. Father ___ A.M. to ___ P.M.
Day 3: Mother ___ A.M. to ___ P.M. Father ____ A.M. to ____ P.M.

❑ **Eid al-Adha**   *Holiday: Date varies*

❑ The ❑ Mother ❑ Father shall have parenting contact for this holiday every year.

❑ During even numbered years, the ❑ Mother ❑ Father has parenting contact. The other parent has parenting contact in odd years.

Time-sharing schedule as follows:

Day 1: Mother ___ A.M. to ___ P.M. Father ___ A.M. to ____ P.M.
Day 2: Mother ___ A.M. to ___ P.M. Father ___ A.M. to ____ P.M.
Day 3: Mother ___ A.M. to ___ P.M. Father ___ A.M. to ____ P.M.

❑ **October 31st (Halloween)**   *Holiday: 31st of October*

❑ The ❑ Mother ❑ Father shall have parenting contact for this holiday every year.

❑ During even numbered years, the ❑ Mother ❑ Father has parenting contact. The other parent has parenting contact in odd years.

Begins: *Check beginning time*
  ❑ _____ P.M. on 31st of October
Ends: *Check ending time*
  ❑ _____ P.M. on 31st of October
  ❑ Beginning of school on 1st of November or, if no school 9:00 A.M.
  ❑ _____ A.M. on 1st of November

❑ **Thanksgiving**   *Holiday: Fourth Thursday in November*

❑ The ❑ Mother ❑ Father shall have parenting contact for this holiday every year.

❑ During even numbered years, the ❑ Mother ❑ Father has parenting contact. The other parent has parenting contact in odd years.

Begins: *Check beginning time*
  ❑ End of school on last day of classes before the holiday
  ❑ _____ A.M. Wednesday _____ P.M. Wednesday
  ❑ _____ A.M. Thursday _____ P.M. Thursday

Ends: *Check ending time*
- ❑ Beginning of school on first day of classes after the holiday
- ❑ _____ A.M. Thursday _____ P.M. Thursday
- ❑ _____ A.M. Friday _____ P.M. Friday
- ❑ _____ A.M. Sunday _____ P.M. Sunday

❑ **Hanukkah**   *Holiday: December*

- ❑ The ❑ Mother ❑ Father shall have parenting contact for this entire holiday every year.
- ❑ During even numbered years, the ❑ Mother ❑ Father has parenting contact. The other parent has parenting contact in odd years.

Time-sharing schedule as follows:

Day 1: Mother _____ A.M. to _____ P.M.
Father _____ A.M. to _____ P.M.
Day 2: Mother _____ A.M. to _____ P.M.
Father _____ A.M. to _____ P.M.
Day 3: Mother _____ A.M. to _____ P.M.
Father _____ A.M. to _____ P.M.
Day 4: Mother _____ A.M. to _____ P.M.
Father _____ A.M. to _____ P.M.
Day 5: Mother _____ A.M. to _____ P.M.
Father _____ A.M. to _____ P.M.
Day 6: Mother _____ A.M. to _____ P.M.
Father _____ A.M. to _____ P.M.
Day 7: Mother _____ A.M. to _____ P.M.
Father _____ A.M. to _____ P.M.
Day 8: Mother _____ A.M. to _____ P.M.
Father _____ A.M. to _____ P.M.

❑ **Winter Break**   ✓ *Check A, B, or C*

- ❑ **A.** During even numbered years, the ❑ Mother ❑ Father has parenting contact during the half of the Winter break that includes Christmas Day. During odd numbered years, the other parent has the half of the Winter Break that includes Christmas Day.

❑ **B.** Parenting contact will be for the entire Winter Break.

Begins: *Check beginning time*

❑ End of school on last day of classes before the break

❑ _____ A.M. Saturday morning after the last day of classes

❑ _____ A.M. Monday after the last day of classes

Ends: *Check ending time*

❑ _____ Saturday before school resumes

❑ Beginning of school on first day of classes after the holiday

❑ _____ P.M. the night before classes resume

❑ **C.** During even numbered years, the Mother Father has parenting contact during the first half and the other parent shall have the second half of the break. This is reversed in odd years.

First Half

Begins: *Check beginning time*

❑ End of school on last day of classes before the break.

❑ _____ A.M. Saturday morning after the last day of classes.

❑ _____ A.M. Monday after the last day of classes.

Ends: *Check ending time*

❑ If the break has an odd number of days, at 2:00 P.M. on the day after the midpoint date. For example if the break is 13 days, the break ends on 13/2 = 6.5, so the first half ends at 2:00 P.M. on the 7th day.

❑ If the break has an even number of days, at 8:00 P.M. on the midpoint date. For example if the break is 12 days, the break ends on 12/2 = 6, so the first half ends at 8:00 P.M. on the 6th day.

Second Half

Begins: *Check beginning time*

❑ If the break has an odd number of days, at 2:00 P.M. on the day after the midpoint date. For example if the break is 13 days, the break ends on 13/2 = 6.5, so the first half ends at 2:00 P.M. on the 7th day.

❑ If the break has an even number of days, at 8:00 P.M. on the midpoint date. For example if the break is 12 days, the break ends on 12/2 = 6, so the first half ends at 8:00 P.M. on the 6th day.

Ends: *Check ending time*
  ❑ Beginning of school on first day of classes after the holiday.
  ❑ _____ P.M. the night before classes resume.

❑ **Christmas Eve**   *Holiday: 24th of December*

❑ The child remains where the Winter Break schedule specifies, OR

❑ The parents shall follow the following schedule:

❑ The ❑ Mother ❑ Father shall have parenting contact for this holiday every year.

❑ During even numbered years, the ❑ Mother ❑ Father has parenting contact. The other parent has parenting contact in odd years.

 Begins: *Check beginning time*
  ❑ The child remains where the Winter Break schedule specifies.
  ❑ _____ A.M. on 24th of December
  ❑ _____ P.M. on 24th of December
 Ends: *Check ending time*
  ❑ _____ P.M. on 24th of December
  ❑ _____ A.M. on 25th of December

❑ **Christmas Day**   *Holiday: 25th of December*

❑ The child remains where the Winter Break schedule specifies, OR

❑ The parents shall follow the following schedule:

❑ The ❑ Mother ❑ Father shall have parenting contact for this holiday every year.

❑ During even numbered years, the ❑ Mother ❑ Father has parenting contact. The other parent has parenting contact in odd years.

 Begins: *Check beginning time*
  ❑ The child remains where the Winter Break schedule specifies
  ❑ _____ A.M. on 25th of December
  ❑ _____ P.M. on 25th of December

Ends: *Check ending time*
    ❑ _____ P.M. on 25th of December
    ❑ _____ A.M. on 26th of December

❑ **Kwanzaa**   *Holiday: December 26/January 1*

  ❑ The ❑ Mother ❑ Father shall have parenting contact for this holiday every year.

  ❑ During even numbered years, the ❑ Mother ❑ Father has parenting contact. The other parent has parenting contact in odd years.

  ❑ Time-sharing schedule as follows:

Note: The last day of this holiday may conflict with New Year's and Winter Break selection.

Dec. 26: Mother:____ A.M. to _____ P.M.
           Father:____ A.M. to _____ P.M.
Dec. 27: Mother:____ A.M. to _____ P.M.
           Father:____ A.M. to _____ P.M.
Dec. 28: Mother:____ A.M. to _____ P.M.
           Father:____ A.M. to _____ P.M.
Dec. 29: Mother:____ A.M. to _____ P.M.
           Father:____ A.M. to _____ P.M.
Dec. 30: Mother:____ A.M. to _____ P.M.
           Father:____ A.M. to _____ P.M.
Dec. 31: Mother:____ A.M. to _____ P.M.
           Father:____ A.M. to _____ P.M.
Jan. 01: Mother:____ A.M. to _____ P.M.
           Father:____ A.M. to _____ P.M.

❑ **New Year's**   *Holiday: December 31 /January*

  ❑ The ❑ Mother ❑ Father shall have parenting contact for this holiday every year.

  ❑ During even numbered years, the ❑ Mother ❑ Father has parenting contact. The other parent has parenting contact in odd years.

Note: This holiday may conflict with the last day of Kwanzaa.

Begins: *Check beginning time*
    ❏ _____ A.M. / _____ P.M. New Year's Eve
    ❏ _____ A.M. / _____ P.M. New Year's Day
Ends: *Check ending time*
    ❏ _____ P.M. New Year's Day

❏ **Mother's Birthday**   *Specify Date:_____*

Begins: *Check beginning time*
    ❏ _____ pm on Mother's Birthday
Ends: *Check ending time*
    ❏ _____ P.M. on Mother's Birthday
    ❏ _____ A.M. the day after the Mother's birthday or at the start of classes the day after the Mother's birthday

---

❏ **Father's Birthday**   *Specify Date:_____*

Begins: *Check beginning time*
    ❏ _____ P.M. on Father's Birthday
Ends: *Check ending time*
    ❏ _____ P.M. on Father's Birthday
    ❏ _____ A.M. the day after the Father's birthday or at the start of classes the day after the Father's birthday

---

❏ **Child(ren)'s Birthday**

Begins: _____ A.M. Child(ren)'s Birthday (Specify Child(ren)'s Name and Date)
    ❏ _____ P.M. Child(ren)'s Birthday

Ends: *Check ending time*

    ❏ _____ A.M. Child(ren)'s Birthday

    ❏ _____ P.M. Child(ren)'s Birthday

    ❏ _____ A.M. Child(ren)'s the day after the birthday

❑ Other Significant Dates: _____

   Begins: _____

   Ends: _____

❑ Other Significant Dates: _____

   Begins: _____

   Ends: _____

EASY REFERENCE CHART

Write Father or Mother only in the periods that apply.
For specific days and times see above.

	Even Years	Odd Years	Every Year
Martin Luther King Jr. Day			
Presidents' Day			
Good Friday			
Easter			
Passover 1st Night			
Passover 2nd Night			
Passover Last Night			
Spring Break			
Memorial Day			
Mother's Day			
Father's Day			
Independence Day			
Labor Day			
Rosh Hashanah			
Yom Kippur			
Columbus Day			

	Even Years	Odd Years	Every Year
Eid al-Fitr Day 1			
Eid al-Fitr Day 2			
Eid al-Fitr Day 3			
Eid al-Adha Day 1			
Eid al-Adha Day 2			
Eid al-Adha Day 3			
October 31			
Thanksgiving			
Hanukkah Day 1			
Hanukkah Day 2			
Hanukkah Day 3			
Hanukkah Day 4			
Hanukkah Day 5			
Hanukkah Day 6			
Hanukkah Day 7			
Hanukkah Day 8			
Winter Break—A			
Winter Break—B			
Winter Break—C			

	Even Years	Odd Years	Every Year
December 24			
December 25			
Kwanzaa December 26			
Kwanzaa December 27			
Kwanzaa December 28			
Kwanzaa December 29			
Kwanzaa December 30			
Kwanzaa December 31			
Kwanzaa January 1			
New Year's Day			
Mother's Birthday			
Father's Birthday			
Child(ren)'s Birthday			
Child(ren)'s Birthday			
Child(ren)'s Birthday			
Child(ren)'s Birthday			
Child(ren)'s Birthday			
Other Holiday			
Other Holiday			

■ DEFAULT HOLIDAY PLAN

IF THE PARTIES CANNOT AGREE THE FOLLOWING SHALL APPLY:

1. <u>In Even Years</u> Parent A shall have the child(ren) for the following holidays:
   Christmas/Winter Holiday—Beginning at 9 A.M. on the day after school ends for seven (7) continuous days.
   Thanksgiving Vacation—No time-sharing.
   Spring Break—Beginning at 9 A.M. on the day after school ends for seven continuous days.
   Other Holidays—If there is one special religious holiday (other than Christmas) that falls into this category, contact shall take place from 7 P.M. the day before the holiday until 6 P.M. on the holiday. If there is more than one special religious holiday, the parents shall alternate and contact shall take place from 7 P.M. the day before the holiday until 6 P.M. on the holiday.
   Parent A shall the child(ren) for Martin Luther King Jr. Day, Good Friday, 4th of July, and October 31, beginning 9 A.M. on the day of the holiday until 9 A.M. the next day or until the time school begins, whichever is earliest.
   The Parent B shall have the child(ren) for Presidents' Day, Memorial Day, and Labor Day, beginning 9 A.M. on the day of the holiday until 9 A.M. the next day or until the time school begins, whichever is earliest.

2. <u>In Odd Years</u> Parent A shall have the child(ren) for the following holidays:
   Christmas/Winter Holiday—Beginning at 9 A.M. on the seventh day after school ends for the holiday break, for seven (7) continuous days.
   Thanksgiving Vacation—Beginning at 9 A.M. on the day after school ends until 6 P.M. on Sunday.
   Spring Break—No contact.
   Other Holidays—If there is one special religious holiday (other than Christmas) that falls into this category, contact shall take place from 7 P.M. the day before the holiday until 6 P.M. on the holiday. If there is more than one special religious holiday, the parents shall alternate and contact shall take place from 7 P.M. the day before the holiday until 6 P.M. on the holiday.

Parent B shall the child(ren) for Martin Luther King Jr. Day, Good Friday, 4th of July and October 31, beginning 9 A.M. on the day of the holiday until 9 A.M. the next day or until the time school begins, whichever is earliest.

Parent A shall have the child(ren) for Presidents' Day, Memorial Day and Labor Day, beginning 9 A.M. on the day of the holiday until 9 A.M. the next day or until the time school begins, whichever is earliest.

3. <u>Every Year</u> the Mother shall have the child(ren) on Mother's Day and the Father shall have the child(ren) on Father's Day. This holiday visit shall begin on Saturday at noon and end at 6 P.M. on Sunday.

17. SUMMER TIME-SHARING

▪ The summer period is defined as starting on the last day of regularly scheduled classes of one school year and ending on the first day of regularly scheduled classes of the next school year.

❑ The parents will keep the ongoing parent contact schedule during summer breaks.

❑ The child(ren) shall spend the month of _____ with: ✓ *Check one*

❑ Parent A

❑ Parent B

❑ The child(ren) shall spend the entire summer vacation, except for the first week and the last 2 weeks of vacation with: ✓ *Check one*

❑ Parent A

❑ Parent B

❑ The child(ren) shall spend _____ weeks of summer vacation with: ✓ *Check one*

❑ Parent A

❑ Parent B

In order to have first choice, this Parent (*specify A or B*)_____ shall provide Parent (*specify A or B*) _____ a date schedule for the summer by April 15th of each year. Otherwise, Parent (*specify A or B*) _____ will have first choice.

❑ The parents have agreed upon the following summer contact schedule:

_____

_____

_____

_____

▪ **Parents shall make alternate arrangements within 2 weeks after the summer school schedule is determined if the child(ren) must attend a summer academic program mandated by the child(ren)'s school district, as follows:** ✓ *Check all that apply*

❑ The child(ren) shall attend summer school in the same district where school is attended during the school year.

❑ The child(ren) shall attend summer school in (specify district)_____school district so long as the child(ren)'s home school district approves it. It shall be the responsibility of Parent (*specify A or B*)_____ to secure approval from the home school district and enroll the child(ren) in summer school in their district prior to scheduling the child(ren)'s alternate summer contact. Parent (*specify A or B*)_____ shall provide the other parent with documentation establishing approval and enrollment if requested.

❑ If the child(ren) must attend summer school, and it limits either parent's contact time, the party who is negatively affected shall be entitled to make–up time over the next twelve months.

18. OPTIONAL TO CONSIDER

If the parents wish to add additional items to their parenting plan, please specify below:

For Example:

Names—*Do the parents agree that only they are to be called "mother" or "father" or like names?*

Driving—*Do the parents agree at what age the child(ren) will drive (jet skies, cars, motorcycles, ATV's)?*

Employment—*Do the parents consent to, and agree as to what age, the child(ren) may be employed?*

Passports—*Do the parents agree the child(ren) can or cannot get a passport?*

Images of the child(ren)—*Are there any restrictions on the child(ren)'s images on internet sites, MySpace, Facebook, etc?*

Cosmetic Surgery/Tattoos/Piercing/Body—*Do the parents consent to these?*

Extended Family—*Do the parents want access for extended family members?*

Special Events—*Are there special family events that need to be agreed upon by the parents?*

No Contact—*Do the parents want to prevent the child's contact with any third parties?*

A. Before _____ the parents must: ❑ Notify the other parent ❑ Agree ❑ Agree in writing.

B. Before _____ the parents must: ❑ Notify the other parent ❑ Agree ❑ Agree in writing.

C. Before _____ the parents must: ❑ Notify the other parent ❑ Agree ❑ Agree in writing.

D. Before _____ the parents must: ❑ Notify the other parent ❑ Agree ❑ Agree in writing.

E. Before _____ the parents must: ❑ Notify the other parent ❑ Agree ❑ Agree in writing.

F. Before _____ the parents must: ❑ Notify the other parent ❑ Agree ❑ Agree in writing.

G. Before _____ the parents must: ❑ Notify the other parent ❑ Agree ❑ Agree in writing.

19. DEPENDENCY EXEMPTION

The dependency exemption for the minor child(ren) shall be assigned to:

- ❏ The Mother
- ❏ The Father
- ❏ The Mother in even numbered years, and the Father in odd number years
- ❏ The Father in even number years, and the Mother in odd number years
- ❏ Divided evenly between the Mother and the Father
- ❏ Other:_____

_____

_____

OTHER (Anything else you want to agree on. Include accommodations for a child's special needs, age, etc.)

_____

_____

INFORMATION SHARING

- ▪ Each parent shall keep the other informed of their current contact information (address, telephone and cell numbers) and inform the other of any change in writing within 3 days.
- ▪ Each parent shall provide the other parent with the contact information for the child's school, sports, extracurricular and religious activities within 3 days of getting that information. Thereafter, it shall be the other parent's responsibility to stay informed of the child's events and activities.

This is part of a Court Order when attached to a signed Judgment. Each party has been put on notice that an intentional failure to follow the rules or a direct violation of this parenting plan is punishable through the contempt of powers of the court. In addition, if the violation poses an immediate threat to the child(ren), the specific parenting time may be stopped by the court. One parent's failure to comply with the rules does not excuse theother party from following the rules.

PARENT INFORMATION

_____   _____
PRINT MOTHER'S NAME   HOME PHONE

_____   _____
STREET ADDRESS   WORK PHONE

_____   _____
CITY, STATE AND ZIP CODE   CELL PHONE

❏ SUBSTITUTE ADDRESS: CHECK BOX   _____
IF YOU HAVE WRITTEN SOMEONE   SUBSTITUTE PHONE NUMBER
ELSE'S ADDRESS BECAUSE YOU FEAR
HARASSMENT OR HARM.

_____   _____
PRINT FATHER'S NAME   HOME PHONE

_____   _____
STREET ADDRESS   WORK PHONE

_____   _____
CITY, STATE AND ZIP CODE   CELL PHONE

❏ SUBSTITUTE ADDRESS: CHECK BOX   _____
IF YOU HAVE WRITTEN SOMEONE   SUBSTITUTE PHONE NUMBER
ELSE'S ADDRESS BECAUSE YOU FEAR
HARASSMENT OR HARM.

By signing this Parenting Plan, I confirm that I have read all of the pages and any attachments, I understand it and I believe that it is in the best interest of my child(ren). I am freely and voluntarily entering into this Agreement and I request that the Judge approve it.

Date Signed: _____   _____
                                  Signature of Mother

_____   _____
Witness   Witness

STATE OF FLORIDA
COUNTY OF _____

I HEREBY CERTIFY that on this day personally appeared before me, an officer duly authorized to administer oaths and take acknowledgements, _____ (MOTHER'S NAME), to me well known to be the person described in or who produced a Florida Driver's License as identification, who executed the foregoing Parenting Plan and acknowledged before me that she executed the same freely and voluntarily and for the purpose therein expressed. WITNESS my hand and official seal in the County and State last aforesaid this _____ day of _____, 20___.

Notary Seal: Notary Signature: _____

By signing this Parenting Plan, I confirm that I have read all of the pages and any attachments, I understand it and I believe that it is in the best interest of my child(ren). I am freely and voluntarily entering into this Agreement and I request that the Judge approve it.

Date Signed:

_____   _____
                                 Signature of Father

_____   _____
Witness   Witness

STATE OF FLORIDA
COUNTY OF _____

I HEREBY CERTIFY that on this day personally appeared before me, an officer duly authorized to administer oaths and take acknowledgements, _____(FATHER'S NAME), to me well known to be the person described in or who produced a Florida Driver's License as identification, who executed the foregoing Parenting Plan and acknowledged before me that she executed the same freely and voluntarily and for the purpose therein expressed. WITNESS my hand and official seal in the County and State last aforesaid this _____ day of _____, 20___.

Notary Seal: Notary Signature: _____

Appendix C

Sample Professional Services Agreement

AGREEMENT BETWEEN_____, AND _____ CLIENT, AND <u>NATIONAL COOPERATIVE PARENTING CENTER (NCPC),</u> CONSULTANT, *REGARDING PARENTING COORDINATION FOR THE MINOR CHILD(REN).*

NCPC agrees to serve as a Parenting Coordinator for the above parties and their minor children in an effort to assist the parties and the children, to promote the children's rights to access to both parents; and to protect the children's best interest in general. NCPC shall be entitled to communicate with the parties, children or any other persons deemed necessary to protect the best interests of the children. The parties will cooperate with NCPC including signing any and all releases of information requested by NCPC for this purpose.

NCPC, as a Parenting Coordinator, has broad responsibilities including:

1. Creating approaches to carrying out a parenting plan that reduces the conflict between the parents;
2. Monitoring any parenting plan or parenting schedule and helping resolve the parent's disputes concerning the plan or schedule of parenting issues;
3. Teaching communication skills, principles of child development and issues facing children when their parents no longer live together;
4. Writing detailed guidelines or rules for communication between the parents and practicing those guidelines or rules with the parents, if necessary. If parenting skills are lacking, the consultant will work with one or both parents to teach those skills;
5. Modifying a parenting plan or parenting schedule when the parents agree to the modification. If an agreement cannot be reached, the family consultant will make recommendations to the parties and their counsel, if necessary, on the changes to the parenting plan or schedule that are recommended;
6. Deciding how a particular element of a parenting plan or parenting schedule will be implemented including, without limitation, the frequency and length of visitation, temporary changes in the

parenting schedule, holiday or vacation planning, logistics of pick up and drop off, suitability of accommodations and issues dealing with the stepparents and significant others;

7. Working with both parents to update and fine tune their parenting schedule over time.

NCPC, as Parenting Coordinator, will maintain communication amongst the parties by serving, if necessary, as a conduit for information. NCPC is not the ally of either parent and is not a neutral mediator. NCPC's role is active and specifically focused on helping parents work together for the benefit of their children. NCPC's fundamental aim is to minimize the conflict to which the children are exposed by continuing hostilities between the parties.

NCPC is not a parenting evaluator. Making the decision about where to place the children most of the time would seriously compromise the family consultant's neutrality. The Parenting Coordinator does not have the power to change the primary residence of the children. NCPC will also not be called as a witness in any court proceedings regarding change of primary residence.

Assistance provided by the Parenting Coordinator is not intended to be a crisis service and the consultant should not be contacted outside of normal working hours. Issues will be brought to the consultant in the ordinary course of business. The Parenting Coordinator's role is to assist the parties in making decisions by teaching both parents resolution techniques and keeping the children in a neutral position in the conflict.

Significant financial matters will not be addressed by the Parenting Coordinator.

The Parenting Coordinator will educate both parents about the sources of their conflict and its effect on the children. Both parents should understand what constitutes a "loyalty bind"; that is, a child being caught in the middle between both parents. When a loyalty bind is occurring, the Parenting Coordinator will point it out and help both parents stop the behavior leading to this dilemma for the children. NCPC, as Parenting Coordinator, will help both parents accept the relevance of the other parent in their children's lives and understand the serious emotional consequences of losing a parent.

The Parenting Coordinator will work with both parents, the children and with others when necessary to observe their communication styles, including any aggressive or defensive attitudes. The Parenting

Coordinator may meet with the parties or the children jointly or separately. The Parenting Coordinator shall determine whether appointments will be joint or separate, by telephone or in person.

Both parents will contact the Parenting Coordinator to schedule and arrange convenient times for meetings with the Parenting Coordinator. Appointments may be scheduled at the request of either parent; however, the Parenting Coordinator will decide when appointments are necessary.

Each parent should direct any disagreements regarding the children to the Parenting Coordinator. The Parenting Coordinator will work with both parents to resolve the conflict and, if necessary, will make a recommendation to the parties' counsel and, if necessary, to the Court.

I have read the above and agree to proceed with parenting coordination services. I, _____ agree to pay **50%** of the retainer consultation fees; and I, _____ agree to pay **50%** of the retainer and consultation fees.

NCPC requires a $1,600.00 retainer in advance of services commencing. Fees will be drawn against this retainer. If the retainer becomes depleted, an additional $1,600.00 will be required before services continue. The fee for Parenting Coordinator is $200.00 for a 1-hour session. All fees and expenses shall be due and paid immediately upon billing. Any amount due, but not paid on the first day of the month at least thirty (30) days subsequent to the billing, shall incur interest at the rate of eighteen per cent (18%) per annum and computed monthly. A lien for the amount of the fee and expenses advanced shall exist in favor of the said Parenting Coordinator, and said lien continues if said Parenting Coordinator is discharged. Failure to pay any amount billed within thirty (30) days will be the basis for the Parenting Coordinator to withdraw from further services, and to do so without objection or complaint from the Client.

APPOINTMENTS NOT CANCELED WITHIN 24 HOURS WILL
RESULT IN A CHARGE FOR THE TIME RESERVED TO
THE CLIENT WHO CANCELED.

_____   _____

Date

_____   _____

Date

_____   _____

Dr. Debra K. Carter, Ph.D. CEO   **Date**

For NCPC (NCPC)

Appendix D

Conflict Identification Questionnaire

NCPC The National Cooperative Parenting Center

Screening Questionnaire for Parent Coordination Services

Name_____ Home Telephone_____
Address_____ Work Telephone_____
What year did you marry? _____ Separate?_____ Divorce? _____
Please list the names, ages and dates of birth of your children:

NAME	AGE	DOB

1. Please rate your current relationship with your child(ren)'s other parent, check one:

   Hostile/Frightening ❑ Bitter/Angry ❑ Distant/Cold ❑ Polite/Respectful ❑ Friendly ❑

2. Please check all the issues, events, or situations which cause problems when you and the child(ren)'s other parent share parenting responsibilities:

   ❑ who pays for what ❑ putting children's needs first

   ❑ pick up/drop-off time ❑ making decisions about school

❑ different standards (e.g., cleanliness, dress) ❑ buyingnecessities
for kids

❑ buying gifts for kids

❑ discipline ❑ vacation time

❑ curfew ❑ stepparent or live-in lover

❑ school performance ❑ wanting more flexibility

❑ last minute changes in schedule ❑ wanting more structure

❑ relationships with in-laws ❑ attendance at school functions (con
(grandparents)   ferences, plays, games)

❑ your ex's personal habits ❑ activities in which your ex involves
(e.g., drinking, cursing)   the children

❑ religious difference ❑ crisis management (e.g., the child has a
problem)

❑ different ideas about seeking medical treatment for child(ren)

❑ division of parenting time

❑ things that bothered you when ❑ your ex's dating habits
you were married

❑ different ideas about diet and exercise for child(ren)

3. I respect the mother/father of my child(ren) as a parent:

Never	Rarely	Sometimes	Usually	Always

4. If I don't agree with my child(ren)'s other parent's approach to child rearing, I can accept that we are different and still support him/her:

Never	Rarely	Sometimes	Usually	Always

5. I restrain myself from talking badly about my child(ren)'s other parent in front of the child(ren):

Never	Rarely	Sometimes	Usually	Always

6. I believe my child(ren)'s other parent restrains him or herself from speaking badly about me in front of the child(ren):

Never	Rarely	Sometimes	Usually	Always

7. I discuss with my child(ren)'s other parent issues which are relevant to the child(ren) (i.e., medical, educational, extracurricular activities, sports activities, family events, awards, etc.):

Never	Rarely	Sometimes	Usually	Always

8. My child(ren)'s other parent is willing to discuss with me any issues which are relevant to the child(ren):

Never	Rarely	Sometimes	Usually	Always

9. I think it is important for my child(ren) to maintain regular contact with their other parent and his/her family (i.e., grandparents) no matter what I think of them:

Never	Rarely	Sometimes	Usually	Always

10. I believe my child(ren)'s other parent feels it is important for my child(ren) to maintain regular contact with me and my extended family no matter what she/he thinks of us:

Never	Rarely	Sometimes	Usually	Always

I would be interested in the following services:

❑ Parent Coordinator ❑ Social Investigation and Parenting Plan Recommendation

❑ Parent Education ❑ Personal/Family Therapy

❑ Mediation ❑ Evaluation to assess needs of child(ren)

❑ Therapy for child(ren)

Scoring Criteria

1. For item #1: if either of the first two choices are marked (Hostile/ Frightening or Bitter/Angry), services are recommended.
2. For item #2: if eight or more items are checked, then services are recommended.
3. If never, rarely, or sometimes is checked for any of items 5 through 10, then services are recommended.
4. Any other services requested at the end of the questionnaire may also be recommended.

Appendix E

Sample Parenting Coordination Report to the Court

Parenting Coordinator Report

Dated the _____day of _____, 201_

Conducted by:_____

Case Name:

In the County of:

Case Number: DR-

Judge Appointing Parenting Coordinator:

Attorneys of Record:

Child(ren):

Dates of Appointments:

Number of hours spent on this case since last report:

Scope of Parenting Coordinator's Authority as Spelled Out in the Order Appointing Parenting Coordinator:

Issues, Observations, and Discussions from Sessions:

Issues Resolved by Consent and Agreement of the Parties:

Issues Resolved by Decision of the Parenting Coordinator, (10 day right to object—or becomes an "Order of the Court"):

Recommendations by the Parenting Coordinator:

Issues To Be Addressed in the Next Session(s):

Next Session To Be Held:

Dated this___day of _____, 201_.

Submitted Respectfully,

Court Appointed Parenting Coordinator

Certificate of Mailing

The undersigned hereby certifies that the above and forgoing Parent Coordinator report was mailed with proper postage thereon to the following: Court Clerk; Plaintiff; Defendant; Other parties; Attorney for the Plaintiff; Attorney for the Defendant.

_____

Parent Coordinator

Bibliography

Ackerman, M. J. (1997). *Does Wednesday mean mom's house or dad's?* New York: John Wiley & Sons.

Ahrons, C. (1995). *The good divorce.* New York: Harper Perennial.

Ainsworth, M. D. S., Bell, S. M., & Stayton, D. (1974). Infant–mother attachment and social development. In M. P. Richards (Ed.), *The introduction of the child into a social world* (pp. 99–135). London: Cambridge University Press.

Ainsworth, M. D. S., & Wittig, B. A. (1969). Attachment and the exploratory behaviour of one-year-olds in a strange situation. In B. M. Foss (Ed.), *Determinants of infant behaviour* (Vol. 4, pp. 113–136), London: Methuen.

Amato, P. R. (1983). Children's adjustment to divorce: Theories, hypotheses and empirical support. *Journal of Marriage and Family, 55,* 23–38.

Amato, P. R. (1994). Life-span adjustment of children to their parents' divorce. *Future of Children, 4*(1), 143–164.

Amato, P. R. (2000). The consequences of divorce for adults and children. *Journal of Marriage and Family, 62,* 1269–1287.

Amato, P. R. (2001). Children of divorce in the 1990s: An update from Amato and Keith (1991) meta-analysis. *Journal of Family Psychology, 15,* 355–370.

Amato, P. R. (2003). Reconciling divergent perspectives: Judith Wallerstein, quantitative family research and children of divorce. *Family Relations, 52,* 322–339.

Amato, P. R. (2005). The impact of family formation change on the cognitive, social, and emotional well-being of the next generation. *The Future of the Children, 15*(2), 75–96. Retrieved from www.futureofchildren.org

Amato, P. R., & Fowler, F. (2002). Parenting practices, child adjustment, and family diversity. *Journal of Marriage and Family, 64,* 703–716.

Amato, P. R., & Gilbreth, J. G. (1999). Nonresident fathers and children's well-being: A meta-analysis. *Journal of Marriage and Family, 61,* 557–573.

Amato, P. R., & Keith, B. (1991). Parental divorce and the well-being of children: A meta-analysis. *Psychological Bulletin, 110*(1), 26–46.

American Academy of Child and Adolescent Psychiatry. (1997). *Practice parameters for child custody evaluation.* Retrieved from http://www.aacap.org/galleries/practiceparameters/custody.pdf

American Arbitration Association, American Bar Association's Section of Dispute Resolution, & Association for Conflict Resolution. (2005). *Model standards of conduct for mediators* (Rev. ed.). Retrieved from http://www.abanet.org/dispute/documents/model_standards_conduct_april2007.pdf

American Bar Association. (2002). *Model rules of professional conduct.*

American Bar Association. (2004). *Family legal guide* (3rd ed.). Retrieved from http://www.abanet.org/publiced/practical/books/family_legal_guide/home.html

American Psychiatric Association. (2000). *Diagnostic and statistical manual of mental disorders (DSM-IV-TR)*. Arlington, VA: American Psychiatric Publishing.

American Psychological Association. (1996). *Violence and the family: Report of the American Psychological Association Presidential task force on Violence and the family.*

American Psychological Association. (2002). *Ethical principles of psychologists and code of conduct.* Retrieved from www.apa.org/ethics/code/index .aspx

American Psychological Association. (2007). Record keeping guidelines. *American Psychologist, 62*(9), 993–1004.

American Psychological Association. (2009). *Guidelines for child custody evaluations in family law proceedings.* Retrieved from www.apa.org/practice/ guidelines/child-custody.pdf

American Psychology-Law Society and Division 41 of the American Psychological Association. (1991). *Specialty guidelines for forensic psychologists.* Retrieved from http://www.ap-ls.org/links/currentforensicguidelines.pdf

Association of Family and Conciliation Courts. (2005). *Guidelines for parenting coordination—AFCC task force on parenting coordination.* Retrieved from www.afccnet.org

Association of Family and Conciliation Courts Guidelines for Parenting Coordination (2005) www.afccnet.org/pdfs/AFCCGuidelinesforParenting coordinationnew.pdf

Association of Family and Conciliation Courts. (2006). *Model standards of practice for child custody evaluations.* Retrieved from http://www.afccnet.org/ pdfs/Model Standards of Practice for Child Custody Evaluation May 2006.pdf

Ayoub, C., Deutsch, R., & Maraganore, N. (1999). Emotional distress in children of high conflict divorce: The impact of marital conflict and violence. *Family and Conciliation Courts Review, 39,* 297–313.

Azar, Edward E. (1990). *The management of protracted social conflict: Theory and cases.* Aldershot, Hampshire, England and Brookfield, VT: Dartmouth.

Bacher, N., Fieldstone, L., & Jonasz, J. (2005). The role of parenting coordination in the family law arena. *Journal of American Family Law, 19*(2), 84–96.

Bacon, B. L., & McKenzie, B. (2004). Parent education after separation/ divorce: Impact of the level of parental conflict on outcomes. *Family Court Review, 45,* 85–98.

Baker, A. J. (2005). The long term effects of parental alienation on adult children: A qualitative research study. *American Journal of Family Therapy, 33,* 289–302.

Barash, D. P., & Webel, C. P. (2002). *Peace and conflict studies* (p. 234). California: Sage Publications.

Baris, M., Coates, C., Duvall, B., Garity, C., Johnson, E., & LaCrosse, E. (2001). *Working with high conflict families of divorce: A guide for professionals.* New Jersey: Jason Aronson Publishers.

Bartlett, B. (2006). Parenting coordination: A new tool for assisting high–conflict families. *Oklahoma Bar Journal.* Retrieved from http://www.okbar.org/objarticles_04/021404.htm

Bartos, O. J., & Wehr, P. (2002). *Using conflict theory* (p. 41). New York: Cambridge University Press.

Baucom, D. H., & Gordon, K. C. (2003). Forgiveness and marriage. *The American Journal of Family Therapy, 31*(3), 179–200.

Baumeister, R. F., Smart, L., & Boden, J. M. (1996). Relation of threatened egotism to violence and aggression: The dark side of high self-esteem. *Psychological Review, 103*, 5–33.

Bauserman, R. (2002). Child adjustment in joint-custody versus sole-custody arrangements: A meta-analysis review. *Journal of Family Psychology, 16*(1), 91–102.

Beck, C. J. A., Putterman, M. D., Sbarra, D. A., & Mehl, M. R. (2008). Parenting coordination roles, program goals and services provided: Insights from the Pima County, Arizona program. *Journal of Child Custody, 5*(1/2), 122–139.

Bender, W. N. (1994). Joint custody: The option of choice. *Journal of Divorce and Remarriage, 21*, 115–131.

Benedek, E. P., & Brown, C. F. (1995). *How to help your child overcome your divorce.* Washington, DC: American Psychiatric Press.

Bennett, D. S. (1996). Security, bargaining, and the end of interstate rivalry. *International Studies Quarterly, 40*, 157–184.

Berk, L. (1991). *Child development.* Boston: Allyn & Bacon.

Berman, W. H., & Sperling, M. B. (1994). *Attachment in adults.* New York: The Guilford Press.

Bernstein, A. (2007). Re-visioning, restructuring, and reconciliation: Clinical practice with complex postdivorce families. *Family Process, 46*(1), 67–78.

Beyer, R., & Winchester, K. (2001). *Juggling act: Handling divorce without dropping the ball.* Minneapolis, MN: Free Spirit Publishing.

Biringin, Z., & Howard, W. (2002). Adult attachment and couple psychotherapy: Secure Base in Practice and Research. In C. Clulow (Ed.), *Couple & relationship therapy* (Vol. 1, pp. 96–99). London, UK: Routledge.

Birnbaum, R., & Fidler, B. J. (2005). Commentary on Epstein and Madsen's Joint custody with a vengeance: The emergence of parallel parenting orders. *Canadian Family Law Quarterly, 24*, 337–349.

Blau, M. (1993). *Families apart: Ten keys to successful co-parenting.* New York: G.P. Putnam's Sons.

Bonnet, G. (2005). *International dictionary of psychoanalysis.* Michigan, IN: Thomas Gale.

Bordow, S., & Gibson, J. (1994). *Evaluation of the family court mediation service.* Sydney, Australia: Family Court of Australia Research and Evaluation Unit.

Bowlby, J. (1969). *Attachment and loss: Vol. 1. Attachment.* New York: Basic Books.

Bowlby, J. (1973). *Attachment and loss: Vol. 2. Separation, anxiety and anger.* New York: Basic Books.

Bowlby, J. (1988). *A secure base: Parentchild attachment and healthy human development*. New York: Basic Books.

Boyan, S. M., & Temini, A. (2004). *The psychotherapist as parenting coordinator in high conflict divorce: Strategies and techniques*. New York: The Haworth Clinical Practice Press.

Boyan, S., & Termini, A. (1999). *Cooperative parenting and divorce: A parent guide to effective coparenting*. Retrieved from www.cooperativeparenting.com

Brahm, E. (2003). Phases of conflict. In G. Burgess & H. Burgess (Eds.). *Beyond intractability*. University of Colorado, Boulder, CO: Conflict Research Consortium.

Braver, S. L., Ellman, I. M., & Fabricius, W. V. (2003). Relocation of children after divorce and children's best interests: New evidence and legal considerations. Tempe, Arizona. *Journal of Family Psychology, 17*(2), 206–219.

Braver, S. L., & O'Connell, D. (1998). *Divorced dads*. New York: Penguin Putnam.

Bray, J. H., & Kelly, J. (1999). *Step families*. Broadway, NY: Broadway Books.

Bridges, A. J., Faust, D., & Ahern, D. C. (2009). Methods for the identification of sexually abused children: Reframing the clinician's task and recognizing disparity with research on indicators. In K. Kuehnle and M. Connell (Eds.), *The evaluation of child sexual abuse allegations* (pp.21–48). Hoboken, NJ: Wiley.

Brisch, K. H. (2002). *Treating attachment disorders: From theory to therapy*. New York: Guilford Press.

Brown, G. W., & Harris, T. O. (1989). *Life events and illness*. New York: Guilford Press.

Brown, N. (2008). *Children of the self-absorbed: a grown-up's guide to getting over narcissistic parents* (2nd ed.). California: New Harbinger Publications.

Brown, T. (2003). Fathers and child abuse allegations in the context of parental separation and divorce. *Family Court Review, 41*, 367–380.

Brown, T., Frederico, M., Hewitt, L., & Sheehan, R. (1998). Problems and solutions in the management of child abuse allegations in custody and access disputes in the family court. *Family Court Review, 36*(4), 431–443.

Brown, T., Frederico, M., Hewitt, L., & Sheehan, R. (2001). The child abuse and divorce myth. *Child Abuse Review, 10*, 113–124.

Buchanan, C. M. (1996). *Adolescents after divorce*. Cambridge, MA: Harvard University Press.

Buchanan, C. M., Maccoby, E., & Dornbusch, S. M. (1991). The parenting of adolescents and adolescents as parents. Retrieved from http://parenthood.library.wisc.edu/Lemer/Lemer.html

Burgess, H. (2004). Parties to intractable conflict. In G. Burgess & H. Burgess (Eds.), *Beyond intractability*. University of Colorado, Boulder, CO: Conflict Research Consortium. Retrieved from http://www.beyondintractability.org/essay/parties/

Burton, J. (1990). *Conflict resolution and prevention*. New York: St. Martin's Press.

Campbell, L. E., & Johnston, J. R. (1988). *Impasses of divorce: The dynamics and resolution of family conflict*. New York: Collier Macmillan Publishers.

Carlson, M. J., & Corcoran, M. E. (2001). Family structure and children's behavioral and cognitive outcomes. *Journal of Marriage and Family, 63*(3), 779–792.

Carter, D. K. (2009). *Best interest of children: Primary roles of parenting coordinators. Good Practice,* DC: American Psychological Association.

Carter, D. K., Bruce, E., Pine Farber, L., Fieldstone, L., Moreland, D., Moring, J., et al. (2010). *Empirically based parenting plans: What professionals need to know.* Sarasota, FL: Professional Resource Press.

Carter, D. K., & Fieldstone, L. (2006). Parenting Coordination: Promote Peace Accord for High Conflict Family Cases, *ACResolution,* Academy of Conflict Resolution, Fall.

Carter, D. K., & Harari, C. (2008). Addressing Myths, Misunderstandings, and Dilemmas About Parenting Coordination. *The Commentator,* Vol. XXIII, No. 1, Family Law Section of The Florida Bar.

Carter, S., Haave, B., & Vandersteen, S. (2008). Family restructuring therapy: Working with high conflict parents and angry children. Workshop presented at the 45th Annual Conference, Association of Family and Conciliation Courts, Vancouver, Canada.

Cashmore, J., Parkinson, P., & Taylor, A. (2008). Overnight stays and children's relationships with resident and nonresident parents after divorce. *Journal of Family Issues, 29*(6), 707–733.

Cassese, A. (1990). *Human rights in a changing world* (p. 63). Philadelphia: Temple University Press.

Cawson, P. (2002). *Child maltreatment in the family: The experience of a national sample of young people.* London: NSPCC.

Cawson, P., Wattam, C., Brooker, S., & Kelly, G. (2000). *Child maltreatment in the United Kingdom: A study of the prevalence of child abuse and neglect* (p. 83). London: NSPCC.

Ceci, S., & Bruck, M. (1995). *Jeopardy in the courtroom: A scientific analysis of children's testimony.* Washington, DC: American Psychological Association.

Child Welfare League of America. (2008). *The relationship between alcohol and other drugs and the child welfare system.* Retrieved from http://www.cwla.org/programs/bhd/aodbrief.htm

Clarke-Stewart, A., & Brentano, A. (2006). *Divorce: Causes and consequences.* New Haven, CT: Yale University Press.

Coates, C. (2003). Parenting coordination: Implementation issues. *Family Court Review, 41*(4), 533–564. Retrieved from afcc@afccnet.org.

Coates, C. A., Deutsch, R., Starnes, H., Sullivan, M. J., & Sydlik, B. L. (2004). Parenting coordination for high conflict families. *Family Court Review, 42,* 246–262.

Coates, C., & LaCrosse, R. (2003). *Learning from divorce: how to take responsibility, stop the blame, and move on.* San Francisco: Jossey-Bass.

Cohen, I. M. (1998). Post decree litigation: Is joint custody to blame? *Family Court Review, 36*(1), 41–53.

Coleman, M., & Pencavel, J. (1993). Trends in market work behavior of women since 1940. *Industrial and Labor Relations Review,* ILR School, Cornell University, 46(4), 653–676.

Coleman, P. T. (2000). Intractable conflict. In M. Deutsch & P. Coleman (Eds.), *The handbook of conflict resolution: Theory and practice* (p. 43, 428, 431, 433). San Francisco: Jossey-Bass.

Coleman, P. T. (2003). Characteristics of protracted, intractable conflict: Towards the development of a meta-framework, peace and conflict. *Journal of Peace Psychology, 9*(1), 1–37.

Coleman, P. T. (2004). Paradigmatic framing of protracted, intractable conflict: Toward the development of a meta-framework-II. *Peace and Conflict: Journal of Peace Psychology, 10*(3), 197–235.

Coleman, P. T. (2006) Conflict, complexity, and change: A meta-framework for addressing protracted, intractable conflicts – III. *Peace and Conflict: Journal of Peace Psychology, 12*(4), 325–348.

Congreve, W. (1697). *The Mourning Bride.* Act III, Scene VIII.

Cookston, J. T., Braver, S. L., Griffin, W. A., de Luse, S. R., & Miles, J. C. (2007). Effects of the dads for life intervention on interparental conflict and coparenting in the two years after divorce. *Family Process, 46*(1), 123–137.

Cowan, C. P., Cowan, P. A., Pruett, M. K., & Pruett, K. (2007). An approach to preventing coparenting conflict and divorce in low-income families: Strengthening couple relationships and fostering fathers' involvement. *Family Process, 46*(1), 109–122.

Crocker, C. A., Hampson, F. O., & Aali, P. (Eds.). (1999). *Herding cats: The management of complex international mediation.* Washington, DC: U.S. Institute of Peace.

Cummings, E., & Davies, P. (1994). *Children and marital conflict.* New York: Guilford Press.

Darling, N., & Steinberg, L. (1993). Parenting style as context: An integrative model. *Psychological Bulletin, 113,* 487–496.

Degarmo, D. S., Patras, J., & Eap, S. (2008). Social support for divorced fathers' parenting: Testing a stress-buffering model. *Family Relations, 57,* 35–48.

Depner, C., Cannata, K., & Ricci, I. (1994). Client evaluation of mediation services. *Family and Conciliation Courts Review, 32,* 306–325.

Depner, C., Leino, E., & Chun, A. (1992). Interparental conflict and child adjustment: A decade review and meta-analysis. *Family and Conciliation Courts Review, 30*(3), 323–341.

Derdeyn, A. P. (1976). Child custody contests in historical perspective. *American Journal of Psychiatry, 133,* 713–29.

Deutsch, M. (1973). *The resolution of conflict.* New Haven, CT: Yale University Press.

Deutsch, M. (2000). Justice and conflict. In M. Deutsch & P. Coleman (Eds.), *The handbook of conflict resolution: Theory and practice.* San Francisco: Jossey-Bass Publishers.

Deutsch, R. (2008). Parenting coordination: A new practice opportunity. *Family Psychologist, 24*(2).

Deutsch, R., & Rotman, A. (2004). Parenting plans: How to settle on appropriate access. *Family Advocate, 26*(4). American Bar Association.

Deutsch, R., Coates, C., & Fieldstone, L. (2007). Parenting coordination: An emerging role. *Interventions with high conflict parents.* Madison, WI: Association of Family and Conciliation Courts.

Dickstein, S. (1998). What's in a family? Review of J. P. McHale and P. A. Cowan (Eds.). Understanding how family level dynamics affect children's development: studies of two-parent families. *Contemporary Psychology, 43,* 768.

Doolittle, D., & Deutsch, R. (1999). Children and high-conflict divorce: Theory, research and intervention. In R. M. Galatzer-Levy & L. Kraus (Eds.), *The scientific basis of child custody decisions.* New York: John Wiley & Sons.

Drozd, L., & Olesen, N. (2004). Is it abuse, alienation, and/or estrangement? A decision tree. *Journal of Child Custody, 1*(3), 65–106.

Eddy, B. (2004). *Splitting: Protecting yourself while divorcing a borderline or narcissist.* Milwaukee, WI: Eggshells Press.

Eddy, B. (2005). Handling high conflict personalities in family mediation. *Conflict Resolution Quarterly, 44*(4), 14–17.

Eddy, B. (2006). *High conflict people in legal disputes.* Canada: Janis Publications.

Eddy, B. (2008). *It's all your fault! 12 Tips for managing people who blame others for everything.* Canada: Janis Publications.

Eddy, B. (2009). New ways for families professional guidebook. Scottsdale, AZ: HCI Press.

Ellis, D., & Stuckless, N. (2006). Domestic violence, DOVE, and divorce mediation. *Family Court Review, 44*(4), 658–671.

Ellis, E. (2007). A stepwise approach to evaluation children for parental alienation syndrome. *Journal of Child Custody, 4*(1/2), 55–78.

Ellis, E. M. (2000). *Divorce wars.* Washington, DC: American Psychological Association.

Elrod, L. (2001). Reforming the system to protect children in high-conflict custody cases. *William Mitchell Law Review, 28,* 495–496.

Emery, R. E. (1994). *Renegotiating family relationships: Divorce, child custody, and mediation.* New York: The Guilford Press.

Emery, R. E. (1998). *Marriage, divorce, and children's adjustment* (2nd ed.). Thousand Oaks, CA: Sage Publications.

Emery, R. E. (1999a). Changing the rules for determining child custody in divorce case. *Clinical Psychology: Science and Practice, 6,* 323–327.

Emery, R. E. (1999b). Postdivorce family life for children: an overview of research and some implications for policy. In P. Amato & R. Thompson (Eds.), *The postdivorce family* (pp. 3–28). Thousand Oaks, CA: Sage Publications.

Emery, R. E. (2004). *The truth about children and divorce.* New York: Viking Press.

Emery, R. E. (2005). Parental alienation syndrome: Proponents bear the burden of proof. *Family Court Review, 42*(1), 8–13.

Emery, R. E., & Forehand, R. (1994). Parental divorce and children's well-being: A focus on resilience.

Enright, R. D. (2001). *Forgiveness is a choice.* Washington, DC: APA Life Tools.

Enright, R. D., & The Human Development Study Group. (1991). The moral development of forgiveness. In W. Kurtines & J. Gerwirtz (Eds.), *Handbook of moral behavior and Development.* Sussex, UK: Psychology Press.

Etzioni, A. (1993). *The spirit of community: Rights, responsibilities, and the communitarian agenda.* New York: Crown Publishers.

Faller, K. C. (1991). Possible explanations for child sexual abuse allegations in divorce. *American Journal of Orthopsychiatry, 61,* 86–91.

Featherstone, B. (2004). *Family life and family support: A feminist analysis.* Basingstoke, UK: Palgrave.

Feinberg, R., & Greene, T. (1997). The intractable client: Guidelines for working with personality disorders in family law. *Family Court Review, 35*(3), 351–365.

Felner, R. D. (1984). Vulnerability in childhood: A preventative framework for understanding children's efforts to cope with life stress and transitions. In M. C. Roberts & L. H. Peterson (Eds.), *Prevention of problems in childhood: psychological research and applications.* New York: Wiley-Interscience.

Felner, R., & Terre, L. (1987). Child custody and children's adaptation following divorce. In L. A. Weithorn (Ed.), *Psychology and child custody determinations: Knowledge, roles, and expertise.* Lincoln, NE: University of Nebraska Press.

Fidler, B., & Bala, N. (2010). Children resisting postseparation contact with a parent: Concepts, controversies, and conundrums. *Family Court Review, 48*(1), 10–47.

Fidler, B. J. (2007). Developing parenting time schedules. Conundrums and considerations. In M. Shaffer (Ed.), *Contemporary issues in family law: Engaging with the legacy of James G. McLeod.* Toronto, ON: Thomson Carswell.

Fidler, B. J., & Epstein, P. (2008). Parenting coordination in Canada: an overview of legal and practice issues. *Journal of Child Custody, 5* (1–2), 53–87.

Finkelhor, D. (Ed.). (1986). *Sourcebook on child sexual abuse.* Beverly Hills, CA: Sage.

Finkelhor, D., Hotaling, G., Lewis, T.A., & Smith, C. (1990). Sexual abuse in a national survey of adult men and women: Prevalence characteristics and risk factors. *Child Abuse and Neglect, 14,* 19–28.

Finley, G. E., & Schwartz, S. J. (2007). Father involvement and long-term young adult outcomes: The differential contributions of divorce and gender. *Family Court Review, 45*(4), 573–587.

Fisher, B., & Alberti, R. (2000). *Rebuilding: When your relationship ends.* Atascadero, CA: Impact Publishers.

Fisher, R., Ury, W., & Patton, B. (1992). *Getting to yes: Negotiating agreement without giving in* (2nd ed.). Boston: Houghton Mifflin.

Florida Bar Continuing Legal Education Committee and the Family Law Section. (1999). *Children's Issues. Seminar presentation.* Miami, FL.

Fonagy, P., Steele, M., & Steele, H. (1991). The capacity for understanding mental states: The reflective self in parent and child and its significance for security of attachment. *Infant Mental Health Journal, 12,* 201–218.

Freed, D., & Walker, T. (1985). Family law in the fifty states: An overview. *Family Law Quarterly, 18*(4), 361–471.

Freeman, R., Abel, D., Cooper-Smith, M., & Stein, L. (2004). Reconnecting children with absent parents: A model for intervention. *Family Court Review, 42,* 439–459.

Friedlander, S., & Walters, M. G. (2010). When a child rejects a parent: Tailoring the intervention to fit the problem. *Family Court Review, 48*(1).

Friedman, M. (2004). The so-called high-conflict couple: A closer look. *American Journal of Family Therapy, 32,* 101–117.

Furstenberg, F. (1994). History and current status of divorce in the United States. *Children and Divorce, 4,* 29–43.

Furstenberg, F. F. (1990). Divorce and the American family. *Annual Review of Sociology, 16,* 379–403.

Furstenberg, F., & Cherlin, A. J. (1991). *Divided families: What happens to children when parents part.* Cambridge, MA: Harvard University Press.

Garber, B. (2007). Conceptualizing visitation resistance and refusal in the context of parental conflict, separation and divorce. *Family Court Review,* (4)1, 588–599.

Garber, B. (2009). *Developmental psychology for family law professionals: Theory, application, and the best interests of the child.* New York: Springer Publishing Company.

Gardner, R. (1970). *The boys and girls book about divorce.* New York: Bantam Books.

Gardner, R. (2002). Rebuttal to Kelly and Johnston's Article. *Children Speak Out for Children, 17*(2), 5–10. Retrieved January 12, 2002 from http://www.rgardner.com/refs/ar16.html.

Gardner, R. (2003, May 23). Articles in peer-review journals and published books on the parental alienation syndrome (PAS). Retrieved June 26, 2003, from http://www.rgardner.com/refs/pas_peerreviewarticles.html

Gardner, R. A. (1987). *The parental alienation syndrome and the differentiation between fabricated and genuine child sex abuse.* Cresskill, NJ: Creative Therapeutics.

Gardner, R. A. (1991). *Psychotherapy with children of divorce.* Northvale, NJ: Jason Aronson.

Gardner, R. A. (1992a). *The parental alienation syndrome.* Cresskill, NJ: Creative Therapeutics.

Gardner, R. A. (1992b). *True and false accusations of child sex abuse.* Cresskill, NJ: Creative Therapeutics.

Gardner, R. A. (1998). *The parental alienation syndrome* (2nd ed.). Cresskill, NJ: Creative Therapeutics.

Gardner, R. A. (2004). Commentary on Kelly and Johnston's the alienated child: A reformulation of parental alienation syndrome. *Family Court Review, 42*(4), 611–621.

Gardner, R. A. (2001a). The parental alienation syndrome: Sixteen years later. *The Academy Forum, 45*(1), 10–12.

Garon, R. J., Donner, D. S., & Peacock, K. (2000). From infants to adolescents a developmental approach to parenting plans. *Family Court Review, 38*(2), 168–191.

Garrity, C. B., & Baris, M. A. (1994). *Caught in the middle: protecting the children of high-conflict divorce.* New York: Lexington Books.

Gerard, J. M., Buehler, C., Franck, K., & Anderson, O. (2005). In the eyes of the beholder: Cognitive appraisals as mediators of the association between interparental conflict and youth maladjustment. *Journal of Family Psychology, 19*(3), 376–384.

Glendon, M. A. (1993). *Rights talk. The impoverishment of political discourse* (reprint ed.). New York: Free Press.

Goodman, M., Bonds, D., Sandler, I., & Braver, S. (2004). Parent psycho-educational programs and reducing the negative effects of interparental conflict following divorce. *Family Court Review, 42*, 263–279.

Gordon, K. C., & Baucom, D. H. (2003). Forgiveness and marriage: Preliminary support for a measure based on a model of recovery from a marital betrayal. *American Journal of Family Therapy, 31*(3), 179–199.

Gordon, K. C., Baucom, D. H., & Snyder, D. K. (2000). *Frontiers of forgiving.* New York: Guilford Press.

Gottman, J. M. (1994a). *What predicts divorce.* New Jersey: Lawrence Erlbaum.

Gottman, J. M. (1994b). *Why marriages succeed or fail and how you can make yours last.* New York: Fireside.

Gottman, J. M., Coan, J., Carrere, S., & Swanson, C. (1998). Predicting marital happiness and stability from newlywed interactions. *Journal of Marriage and the Family, 60*, 5–22.

Gottman, J. M., & DeClaire, J. (2001). *The relationship cure: A 5 step guide to strengthening your marriage, family, and friendships.* New York: Three Rivers Press.

Gottman, J. M., & Levenson, R. W. (1999). What predicts change in marital interaction over time? A study of alternative models. *Family Process, 38*(2), 143–158.

Gottman, J. M., & Notarius, C. I. (2001). Decade review: Observing marital interaction. In R. M. Molardo (Ed.), *Understanding families into the new millennium: A decade in review* (pp. 146–166). Kansas: National Council on Family Relations.

Gottman, J. M., & Silver, N. (1999). The seven principles for making marriage work. New York: Three Rivers Press.

Grych, J. H. (2005). Interparental conflict as a risk factor for child maladjustment: implications for the development of prevention programs. *Family Court Review, 43*(1), 97–108.

Grych, J. H., & Fincham, F. D. (2001). *Interparental conflict and child development: Theory, research, and applications.* New York: Cambridge University Press.

Hargrave, T. D., & Sells, J. N. (1997). The development of a forgiveness scale. *Journal of Marital and Family Therapy and development.* Hillsdale, NJ: Lawrence Erlbaum.

Hetherington, E. M. (1999). *Coping with divorce, single parenting, and remarriage.* Mahwah, NJ: Lawrence Erlbaum Associates.

Hetherington, E. M. (2003). Intimate pathways: Changing patterns in close personal relationships across time. *Family Relations, 51*, 318–331.

Hetherington, E. M., & Kelly, J. (2002). *For better or for worse: Divorce reconsidered.* New York: W. W. Norton & Company.

Horowitz, D. L. (1985). *Ethnic groups in conflict.* Berkeley, CA: University of California Press.

Horowitz, M. J., Stinson, C., & Field, N. (1991). Natural disasters and stress response syndromes. *Psychiatric Annals, 21*(9), 556–562.

Human rights today: A United Nations priority. (2000). The United Nations. Retrieved from http://www.un.org/rights/HRToday/

Hynan, D. J. (1998). Interviewing children in custody evaluations. *Family Court Review, 36*(4), 466–478.

Irving, H., & Benjamin, M. (1992). An evaluation of process and outcome in a private family mediation service. *Mediation Quarterly, 24,* 71–88.

Jacobs, N., & Jaffe, R. (2010). Investigating the Efficacy of CoMeT, a new mediation model for high conflict separating parents. *The American Journal of Family Therapy, 38*(10), 16–31.

Jaffe, P. G., Johnston, J. R., Crooks, C. V., & Bala, N. (2008). Custody disputes involving allegations of domestic violence: The need for differentiated approaches to parenting plans. *Family Court Review, 46*(3), 500–522.

Johnston, J. R. (1994). The future of children. *Children and Divorce, 4*(1).

Johnston, J. R. (1995). Research update: Children's adjustment in sole custody compared to joint custody families and principles for custody decision making. *Family and Conciliation Courts Review, 33,* 415–425.

Johnston, J. R. (2000, Spring). Building multidisciplinary professional partnerships with the court on behalf of high-conflict divorcing families and their children; who needs what kind of help? *University of Arkansas at Little Rock Law Review, 22,* 453.

Johnston, J. R. (2003). Parental alignments and rejection: An empirical study of alienation in children of divorce. *Journal of the American Academy of Psychiatry & Law, 31,* 158–170.

Johnston, J. R. (2005). Children of divorce who reject a parent and refuse visitation: Recent research and social policy implications for the alienated child. *Family Law Quarterly, 38*(4), 757–775.

Johnston, J. R., & Campbell, L. E. (1988). *Impasses of divorce: The dynamics and resolution of family conflict.* New York: Free Press.

Johnston, J. R., & Campbell, L. E. (1993). A clinical typology of interparental violence in dispute-custody divorces. *American Journal of Orthopsychiatry, 63*(2), 190–199.

Johnston, J. R., & Kelly, J. B. (2004a). Commentary on Walker, Brantley and Rigsbee's a critical analysis of parental alienation and its admissibility in the family court. *Journal of Child Custody, 1*(4), 77–89.

Johnston, J. R., & Kelly, J. B. (2004b). Rejoinder to Gardner's Commentary on Kelly and Johnston's the alienated child: A reformulation of parental alienation syndrome. *Family Court Review, 42*(4), 622–628.

Johnston, J. R., Kline, M., & Tschann, J. M. (1989). Ongoing postdivorce conflict: Effects on children of joint custody and frequent access. *American Journal of Orthopsychiatry, 59,* 576–592.

Johnston, J. R., Lee, S., Olesen, N. W., & Walters, M. G. (2005). Allegations and substantiations of abuse in custody disputing families. *Family Court Review, 43*(2), 283–294.

Johnston, J. R., & Roseby, V. (1997). *In the name of the child. A developmental approach to understanding and helping children of conflict and violent divorce.* New York: Free Press.

Johnston, J. R., Roseby, V., & Kuehnle, K. (2009). *In the name of the child: A developmental approach to understanding and helping children of conflicted and violent divorce.* New York: Springer Publishing Company.

Johnston, J. R., Walters, M. G., & Friedlander, S. (2001). Therapeutic work with alienated children and their families. *Family Court Review, 39*(3), 316–333.

Johnston, J. R., Walters, M. G., & Olesen, N. W. (2005a). Clinical ratings of parenting capacity and Rorschach protocols of custody-disputing parents: An exploratory study. *Journal of Child Custody, 2,* 159–178.

Johnston, J. R., Walters, M. G., & Olesen, N. W. (2005b). Is it alienating parenting, role reversal or child abuse? An empirical study of children's rejection of a parent in child custody disputes. *Journal of Emotional Abuse, 5*(4), 191–218.

Johnston, J. R., Walters, M. G., & Olesen, N. W. (2005c). The psychological functioning of alienated children in custody disputing families: An exploratory study. *American Journal of Forensic Psychology, 39*(3), 39–64.

Kalter, N., Kioner, A., Schreier, S., & Okla, M. A. (1989). Predictors of children's post-divorce adjustment. *American Journal of Orthopsychiatry, 59,* 605–618.

Karen, R. (1994). *Becoming attached.* New York: Warner Books.

Kaslow, F. W., & Schwartz, L. L. (1987). *The dynamics of divorce.* New York: Brunner/Mazel.

Kelly, J. B. (1990). Is mediation less expensive? Comparison of mediated and adversarial divorce costs. *Mediation Quarterly, 8*(1), 15–26.

Kelly, J. B. (1996). A decade of divorce mediation research: Some answers and questions. *Family and Conciliation Courts Review, 34*(3), 373–385.

Kelly, J. B. (2000). Children's adjustment in conflicted marriage and divorce: A decade review of research. *Journal of Child and Adolescent Psychiatry, 39*(8), 963–973.

Kelly, J. B. (2002). Psychological and legal interventions for parents and children in custody and access disputes: Current research and practice. *Virginia Journal of Social Policy and Law, 10*(1), 129–163.

Kelly, J. B. (2003). Parents with enduring child disputes: Focused interventions with parents in enduring disputes. *Journal of Family Studies, 9*(1), 51–62.

Kelly, J. B. (2005). Developing beneficial parenting plan models for children following separation and divorce. *Journal of American Academy of Matrimonial Lawyers.*

Kelly, J. B. (2006). Children's living arrangements following separation and divorce: Insights from empirical and clinical research. *Family Process, 46*(1), 35–55.

Kelly, J. B. (2007). Children's living arrangements following separation and divorce: Insights from empirical and clinical research. *Family Process, 46*(1), 35–52.

Kelly, J. B. (2008). Preparing for the parenting coordination role: Training needs for mental health and legal professionals. *Journal of Child Custody, 5*(1–2), 140–159.

Kelly, J. B., & Duryee, M. (1992). Women's and men's views of mediation in voluntary and mandatory mediation settings. *Family and Conciliation Courts Review, 30*, 34–49.

Kelly, J. B., & Emery, R. (2003). Children's adjustment following divorce: Risk and resilience perspectives. *Family Relations, 52*(4), 352–362.

Kelly, J. B., & Johnston, J. R. (2001). The alienated child: A reformulation of parental alienation syndrome. *Family Courts Review, 39*(3), 249–266.

Kelly, J. B., & Johnson, M. P. (2008). Differentiation among types of domestic violence: Research update and implications for interventions. *Family Court Review, 46*(3), 476–499.

Kelly, J. B., & Lamb, M. E. (2000). Using child development research to make appropriate custody and access decisions. *Family & Conciliation Courts Review, 38*(3), 297–311.

Kelly, J. B., & Lamb, M. E. (2003). Developmental issues in relocation cases involving young children: When, whether, and how? *Journal of Family Psychology, 17*, 193–205.

Kelly, J. B., & Wallerstein, J. S. (1976). The effects of parental divorce: Experiences of the child in early latency. *The American Journal of orthopsychiatry, 46*(1), 20–32

Kendall-Tackett, K. A., Williams, L. M., & Finkelhor, D. (1993). Impact of sexual abuse on children: A review and synthesis of recent empirical studies. *Psychological Bulletin, 113*(1), 164–180.

Kendler, K. S., Kessler, R. C., Walters, E. E., MacLean, C., Neale, M. C., Heath, A. C., et al. (1995). Stressful life events, genetic liability, and onset of an episode of major depression in women. *American Journal of Psychiatry, 152*, 833–842.

Kenney, L. M. (1996, Summer). A lawyers guide to therapeutic interventions in domestic relations court. *Arizona State Law Journal, 28*, 629.

Kibler, S., Sanchez, E., & Baker-Jackson, M. (1994). Precontempt/contemnors group diversion counseling program: A program to address parental frustration of custody and visitation orders. *Family & Conciliation Courts Review, 32*, 62–63.

Kirkland, K. (2008). Parenting coordination (PC) laws, rules, and regulations: A jurisdictional comparison. *Journal of Child Custody, 5*(1–2), 25–52.

Kirkland, K., & Kirkland, K. E. (2006). Risk management and aspirational ethics for parenting coordinators. *Journal of Child Custody, 3*(2), 23–47.

Kline, M., Tschann, J. M., Johnston, J. R. & Wallerstein, J. S. (1989). Children's adjustment in joint and sole custody families. *Developmental Psychology, 25*, 430–438.

Kriesberg, L. (1998). Intractable conflicts. In E. Weiner (Ed.), *The handbook of interethnic coexistence*. New York: Continuum Publishing.

Kriesberg, L. (2005). Nature, dynamics, and phases of intractability. In C. A. Crocker, F. O. Hampson, & P. Aall (Eds.), *Grasping the nettle: Analyzing cases of intractable conflict* (pp. 65–97). United States Institute of Peace Press.

Kuehnle, K. F., & Connell, M. (Eds.). (2009). *The evaluation of child sexual abuse allegations: A comprehensive guide to assessment and testimony.* Hoboken, NJ.: Wiley & Sons.

Lally, S. J., & Higuchi, S. A. (2008). The American Psychological Association Parenting Coordination Project: Development of the project and initial review of the first two years. *Journal of Child Custody, 5*(1–2), 101–121.

Lamb, M. E. (Ed.). (1997). *The role of the father in child development* (3rd ed.). New York: Wiley.

Lamb, M. E. (Ed.). (1999). *Parenting and child development in nontraditional families.* Mahwah, NJ: Lawrence Erlbaum Associates.

Lamb, M. E., Bornstein, M., & Teti, D. (2002). *Development in infancy* (4th ed.). Mahwah, NJ: Erlbaum.

Lamb, M. E., & Kelly, J. B. (2001). Using the empirical literature to guide the development of parenting plans for young children: A rejoinder to Solomon and Biringen. *Family Court Review, 39*(4).

Lamb, M. E., Sternberg, K. J., & Thompson, R. A. (1997). The effects of divorce and custody arrangements on children's behavior, development, and adjustment. *Family and Conciliation Courts Review, 35,* 393–404.

Lample, A. K. (2002), Assessing for alienation and access in child custody cases. *Family Court Review, 40,* 232–235.

Lazarus, R. S., & Folkman, S. (1984). *Stress, appraisal and coping.* New York: Springer.

Lebow, J., & Rekart, K. N. (2007). Integrative family therapy for high conflict divorce with disputes over child custody and visitation. *Family Process, 46*(1), 79–92.

Lee, S. M., & Olesen, N. W. (2001). Assessing for alienation in child custody and access evaluations. *Family Court Review, 39,* 282–298.

Leis, R., & Rosenbloom, D. (2009). *Family Court Review, 47*(2), 274–285.

Love, A., Moloney, L., & Fisher, T. (1995). *Federally-funded family mediation in Melbourne: Outcomes, costs, and client satisfaction.* Office of Legal Aid and Family Services, Attorney-General's Department, Barton, ACT 2600.

Maccoby, E. E., & Mnookin, R. H. (1992). *Dividing the child: social and legal dilemmas of custody.* Cambridge, MA: Harvard University Press.

Margolin, G., Gordis, E. B., & John, R. S. (2001). Coparenting: A link between marital conflict and parenting in two-parent families, *Journal of Family Psychology, 15*(1), 3–21.

Marshall, M. G., & Gurr, T. R. (2005). *Peace and conflict 2005: A global survey of armed conflicts, self-determination movements, and democracy.* College Park, MD: Center for International Development and Conflict Management, University of Maryland. Chapters authored include "Peace and Conflict Ledger," "Global Trends in Violent Conflict," "Global Trends in Democratization," "Focus on Political Instability in Africa," and "Global Terrorism." HYPERLINK "http://members.aol.com/cspmgm/PC2005.pdf" "http://HYPERLINK "http://www.systemicpeace.org/PC2005.pdf" www.systemicpeace.org HYPERLINK "http://members.aol.com/cspmgm/PC2005.pdf"/PC2005.pdf

Martinez, C. R., Jr., & Forgatch, M. S. (2002). Adjusting to change: Linking family structure transitions with parenting and child adjustment. *Journal of Family Psychology, 16*(2), 107–117.

Maundi, M., Khadiagala, G., Nuemah, K., Touval, S., & Zartman, I. W. (2000). *Entry and access in mediation.* Washington, DC: U.S. Institute of Peace.

McCann, I. L., Sakheim, D., & Abrahamson, D. (1988). Trauma and victimization: A model of psychological adaptation. *The Counseling Psychologist.*

McIntosh, J. (2009). Legislating for shared parenting: Exploring some underlying assumptions. *Family Court Review, 47,* 389–400.

McIntosh, J., & Long, C. (2005). Current findings on Australian children in post-separation disputes: outer conflict, inner discord. *Journal of Family Studies, 11*(1), 99–109.

McIntosh, J., Long, C., & Moloney, L. (2004). Child-focused and child-inclusive mediation: A comparative study of outcomes. *Journal of Family Studies, 10*(1), 87–96.

Mezulis, A. H., Hyde, J. S., & Clark, R. (2004). Father involvement moderates the effect of maternal depression during a child's infancy on child behavior problems in kindergarten. *Journal of Family Psychology, 18,* 575–588.

Moloney, L. (2005). Children's voices: Reflections on the telling and the listening. *Journal of Family Studies, 11*(2), 216–226.

Moloney, L., & McIntosh, J. (2004). Child-responsive practices in Australian Family Law: Past problems and future directions. *Journal of Family Studies, 10*(1), 71–86.

Muha, T., & Vernon, M. (1996). *Divorce is the pits: So stop digging.* Annapolis, MD: Looking Glass Productions.

Naess, A. (1958). A systemization of Gandhian ethics of conflict resolution. *Journal of Conflict Resolution, 1,* 140–155.

National Survey of Family Growth. (2002). Retrieved from http://www.cdc.gov/nchs/nsfg.htm

Neighbors, B., Forhand, R., & McVicar, D. (1993). *Resilient adolescents and interparental conflict.* Retrieved from http://onlinelibrary.wiley.com/doi/10.1111/ajop.1993.63.issue-3/issuetoc

Nelson, R. (1989). Parental hostility, conflict and communication in joint and sole custody families. *Journal of Divorce, 13,* 145–157.

Northrup, T. A. (1989). The dynamic of identity in personal and social conflict. In L. Kriesberg, T. A. Northrup, & J. T. Stuart (Eds.), *Intractable conflicts and their transformation.* Syracuse, NY: Syracuse University Press.

Pearce, B. W., & Littlejohn, S. (1997). *Moral conflict: When social worlds collide.* Thousand Oaks, CA: Sage Publications.

Pearson, P. (1998). *Splitting up.* New York: The Guilford Press.

Pearson, J., & Thoennes, N. (1990). Custody after divorce: Demographic and attitudinal patterns. *American Journal of Orthopsychiatry, 60,* 233–249.

Peterson, G., Leigh, G., & Day, R. (1984). Family stress theory and the impact of divorce on children. *Journal of Divorce, 7,* 1–20.

Poole, D. A., & Lamb, M. E. (1998). *Investigative interviews of children. A guide for helping professionals.* Washington, DC: American Psychological Association. See Chapters 3, 4, 5.

Pruett, M. K., Ebling, R., & Insabella, G. (2004). Parenting plans and visitation: Critical aspects of parenting plans for young children interjecting data into the debate about overnights. *Family Court Review, 42,* 39–59.

Pruett, M. K., Williams, T. Y., Insabella, G., & Little, T. D. (2003). *Family and legal indicators of child adjustment to divorce among families with young children.* Retrieved from http://www.agencylab.ku.edu/~agencylab/manuscripts/ (Pruett,%20Williams,%20Insebella,%20and%20Little%202003).pdf

Pruitt, D. G. (1997). Ripeness theory and the Oslo talks. *International Negotiation, II*(2), 237–250.

Rand, D. (1997a). The spectrum of parental alienation syndrome, Part I. *American Journal of Forensic Psychology, 15*(3), 23–52.

Rand, D. (1997b). The spectrum of parental alienation syndrome, Part II. *American Journal of Forensic Psychology, 15*(4), 39–92.

Rand, D., Rand, R., & Kopetski, L. (2005). The spectrum of parental alienation syndrome: Part III: The Kopetski Follow-up Study. *American Journal of Forensic Psychology, 34*(1), 15–43.

Resick, P. A., & Calhoun, K. S. (2001). Posttraumatic stress disorder. In D. H. Barlow, (Ed.), *Clinical handbook of psychological disorders* (3rd ed.). New York: Guilford Press.

Ricci, I. (1997). *Mom's house, dad's house: Making two homes for your child.* New York: Fireside.

Rokeach, M. (1973). *The nature of human values.* New York: Free Press.

Rosenak, C. M., & Harnden, G. M. (1992). Forgiveness in the psychotherapeutic process: Clinical applications. *Journal of Psychology and Christianity, 11,* 188–197.

Rothman, J. (1997). *Resolving identity-based conflict in nations, organizations, and communities.* San Francisco: Jossey-Bass Publishers.

Rowe, J. O., Halling, S., Davies, E., & Leifer, M. (1989). The psychology of forgiving another: A dialogal research approach. In R. S. Valle & S. Halling (Eds.), *Existential-phenomenological perspectives in psychology: Exploring the breadth of human experience* (pp. 233–244). New York: Plenum Press.

Rutter, M. (1981). Stress, coping and development: Some issues and some questions. *Journal of Child Psychology and Psychiatry, 22,* 323–356.

Sandler, I., Miles, J., Cookston, J., & Braver, S. (2008). Effects of father and mother parenting on children's mental health in high and low conflict divorces. *Family Court Review, 46,* 282–296.

Saposnek, D. (1998). *Mediating child custody disputes: A strategic approach* (Rev. ed.). San Francisco: Jossey-Bass Publishers.

Saywitz, K. J. (2002). Developmental underpinnings of children's testimony. In H. L. Wescott, G. M. Davies, & R. H. C. Bull (Eds.), *Children's testimony.* New York: Wiley.

Saywitz, K. J. (2008). The art of interviewing young children in custody disputes. *Family Advocate, 30*(4).

Schulman, J. (1982). Who's looking after the children? *Family Advocate, 5,* 31–37, 43.

Schutz, B. M., Dixon, E. B., Lindenberger, J. C., & Ruther, N, J. (1989). *Solomon's sword: A practical guide to conducting child custody evaluations.* San Francisco: Jossey-Bass Publishers.

Seuss, Dr. (1990). *Oh, the places you'll go.* New York: Random House.

Shaw, D. S., & Emery, R. E. (1987). Parental conflict and other correlates of the adjustment of school-age children whose parents have separated. *Journal of Abnormal Child Psychology, 15*(2), 269–281.

Shi, L. (2003). The association between adult attachment styles and conflict resolution in romantic relationships. *The American Journal of Family Therapy, 31*(3), 143–157.

Siegel, J. P. (2000). *What children learn from their parents' marriage.* New York: Harper Collins Publishers.

Simons, R. L., & Associates. (1996). *Understanding differences between divorced and intact families: Stress, interaction, and child outcome.* Thousand Oaks, CA: Sage Publications.

Smedes, L. B. (1984). *Forgive and forget: Healing the hurts we don't deserve.* New York: Harper & Row.

Smyth, B. (2009). A 5 year retrospective of post-separation shared care research in Australia. *Journal of Family Studies, 15,* 36–59.

Solomon, J., & Biringen, Z. (2001). The continuing debate about overnight visitation: Another look at the developmental research: Commentary on Kelly and Lamb's Using child development research to make appropriate custody and access decisions for young children. *Family Court Review, 39,* 355–364.

Solomon, J., & George, C. (1999). The development of attachment in separated and divorced families: Effects of overnight visitation, parent and couple variable. *Attachment & Human Development, 1,* 2–33.

Sperling, M. B., & Berman, W. H. (1994). *Attachment in adults.* New York: The Guilford Press.

Stahl, P. (1994). *Conducting child custody evaluations.* Thousand Oaks, CA: Sage Publications.

Stahl, P. (1999). *Complex issues in child custody evaluations.* Thousand Oaks, CA: Sage Publications.

Stewart, A. J., Copeland, A. P., Chester, N. L., & Malley, J. E. (1997). *Separating together: How divorce transforms families.* New York: The Guilford Press.

Stewart, R. (2001). *The early identification and streaming of cases of high-conflict separation and divorce: A review.* Ottawa, ON: Department of Justice Canada (2001-FCY-7E/7F).

Stimmel, B. (2009). From addiction to abstinence: maximizing the chances of success. *Family Court Review, 47,* 265–273.

Stolberg, A. L., Camplair, C., Currier, K., & Wells, M. J. (1987). Individual, familial and environmental determinants of children's post-divorce adjustment and maladjustment. *Journal of Divorce, 11,* 51–70.

Stolz, J. M., & Ney, T. (2002). Resistance to visitation: Rethinking parental and child alienation. *Family Court Review, 40*(2), 220–231.

Sullivan, M. J. (2004). Ethical, legal and professional practice issues in acting as a psychologist coordinator in child custody cases. *Family Court Review, 42*(3), 576–582.

Sullivan, M. J. (2008). Coparenting and the parenting coordination process. *Journal of Child Custody, 5*(1–2), 4–24.

Sullivan, M. J., & Kelly, J. B. (2001). Legal and psychological management of cases with an alienated child. *Family Courts Review, 39*(3), 299–315.

Sydlik, B. *Parenting coordination: implementation issue.* This is the comprehensive report from AFCCs (Association of Family & Conciliation Courts). Task Force on Parenting Coordination & Special Masters. Available to members of AFCC at their website www.afccnet.org.

Sydlik, B., & Phalan, A. B. (1999). *Interventions for high conflict families: A national perspective.* Oregon : Office of the State Court Administrator, Oregon Judicial Department.

Teicher, M. H. (2002). Scars that won't heal: The neurobiology of child abuse. *Scientific American, 286*(3), 68–75.

Tessman, L. H. (1996). *Helping children cope with parting parents.* Northvale, NJ: Jason Aronson.

Textor, M. (1989). *The divorce and divorce therapy handbook.* Northvale, NJ: Jason Aronson.

Thayer, E., & Zimmerman, J. (2001). *The co-parenting survival guide: letting go of conflict after a difficult divorce.* Oakland, CA: New Harbinger Publications.

Tillett, G. (1999). *Resolving conflict: A practical approach.* New York: Oxford University Press.

Tomison, A. M. (1995). *Update on child sexual abuse,* NCPCH Issues Paper no.5, AIFS, Melbourne.

Turner, H. A., & Kopiec, K. (2006). Exposure to interparental conflict and psychological disorder among young adults. *Journal of Family Issues, 27*(2), 131–158.

Ury, W. (2000). *The third side: Why we fight and how we can stop.* New York: Penguin Books. Retrieved from http://www.thirdside.org/roles.cfm

Ury, W., Brett, J., & Goldberg, S. (1988). *Getting disputes resolved: Designing systems to cut the cost of conflict.* San Francisco: Jossey-Bass.

US Dept of Health and Human Services. (2000). Substance abuse treatment for persons with child abuse and neglect issues. *Treatment Improvement Protocol Series, 36.* Retrieved from http://ncadi,samhsa,gov/govpubs/BKD343/36c.aspx

Vandewater, E. A., & Lansford, J. E. (1998). Infl uences of family structure and parental conflict on children's well-being. *Family Relations, 47,* 323–330. Retrieved from http://www.jstor.org/pss/585263

Veuthey, M. (1998). International humanitarian law and the restoration and maintenance of peace. *African Security Review, 7*(5), Institute for Security Studies. Retrieved from http://www.iss.co.za/Pubs/ASR/7No5/InternationalHumanitarian.html

Vic, M. H., & Backerman, R. (1996). *Mediation/arbitration: surveys of professionals and clients.* Paper presented at the Boulder Interdisciplinary Committee on Child Custody, Boulder.

Visher, E., & Visher, J. S. (1991). *How to win as a step family.* Levittown, PA: Brunner/Mazel.

Walker, L. E. A., Brantley, K. L., & Rigsbee, J. A. (2004). A critical analysis of parental alienation syndrome and its admissibility in the family court. *Journal of Child Custody.*

Wallerstein, J. S., & Blakeslee, S. (1996). *Second chances.* New York: Houghton-Mifflin.

Wallerstein, J. S., & Kelly, J. B. (1980). *Surviving the breakup: How children and parents cope with divorce.* New York: Basic Books.

Wallerstein, J. S., & Lewis, J. M. (1998). The long-term impact of divorce on children: A first report from a 25-year study. *Family and Conciliation Courts Review, 36,* 368–383.

Wallerstein, J. S., Lewis, J. M., & Blakeslee, S. (2000). *The unexpected legacy of divorce. A 25 year landmark study.* Hyperion Press.

Warshak, R. A. (1992). *The custody revolution: The father factor and the motherhood mystique.* New York: Poseidon Press.

Warshak, R. A. (2000). Blanket restrictions: Overnight contact between divorced parents and young children. *Family and Conciliation Courts Review, 38*(4), 422–445.

Warshak, R. A. (2001). *Divorce poison: Protecting the parent–child bond from a vindictive ex.* New York: Regan Books.

Warshak, R. A. (2002). Who will be there when I cry in the night? *Family Court Review, 40*(2), 208–219.

Warshak, R. A. (2003a). Bringing sense to parental alienation: A look at the dispute and the evidence. *Family Law Quarterly, 37,* 273–301.

Warshak, R. A. (2003b). Payoffs and pitfalls of listening to children. *Family Relations, 52*(4), 373–384.

Weeks, D. (1992). *The eight essential steps to conflict resolution.* New York: Penguin Putnam.

Wehr, P. (1979). Self-limiting conflict: The Gandhian style. In *Conflict regulation* (pp. 55–68). Boulder, CO: Westview Press.

Weitzman, L. J. J. (1985). *Divorce revolution: the unexpected social and economic consequences for women and children in America.* New York: Simon & Schuster.

Whiteside, M. F. (1998), The parental alliance following divorce: An overview. *Journal of Marital and Family Therapy.*

Whiteside, M. F. (1998). Custody for children age fi ve and younger. *Family and Conciliation Courts Review, 36*(4), 479–502.

Wiese, S., Vallacher, R., & Starawinska, U. (2010). Dynamic social psychology: Complexity and coherence in human experience. *Social and Personality Psychology Compass, 4*(11), 1018–1030.

Winkler, A. E. (1998). Earnings of husbands and wives in dual-earner families. *Monthy Labor Review, 121.*

Winsdale, J., & Monk, G. (2000). *Narrative mediation: A new approach to conflict resolution.* San Francisco: John Wiley & Sons.

Wittman, J. P. (2001). *Custody chaos, personal peace: sharing custody with an ex who drives you crazy.* New York: The Berkley Publishing Group.

Wyer, S., Gaylord, J., & Grove, E. (1987). The legal context of child custody evaluations. In*Psychology and child custody determinations* (Vol. 3, pp. 8–14).

Zartman, I. W. (1989). *Ripe for resolution.* New York: Oxford University Press.

Zartman, I. W. (2000). Ripeness: The hurting stalemate and beyond. In P. C. Stern & D. Druckman (Eds.), *International conflict resolution after the cold war* (pp. 225–250). Committee on International Conflict Resolution. Washington, DC: National Academy Press.

Zartman, I. W., & Berman, M. (1982). *The practical negotiator.* New Haven, CT: Yale University Press.

MATERIALS AND VIDEOS:

AFCC Domestic Violence Visitation Risk Assessment. (1994, October). afcc@afccnet.org.

AFCC Guidelines for Parenting Coordination. (2006). Developed by the AFCC task force on parenting coordination. May 2005. *Family Court Review, 44,* 164–181. Retrieved from http://www.afcc.net.org/resources/standards_practice.asp.

AFCC Parenting Coordination Guidelines. (2005, May). afcc@afccnet.org.

AFCC. (2004). *Planning for shared parenting: a guide for parents living apart.* Available from www.afccnet.org.

After the storm: resolving post-separation conflict. Video, manuals. Center for Divorce Education, Athens, OH 45701. www.divorce-education.com.

Alaska Court System Model Parenting Agreement. www.state.ak.us/courts/dr-475.doc.

Brahm, E. Conflict stages. In G. Burgess & H. Burgess (Eds.). *Beyond intractability.* Conflict Research Consortium, University of Colorado, Boulder. Posted: September 2003 http://www.beyondintractability.org/essay/conflict_stages/

Guidelines for Parenting Coordination—AFCC Task Force on Parenting Coordination, 2005. www.afccnet.org. And in *Family Court Review,* 2006.

Idaho Bench book *To Protect Children of High-Conflict Divorce.* Idaho State Bar (208). 334–4500.

Matthew J. Sullivan has two (2) 6-hour videotapes and materials for training Parenting Coordinators. (650) 493-6282 or sullydoc@aol.com.

Model parenting time plans for parent/child access. Arizona Supreme Court. www.supreme.state.az.us (go to Public Information, Divorce/Parenting Issues, Custody and Parenting Time).

Rodriguez-Garcia, R., Macinko, J., Solorzano, X., & Schlesser, M. How can health serve as a bridge for peace? *The George Washington University School of Public Health and Health Services.* Available online at http://www.certi.org/publications/policy/gwc-12-a-brief.htm.

The Conflict Database, http://www.usc.edu/dept/LAS/ir/cews/html_pages/conflictdatabase.htm

Wingspread Report and Action Plan. (2002). High conflict custody cases: reforming the system for children. *Family Court Review, 39,* 146–152.

Index